Wharton Esherick
Studio and Collection

Edited by Paul Eisenhauer, Ph. D.
Curator, Wharton Esherick Museum

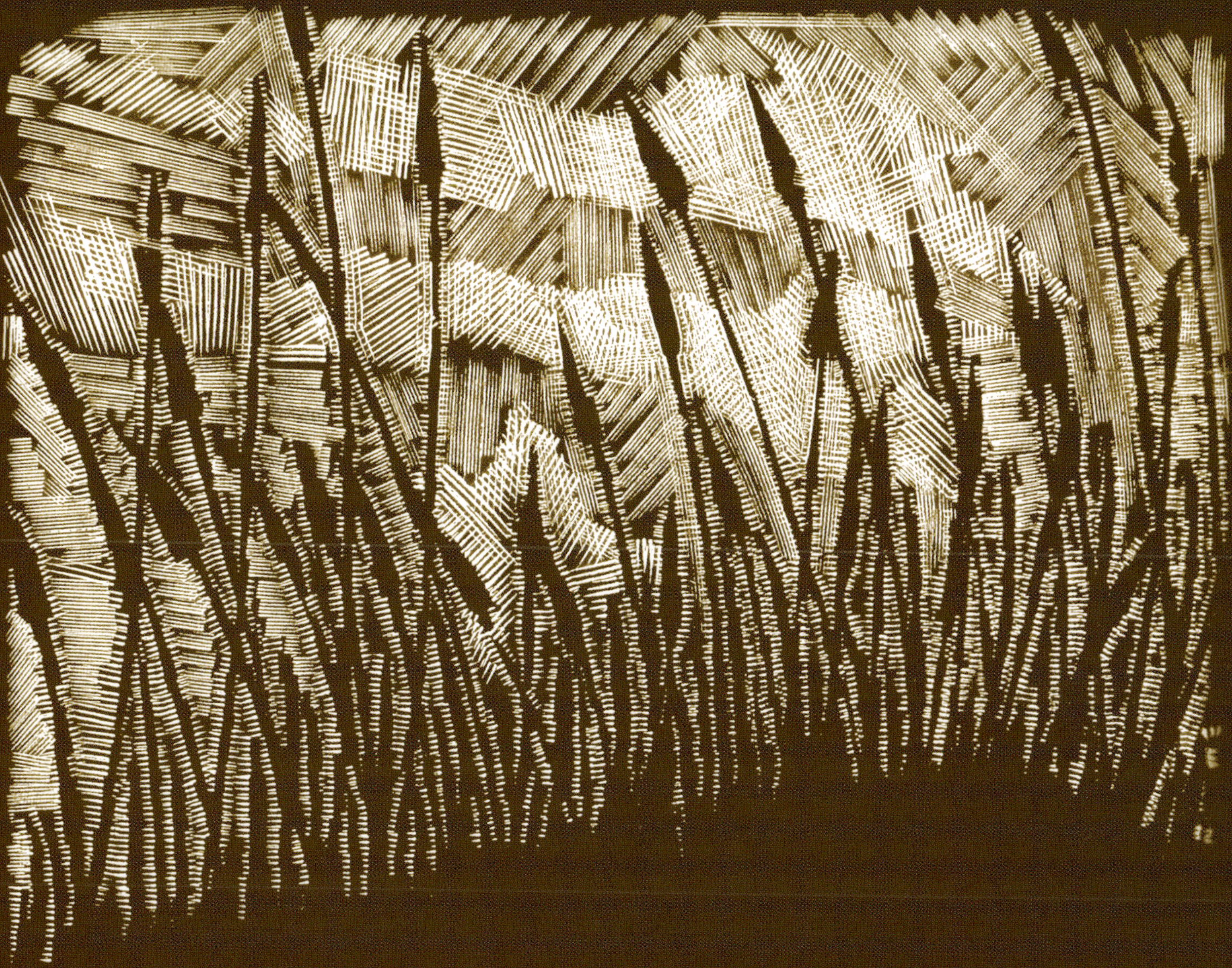

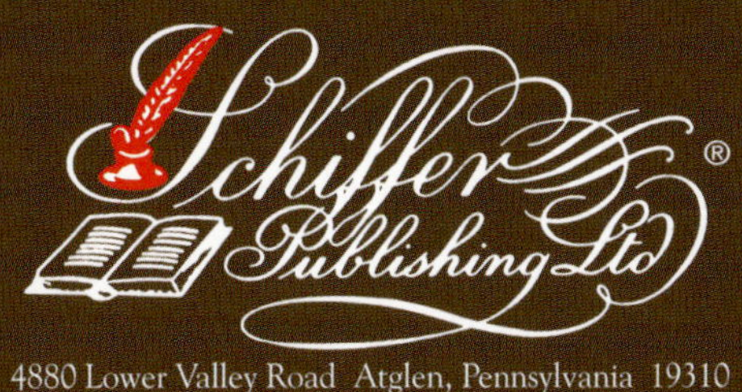

4880 Lower Valley Road Atglen, Pennsylvania 19310
Printed in China

The Wharton Esherick is open daily for tours by reservation between March 1 and December 31. For information visit www.whartonesherickmuseum.org or call 610-644-5822.

Library of Congress Control Number: 2009939610

Cover and book designed by: Bruce Waters
Type set in Zurich BT

ISBN: 978-0-7643-3449-8
Printed in China

Published by Schiffer Publishing Ltd.
4880 Lower Valley Road
Atglen, PA 19310
Phone: (610) 593-1777; Fax: (610) 593-2002
E-mail: Info@schifferbooks.com

In Europe, Schiffer books are distributed by
Bushwood Books
6 Marksbury Ave.
Kew Gardens
Surrey TW9 4JF England
Phone: 44 (0) 20 8392 8585; Fax: 44 (0) 20 8392 9876
E-mail: info@bushwoodbooks.co.uk
Website: www.bushwoodbooks.co.uk

Contents

Foreword and Acknowledgements

This catalog was made possible by a generous grant from The Meacham Family Foundation

Since 1972, the Wharton Esherick Museum has been delighting and inspiring visitors by allowing them to peer into the life and world of Wharton Esherick. Visitors' experiences are as diverse as their reasons for coming. Some find tranquility on the wooded hillside. Others laugh at Wharton's humor and joy of living. Some are moved by his connection to nature and his attempts to build and create in harmony with that world. Many are impressed with Wharton's ingenuity. Indeed, one of the joys of working at the Museum is watching visitors' reactions and talking with them about their experience. Invariably they want to take some of the feeling home with them and they want to spread the word about the Museum. We hope this catalog will enable them to do so.

The Museum produced the first edition of this catalog in 1977 and a second edition in 1984. Between the printing of the second edition and our selling the last copy, printing technology changed radically with the coming of the digital age. That meant we had to start from scratch on the third edition, delaying publication by several years. However digital technology allows us to print many more pictures – and more in color – than we were able to afford to print in the past.

For this new edition, we have kept Anne d'Harnoncourt's preface as a tribute. Her passing has been felt by the entire museum community. Anne was an early supporter of the Wharton Esherick Museum and served as a mentor during the early years. Her essay, though brief, captures the essence of Esherick's genius. There is one point in her essay that is out of date – the Curtis Bok house no longer exists, but through Anne's efforts, the Philadelphia Museum of Art now owns and displays several Esherick elements from the house.

Mansfield Bascom has written a new biographical sketch of Wharton Esherick for this edition. There is no one better for the task. He was one of the founders of the Museum, has served as Executive Director and Curator, and has written Esherick's biography. This catalog could not have been written without his help. He and his wife, Ruth Esherick Bascom, have generously shared their knowledge throughout the process.

Many people have helped in the production of this book. James Mario, a local artist and photographer, donated his services to the Museum and took most of the photographs used in this book. The many hours he spent getting to know the Museum and the collection are reflected in the quality of the images he produced. Mark Sfirri also provided photographs from his extensive collection. Tina Skinner and Pete Schiffer of Schiffer Publishing have been supportive of both the Museum and this catalog. Lisa Lapp worked her editorial and proof-reading magic on the book (though the errors that still slip through are my fault, not hers). Rob Leonard, our Executive Director, and our many volunteers helped me have the time to pull a project like this together. My sons, Jake and Jesse helped me solve computer problems. Marion Post has been the kind of supportive partner that everyone should have.

– Paul Eisenhauer, Curator
July, 2009

Preface

When Ford Maddox Ford traveled half way around the world in the mid 1930s, he broke his journey on a Pennsylvania hillside near Paoli and described his friend Esherick's workshop as a kind of sanctuary for the human spirit:

> A dim studio in which blocks of rare woods, carver's tools, medieval looking carving gadgets, looms, printing presses, rise up like ghosts in the twilight while the slow fire dies in the brands...Such a studio built by the craftsman's own hands out of chunks of rock and great balks of timber, sinking back into the quiet woods on a quiet crag with, below its long windows, quiet fields parceled out by the string-courses of hedges and running to a quietly rising horizon...such a quiet spot is the best place to think in.
>
> And let Esherick be moving noiselessly about in the shadows, with a plane and a piece of boxwood, or swinging backwards the lever of his press, printing off his engravings. Or pouring, a hundred times, heavy oil and emery powder on one of the tables he has designed, and rubbing it off with cloths to get the polish exactly true, and bending down again and again to see the sheen of the light along the polished wood...Those are the conditions you need for thought. Because they present your mind neither success or failure, but conditions coeval with the standing rocks and the life of a man. There have always been craftsmen and the craftsmen have always been the best men of their time because a handicraft goes at a pace commensurate with the thoughts in a man's head. (*Great Trade Route*, New York, Oxford University Press, 1937, page 202)

As his studio was a peaceful retreat, high in the woods overlooking the Great Valley, so Esherick was something of a loner. His long and productive career is curiously resistant to description in art historical terms. Like Ford Maddox Ford, many of his closest friends were not artists but men of letters: Theodore Dreiser worked over the stage version of *An American Tragedy* in Esherick's kitchen; *Spiral Pole*, one of Esherick's finest abstract sculptures, was carved during a visit to Sherwood Anderson (who later asked that his friend be commissioned to design his tombstone). Despite his beginnings as a Pennsylvania Academy trained painter, and his ability to produce conventional figurative sculpture in an academic vein, Esherick's evolution as an artist seems to have sprung directly from the physical experience of working with wood. His profound belief in handwork, honest construction, and truth to natural materials may well have been reinforced by his early contact with the arts and crafts community at Rose Valley, Pennsylvania: the buildings and simple oak furniture designed by William Price; the lively mingling of visual and dramatic arts at the Hedgerow Theatre. Certainly he was aware of Shaker furniture and the austere, functional shapes of rural Pennsylvania architecture. As for the broader picture of contemporary design, we know he visited Scandinavia on a trip to Europe in 1931, but was apparently more preoccupied with studying sculpture than the work of the young furniture designers.

In his preoccupation with treating every aspect of an interior as an organic whole, including sculpture, furniture and plane surfaces, Esherick suggests reference to the work of Frank Lloyd Wright. The almost fanatical integration of details into the whole, and the house into the landscape, were shared concerns. Esherick's friendship with other architects led to two important collaborations: with George Howe on the "Pennsylvania Hill House" for the 1939-1940 World's Fair, and with Louis Kahn for Esherick's workshop in 1956. In each case, the architects paid their friend the rare tribute of subsuming their own distinctive styles into his idiosyncratic and creative imagination.

Chronology does not seem crucial here. Although Esherick shared his interest in direct carving with a generation of American sculptors such as John Flannagan, Chaim Gross and José de Creeft, his work has little in common with theirs. If Robert Laurent's wood carved *Flame* of 1918 (Whitney Museum of Art) presages Esherick's interest in fluid wooden forms, it proves to be a passing phase in the career of the older artist and a prolonged passion with Esherick. As is the case with many great craftsmen, he had no hesitation in repeating a given design over a period of decades if it demonstrated its worth in use and if he found pleasure in the slight variations that made each piece individual: a chair conceived in 1940 might be made again in 1965. Esherick's most profound study was the nature of his materials themselves – the trees outside his studio windows. As his career advanced he drew further from any theoretical or even stylistic approach to design, taking increased delight in drawing upon the intrinsic properties and eccentricities of each piece of wood.

The masterpiece of the Museum, the red oak spiral stair that twists up through the space of the house linking ground floor with the second level, suggests the core of Esherick's character as an artist. Carved in 1930, before his trip to Europe and after his initial ventures with objects distinctly related to the arts and crafts movement, it declares his gift for combining the sculptural with the functional. Its rough-hewn steps and boldly cantilevered design have a rugged "American" quality like the poetry of Walt Whitman, which Esherick loved to illustrate.

The twentieth century has seen the development of the widest range of new methods and materials adapted to the making of sculpture and furniture, from the tubular steel of Mies van der Rohe's MR chair, to Charles Eames' pressed plywood and molded fiberglass, to the polyurethane foam favored by many recent designers. Not averse to mass production in principle, Esherick simply took too much delight in the process of making things himself to tackle the problem of design for a vast market. Discovering the pleasure of carving useful objects as early as 1920, he was in many ways a pioneer of the revival of handicrafts, which has now taken such a powerful hold on this country. Many others have followed, each pursuing a distinctive personal style: Sam Maloof, Wendell Castle and Arthur Espinet Carpenter to mention only a few of the best known.

Esherick's work is now scattered across the United States, from New York to California, and is already handed down from one generation to the next as prized possessions. The Philadelphia area is rich in examples of his best sculpture and furniture: his portrait of Dreiser and a study table have a place in the Rare Book room of the Van Pelt Library at the University of Pennsylvania; the distinguished interior designed for Curtis Bok still exists in the Gulph Mills house, several works have entered the public collections and many more are still in private hands.

The Wharton Esherick Museum, like Henry Chapman Mercer's home "Fonthill" in Doylestown, some 30 miles away, belongs to that rare variety of historic house, which is a complete expression of one man's intensely personal fusion of fine craftsmanship with the wild flights of the imagination. There are few museums in which a sense of the artist's character remains so vivid: Ford's words, quoted above, evoke an image of Esherick, which the visitor will find like a benign if crusty presence in every room.

— Anne d'Harnoncourt

WHARTON ESHERICK: A LIFE IN ART

by Mansfield Bascom

Wharton Esherick was one of a small group of artists credited with developing an American sculpture style early in the twentieth century. Working primarily in wood, he readily extended his innovative forms to furniture, furnishings, interiors and buildings, envisioning a sculptural environment. He developed an affinity for wood – its tactile qualities, its visual warmth, its decorative grain figures, its ease in working, and its plentiful supply in the woodlands at his door. When he began sculpting in 1920, wood was considered to be only a craft medium, but the acceptance in 1924 of his work at the Whitney Gallery in New York (later the Whitney Museum of Art) recognized that wood could be a fine art medium as well. There was little market at the time for wood sculpture, but the unusual furniture he made for himself began to attract attention and a few buyers. With the acceptance of his furniture as fine art, he bridged the gap between art and craft.

He was born with a creative mind that constantly sought more interesting, yet always functional, ways of shaping items of everyday use. He saw his commissions not so much as sources of income, but as opportunities to create new designs. Through the 1920s, '30s, and '40s, he was a solitary furniture maker, continuing the spirit – but not the designs – of the Arts and Crafts Movement that had failed commercially earlier in the century. There were no societies of furniture makers or craftsmen as there are today, and few galleries would consider displaying contemporary 'art' furniture. But he was well read and aware of what other artists were doing in this country and abroad. To him their work was more of a challenge, the introduction of a concept, than an influence.

In 1958, when Wharton was in his 60s, the newly opened Museum of Contemporary Craft in New York mounted a retrospective exhibition of his work, recognizing it as the link between the Arts and Crafts Movement and the resurgent interest in furniture making in the 1950s. A year after his death at age 83, the Renwick Gallery of the Smithsonian Institution produced "Wooden Works," a collection of Wharton's work surrounded by similar pieces by the four leading furniture makers of this new generation.

Since then he has been called the dean of American craftsmen and the godfather of the Studio Furniture Movement for having pioneered the way for today's furniture makers to market work of their own design. His designs were too personal to produce a 'style,' nor would he have wanted to. His legacy is the encouragement his success gave to others to abandon traditional designs and develop their own. For this reason, many consider him to be the most important American furniture designer of the twentieth century.

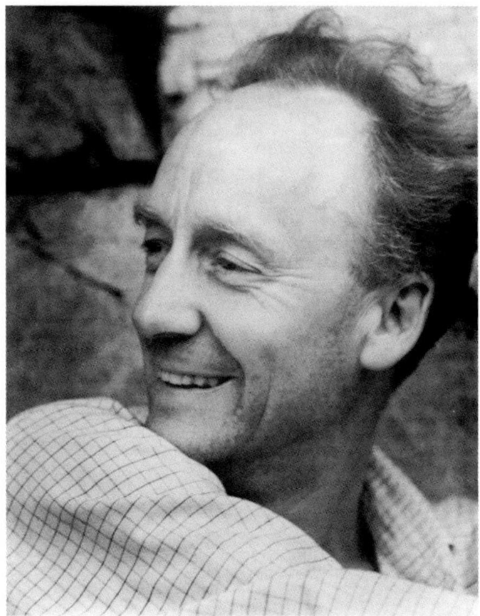

Wharton Esherick, c.1930. Photograph believed to be taken by Consuelo Kanaga.

An Artist's Beginning

Wharton Esherick was born on July 15, 1887 to a moderately prosperous family in a large house in West Philadelphia, the city's new suburb. As a child he was fascinated with drawing and he quickly realized he would be an artist when he grew up. His father tried to dissuade him, saying, "Wharton, you'll never make any money as an artist," but reluctantly let him attend Manual Training High School and then the Philadelphia Museum School of Industrial Art. There he learned wood and metal working, graphic arts, silk screening, and printmaking. But his main interest still was drawing, and he spent hours studying noses, ears, and mouths.

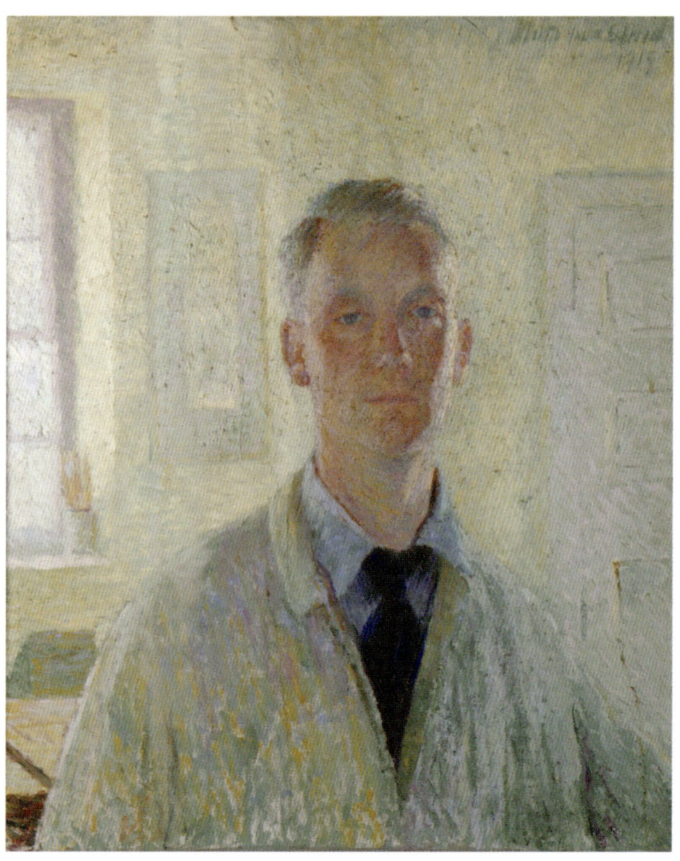

Self Portrait, 1919. Oil on canvas, 29.9 in. X 25.2 in. Signed "Wharton Harris Esherick 1919."

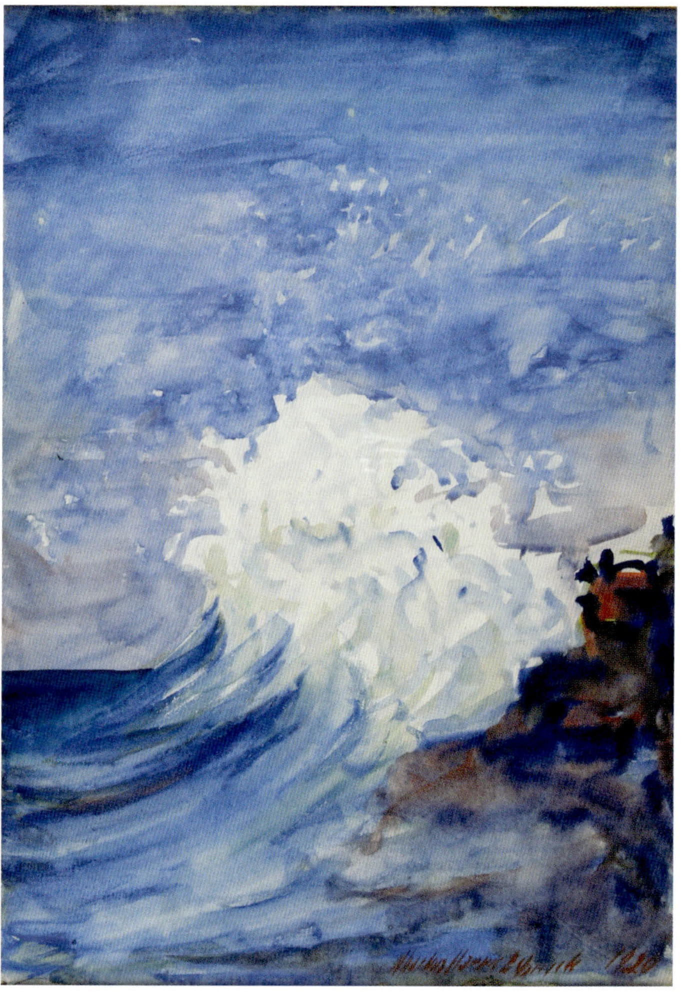

The Wave, 1920. Watercolor, 13.8 in. X 9.8 in. Signed "Wharton Harris Esherick 1920."

In 1908 Wharton won a scholarship to the two-year, non-degree painting program at the Pennsylvania Academy of the Fine Arts. American Impressionism was at its peak, and he studied under such well-known artists as William Merit Chase, Cecilia Beaux, and Thomas Anshutz. He learned the skills of mixing colors, of working with light, and the painting techniques and styles of respected artists. But he yearned to get away from his teachers' influence and develop his own style, and left the academy six weeks before the program was completed. He soon learned how right his father had been; there was no market for the work of an unknown painter.

Relying on his drawing skills, he worked with the local newspapers translating photographs to line drawings and lithographs so the images could be printed. It didn't pay much, but he could still live at home. Then, he was offered a job with the Victor Talking Machine Company, one of the country's largest manufacturers, designing posters to be silk screened and sent to the hundreds of retail stores that sold Victrola records. It was a bit more creative, working from photographs of famous opera singers in their many roles. And, it paid well – well enough for marriage. Returning with his bride, Letty (Leticia Nofer), from their honeymoon sailing up the coast and the Hudson aboard a borrowed boat, he learned the company had acquired the equipment for the half-tone process enabling it to print posters directly from photographs without the need for silkscreens, or him. And so had the newspapers. At age twenty five his income producing talents were obsolete.

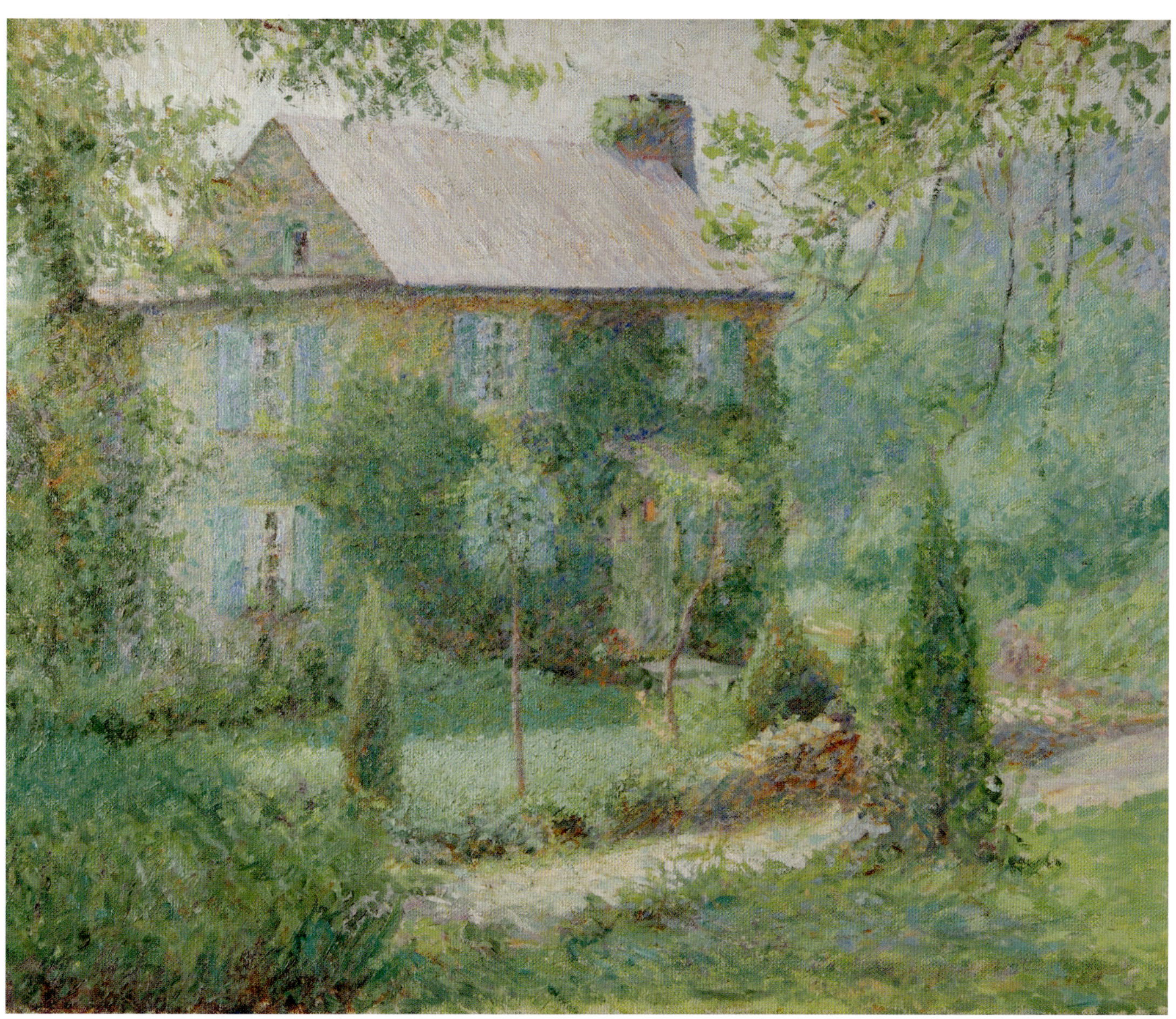

The Farmhouse, 1924. Oil on canvas, 25.2 in. X 29.9 in. Signed "Wharton Harris Esherick 1924." The farmhouse with its large cherry tree that Esherick's purchased in 1913.

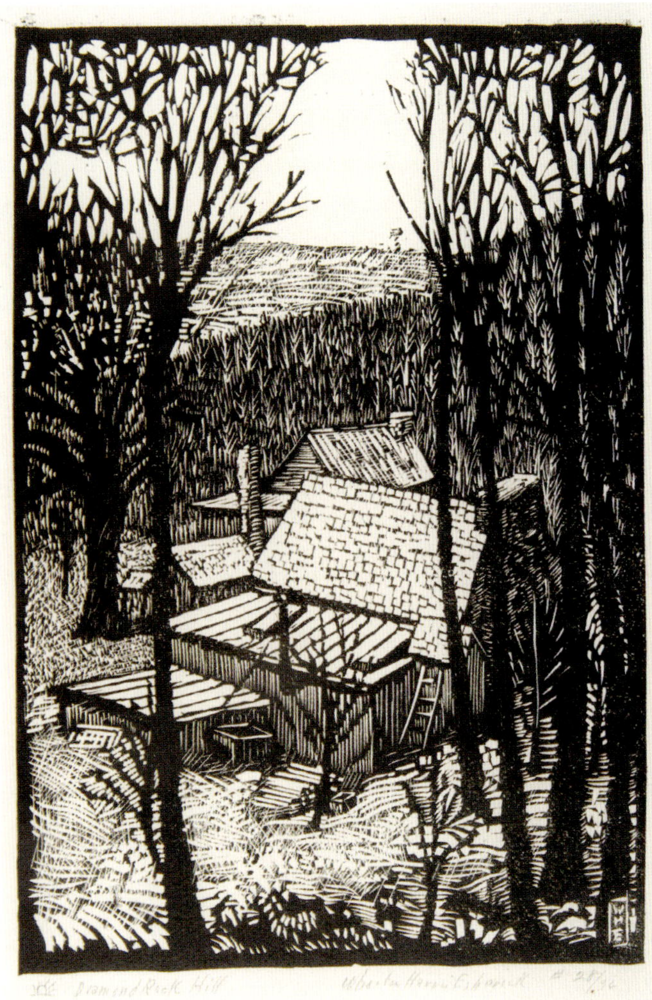

Diamond Rock Hill, 1923. Wood engraving, 8.75 in. X 6 in. Esherick's view from Diamond Rock Hill looking down at the farmhouse and barn.

Impressionist painters were moving from portraiture to landscape painting, forsaking their studios for open fields. Several graduates of the academy had moved to the country establishing a small colony at New Hope, up the Delaware River from Philadelphia. Using a small inheritance from his grandmother, Wharton and Letty decided to join them, and began looking at places along the river. But the best they could afford was a five-acre farm on a wooded hillside overlooking the Great Chester Valley near Paoli, some twenty-five miles west of Philadelphia. It was a place where they could live organically and raise a family close to nature. And it had an enormous wild cherry tree that shaded an old stone farmhouse and enough level, tillable land to grow their food if his paintings didn't sell. For the next several years, Wharton spent as much time farming as painting.

They called the farm *Sunekrest,* and Wharton carved a rising sun logo in the shutters. He painted murals on the walls, and when their daughter, Mary, was born, he covered the nursery walls with farm animals. Letty became interested in the concepts of 'progressive education' as practiced at the recently opened School for Organic Education in Fairhope, Alabama, and they spent the winter of 1919-1920 there. Wharton painted while Letty helped in the school. When Wharton complained of the type of art the children were being taught, the head of the school challenged him to do better, and he volunteered to teach a few hours one day each week.

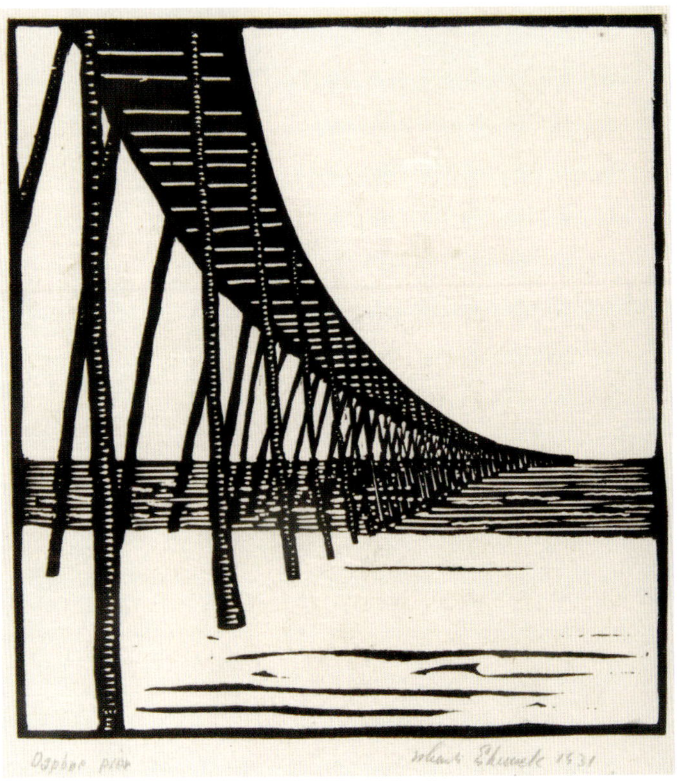

Daphne Pier, 1931. Wood engraving, 6.5 in. X 6 in. A pier on Mobile Bay near Fairhope, Alabama.

As the school year was ending, Wharton held an exhibition of the paintings he had done at Fairhope. It had become customary for the artists at New Hope to carve the frames for their oils, so Wharton acquired some woodcarving tools and began carving on simple flat frames. Unlike the New Hope frames, Wharton's designs truly related to the subjects of the paintings – a painting of pine trees would be framed by pinecones and needles. His later carved frames were more geometric than representational. Fairhope was a winter gathering place for writers, painters, and musicians and the Eshericks had made many friends among them. One of these, Mary Marcy, wrote asking Wharton to illustrate a children's book she was writing on evolution, a controversial subject then.

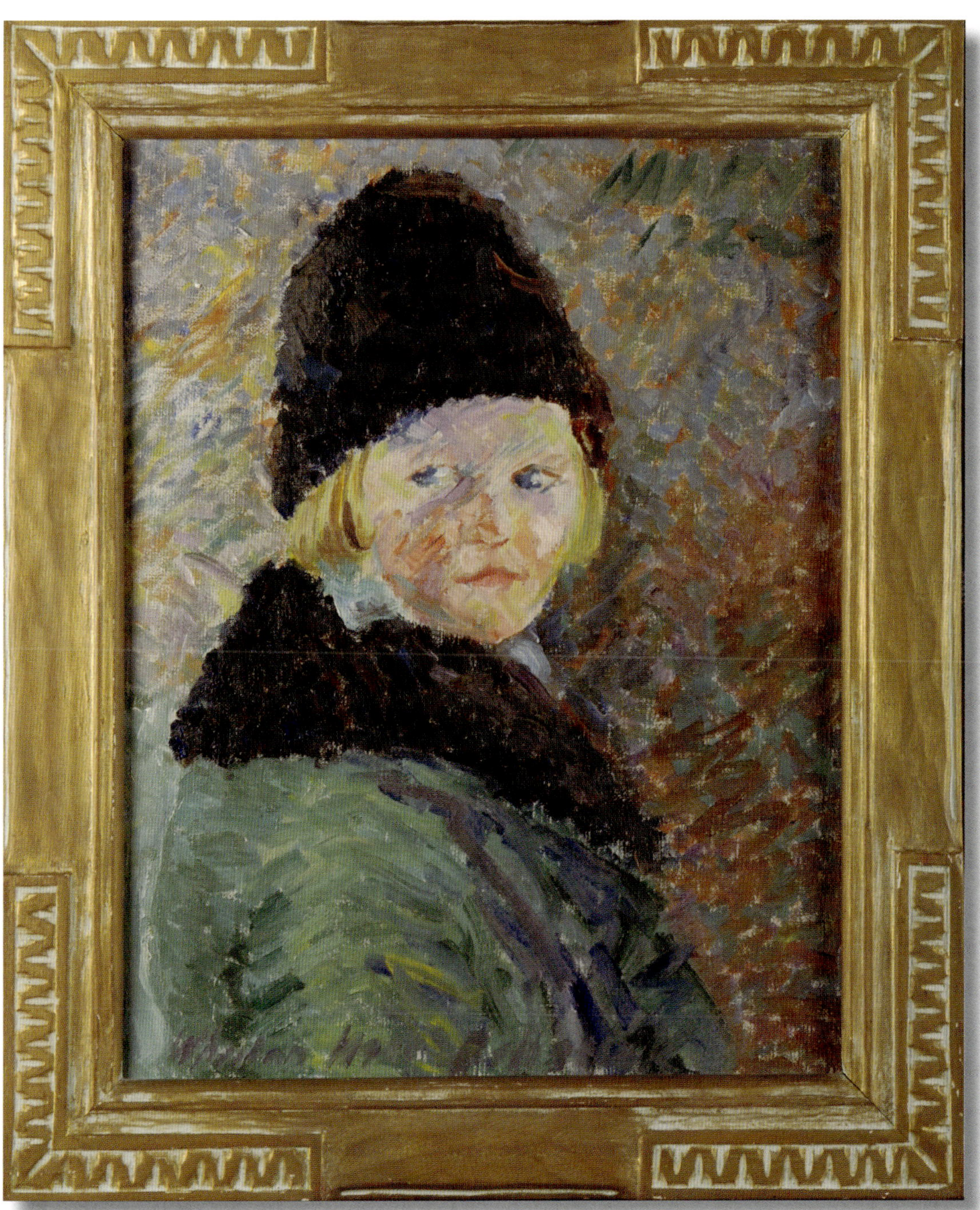

Mary, 1922. Oil on canvas, 20.1 in. X 16 in. Signed "Wharton Harris Esherick 1922." Frame carved and gilded by Esherick.

From Painter to Sculptor

On their return to Paoli, Wharton enlarged their small barn to make a well-lighted painting studio with an adjoining carving shop. He then set to work using his carving tools to illustrate Marcy's *Rhymes of Early Jungle Folk* with 70 woodcuts. Recognizing the artistic merit of the illustrations, Harold Mason, owner of the Centaur Bookshop in Philadelphia, commissioned him to illustrate Walt Whitman's *Song of the Broad-Axe,* followed by *Song of Solomon,* as art books printed on deckle-edged handmade paper in editions of 450 signed and numbered copies.

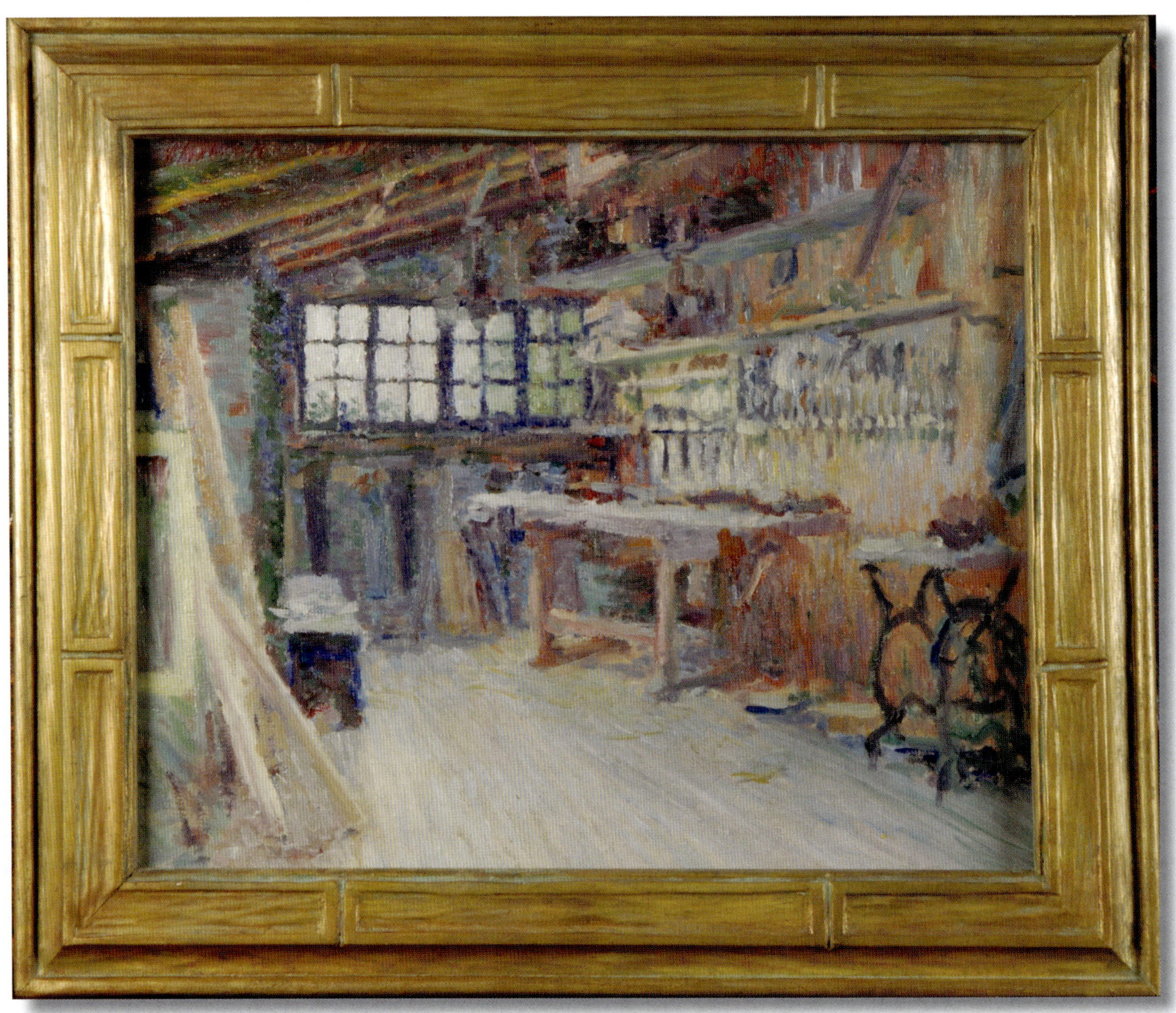

The Wood Carver's Shop, 1922. Oil on canvas, 16.1 in. X 20.1 in. Signed "Wharton Harris Esherick 1922." Esherick's carving shop in the barn at the farmhouse.

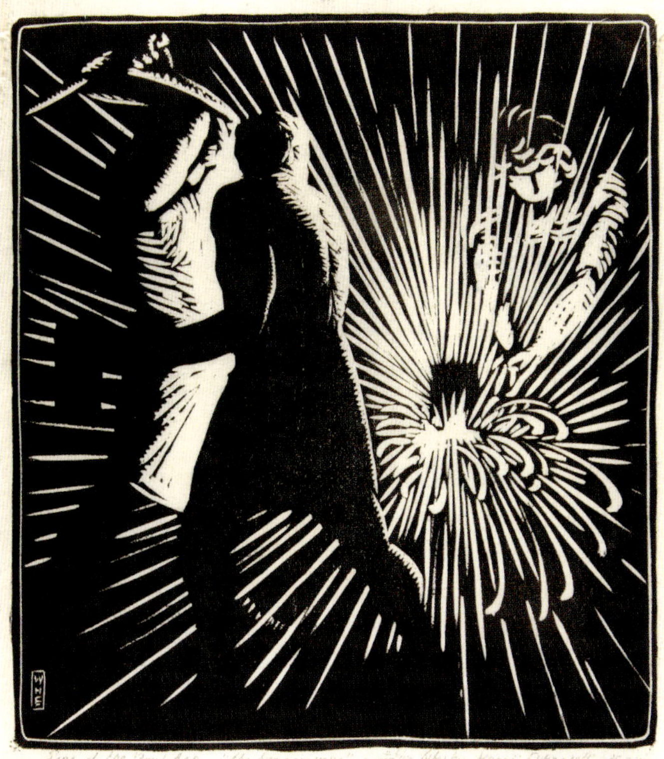

The Hammersmen, 1924. Woodcut print, 10 in. X 9.1 in. Woodcut made for the Centaur Press's 1924 edition of Walt Whitman's *Song of the Broad-Axe*, illustrated by Wharton Esherick.

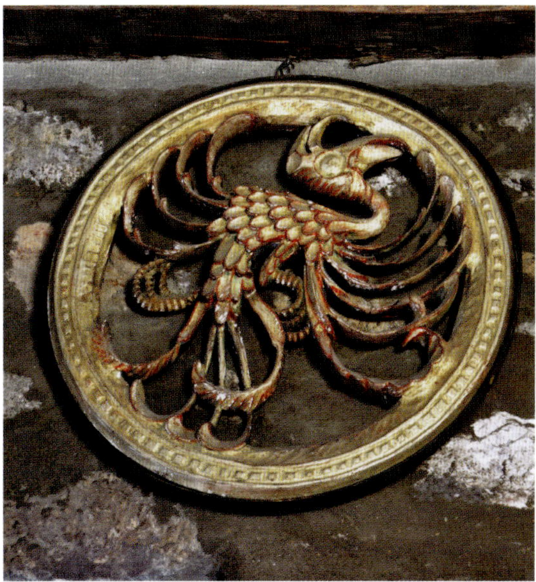

My Zhar Ptitsa (Firebird), 1925. Gilded poplar in iron frame, 25 in. diameter. Signed "Wharton Esherick 1925." Inspired by Stravinsky's musical score, *The Fire Bird*, this piece was used as a grille over a high opening in the wall separating the painting and carving rooms in Wharton's barn studio. *Photo courtesy of James Mario.*

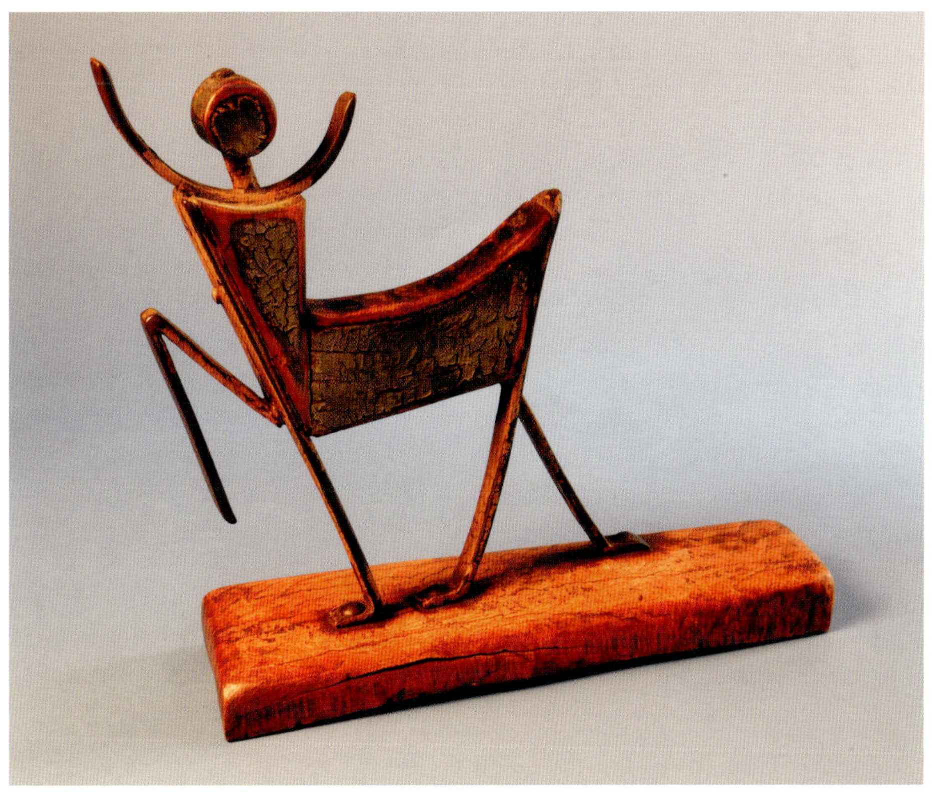

Centaur, 1924. Iron and wood, 15.62 in. X 5.5 in. X 16 in. Inscribed "W.E. to H.M. MCMXXIV." Sign made for the Centaur Book Shop. *Photo courtesy of James Mario.*

Woodcuts were popular at the time and saleable. Over the next several years, Wharton would carve 400 blocks and illustrate nine books. By 1925 he had carved and printed more than 250 blocks and had begun work on a large drop-leaf desk with sliding trays below to hold all those prints and compartments above for the books. It was very much an Arts and Crafts Movement piece with its hand-tooled surfaces, non-uniform dovetails, wooden hinges, and rather Medieval design. On the leaf and doors he carved bas-relief stylized depictions of the trees in the surrounding woods, bare winter branches and turkey buzzards soaring overhead. His influence came from the Rose Valley neighborhood about fifteen miles to the south, where an Arts and Crafts community had been active at the turn of the century, with potters, weavers, painters, and furniture makers sharing studios in an old mill and living in the old workers' houses. The desk was a major undertaking, not signed and dated until 1927. By then, he considered such representational carving to be 'unnecessary literature,' saying, "Furniture, like sculpture, should depend on form, not surface decoration."

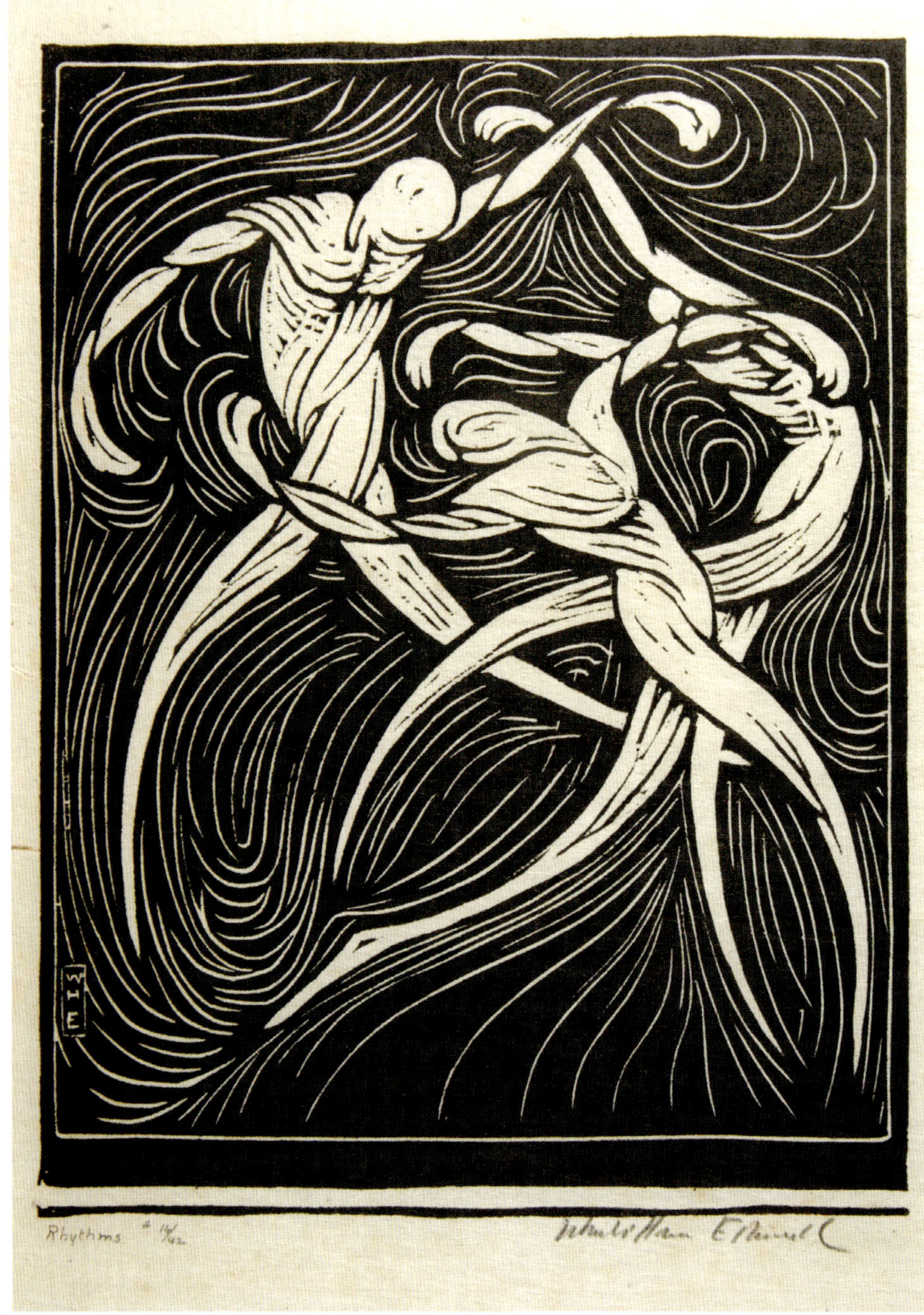

Rhythms, 1922. Woodcut print
6.6 in. X 4.9 in.

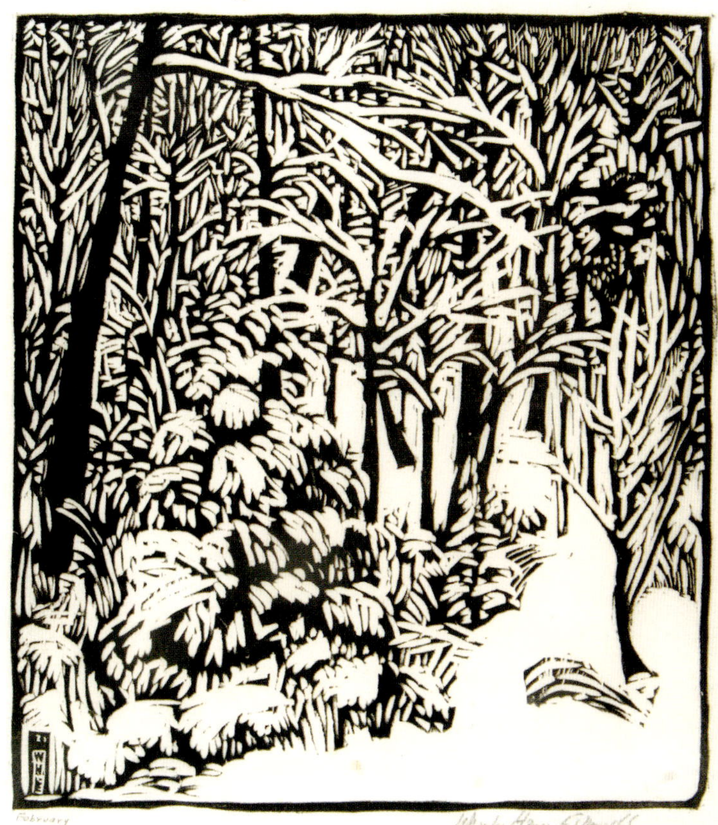

February, 1922. Woodcut print 9.4 in. X 8.5 in. Signed "Wharton Harris Esherick."

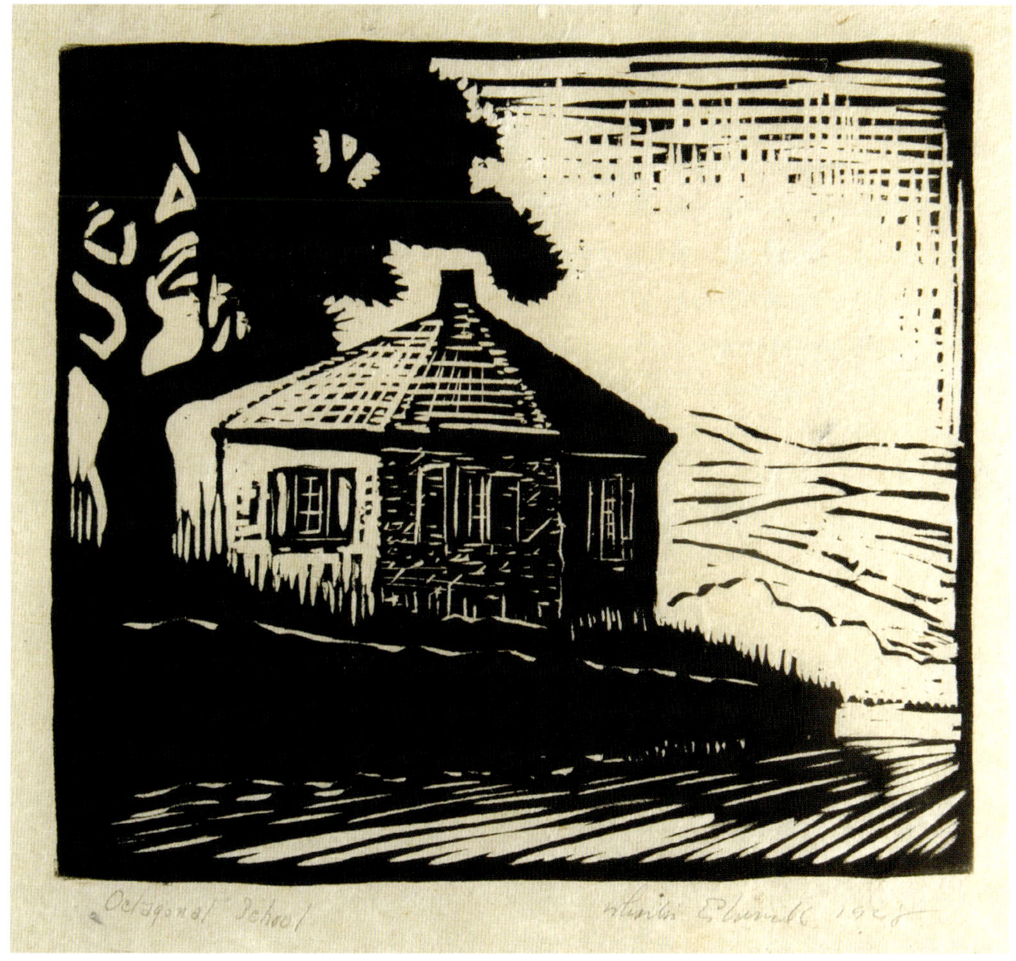

Octagonal School, 1928. Wood engraving, 7 in. X 8 in. Wharton used this octagonal schoolhouse at the foot of Diamond Rock Hill as a painting studio in 1918-19, painting his *Self Portrait* here.

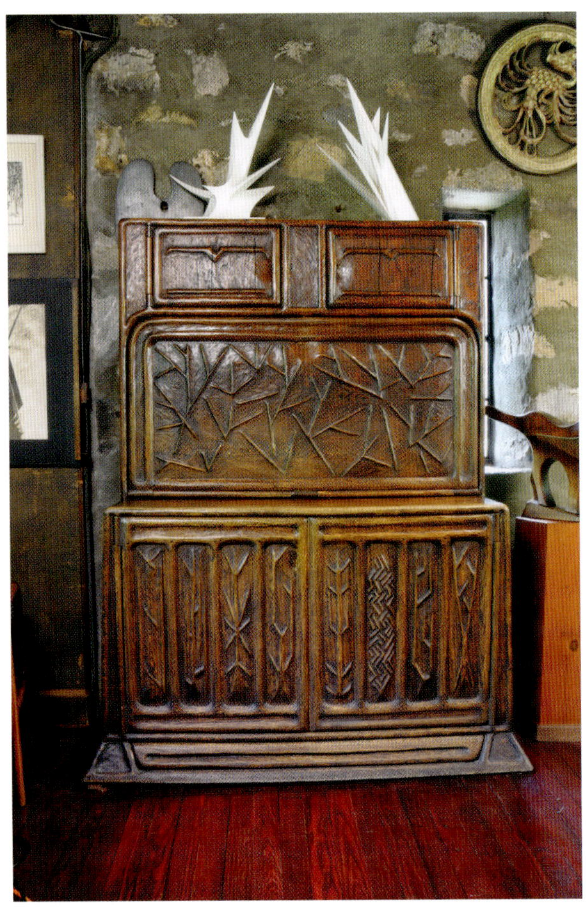

Drop Leaf Desk, 1925-1927. Red oak, 78 in. X 54 in. X 26 in. Signed "W.E. MCMXXVII." *Photo courtesy of James Mario.*

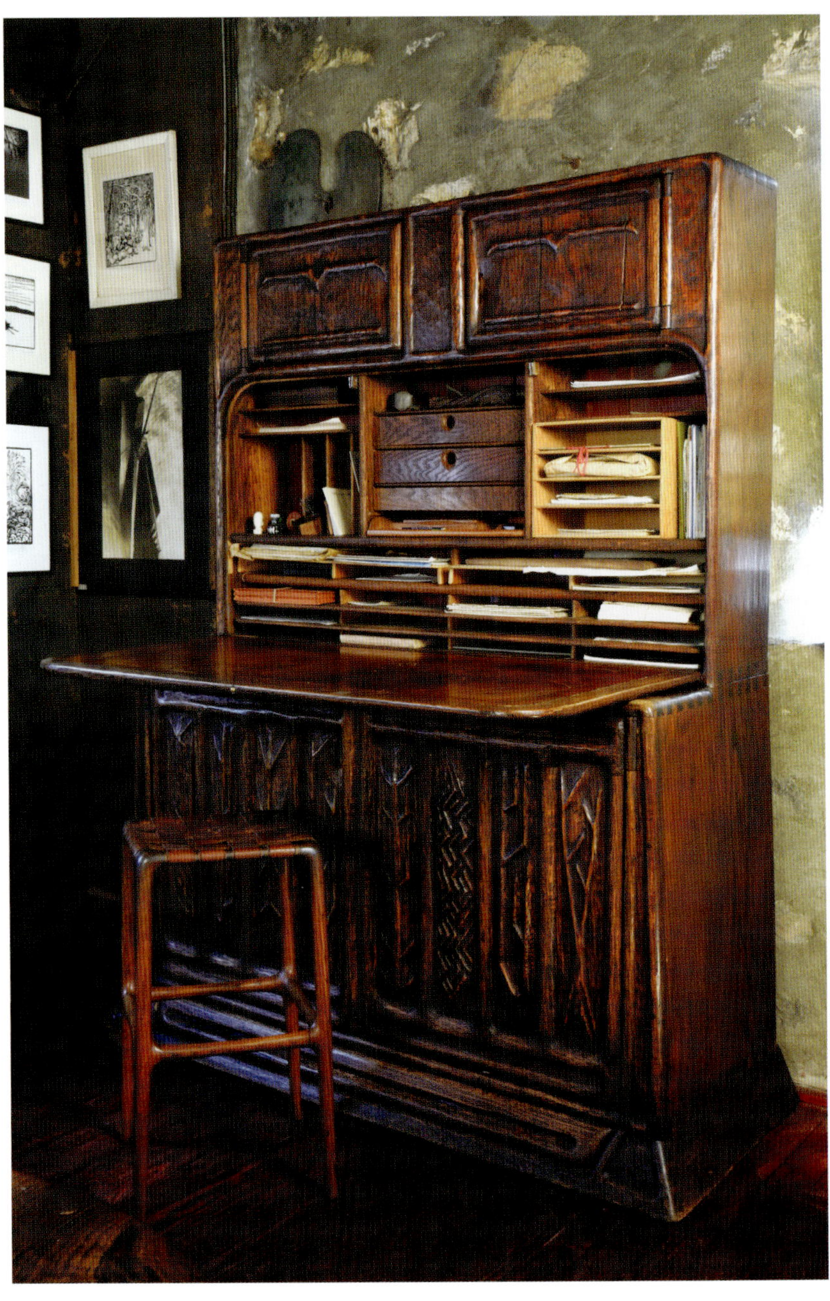

Drop Leaf Desk, open. *Photo courtesy of James Mario.*

In 1923, a group of actors from the Provincetown Players, under the leadership of Jasper Deeter, opened Hedgerow Theatre in an old mill in Rose Valley. Wharton immediately became involved with Deeter's repertory theater, designing stage sets and lighting and carving woodcut posters to promote the shows, and, later, two spiral stairs. Earlier, through friends they had made at Fairhope, Wharton and Letty had been introduced to a rhythmic dance camp in the Adirondacks, and through the Anthroposophists at the camp to the theories of Rudolf Steiner and German Abstract Expressionism. As Wharton's interest in Expressionism turned to fascination, the fantasy of the theater provided him a stage for experimenting. Over the years, Hedgerow Theatre would play a major role in his life, ultimately involving his entire family.

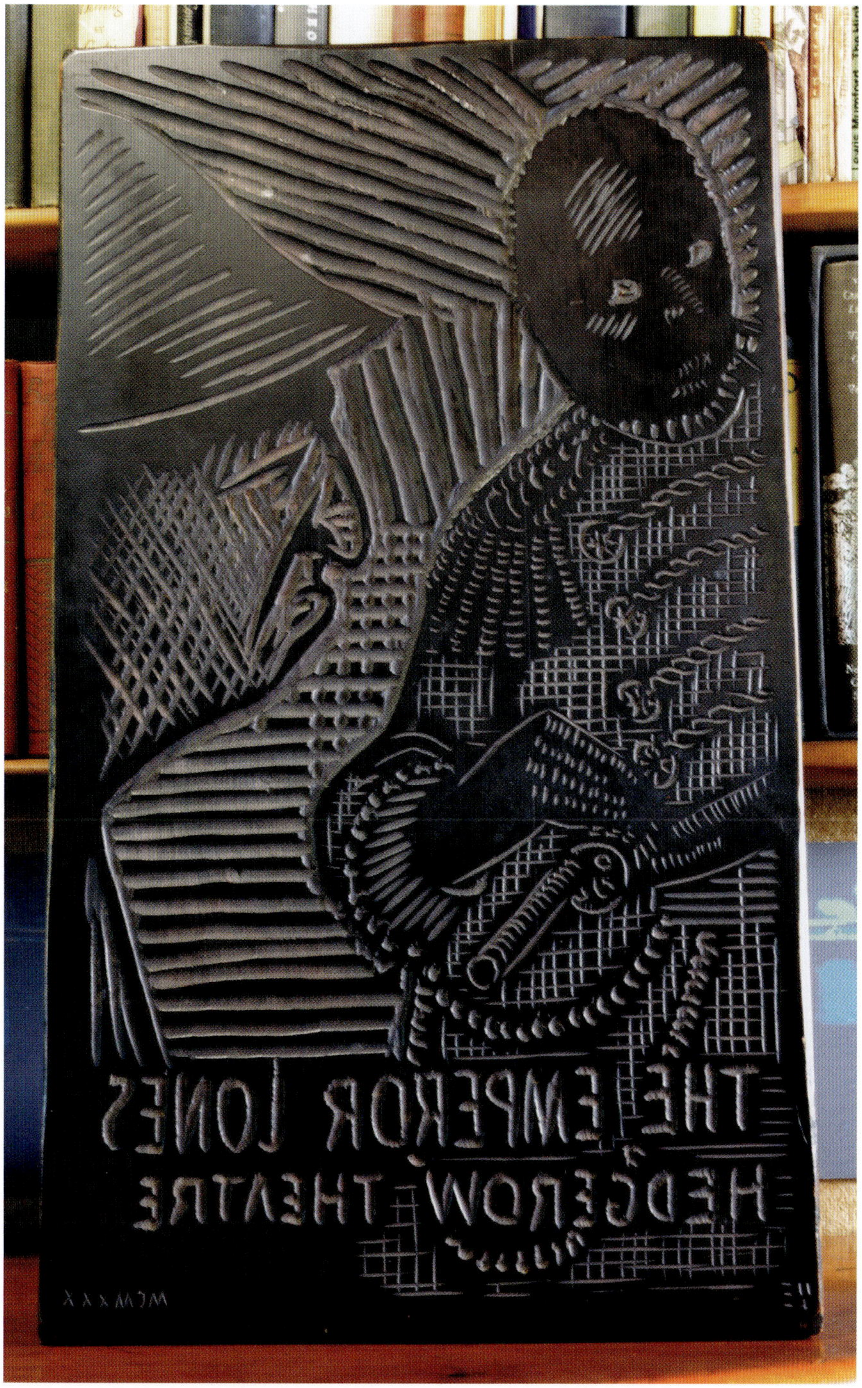

The Emperor Jones, 1930. Wood block 26.6 in. X 15.6 in. Block for posters for Hedgerow Theatre's production of Eugene O'Neill's play; used by Esherick as a headboard. *Photo courtesy of James Mario.*

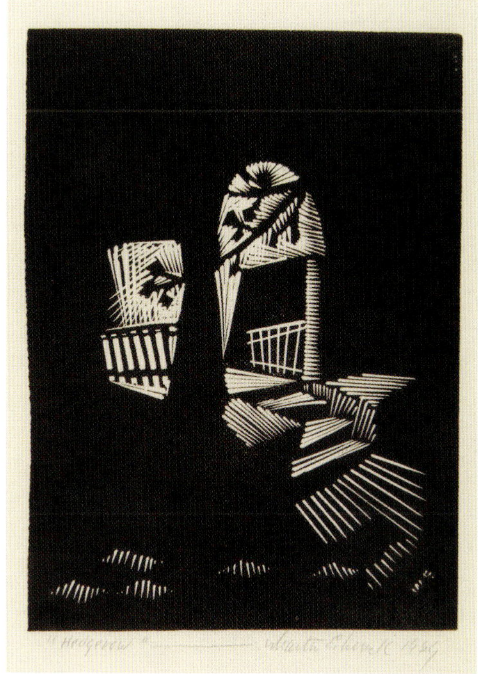

Hedgerow Theatre Entrance, c.1929. Wood Engraving, 7 in. X 5.5 in.

As Wharton became recognized for his woodcuts, sculpture, and furniture, he stacked the paintings and their frames in the barn attic, muttering, "If I can't paint like Esherick, I can, at least, sculpt like Esherick." He had worked at painting, too bound by his training to experiment, but with sculpting he was free and enjoying that freedom and the success it was bringing. Accepting this new reality his motto became "If it isn't fun it isn't worth doing." But In the cramped barn he was able to carve only small pieces, desk-top sculptures, chess sets, and a horse-race game; his commitment to sculpting required a much larger studio. In 1926, at age 39, he acquired the wooded hillside behind the farmhouse and began construction of an Arts and Crafts influenced, barn-like building with stone walls and hand-hewn beams. It combined Frank Lloyd Wright's ideas about organic architecture – of buildings seeming to grow from their sites – with Rudolf Steiner's free curves. The thick stone walls, with deeply raked joints, tapered and curved out at their bases as a tree trunk grows. Where the farmer would have had a large door for the hay wagon he put a window with ribbed glass panes – his north light – that spread an even, non-glare light throughout the room.

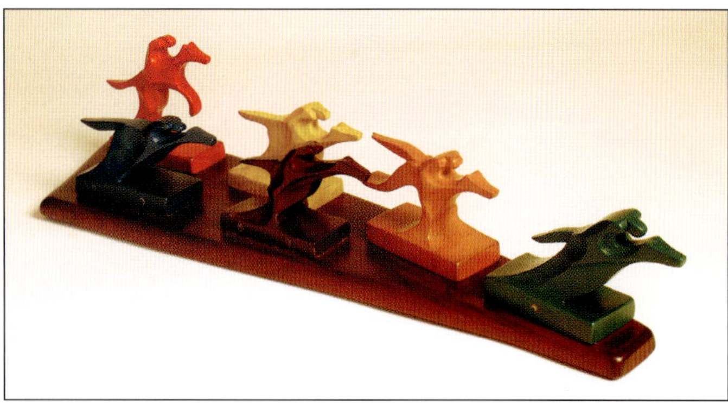

The Race, 1925. Painted wood on walnut base, 6.8 in. X 30.7 in. X 8.5 in. Signed "W.E. 1920," the year the Eshericks played a horse race game aboard the boat on their trip to Fairhope, Alabama. Wharton said that the horses looked like they were asleep in their barn. He carved this game to see if he could make horses that showed some speed. Wharton did not date his pieces consistently. In this case, the date was put on much later when he mounted the game pieces to the base. *Photo courtesy of Mark Sfirri.*

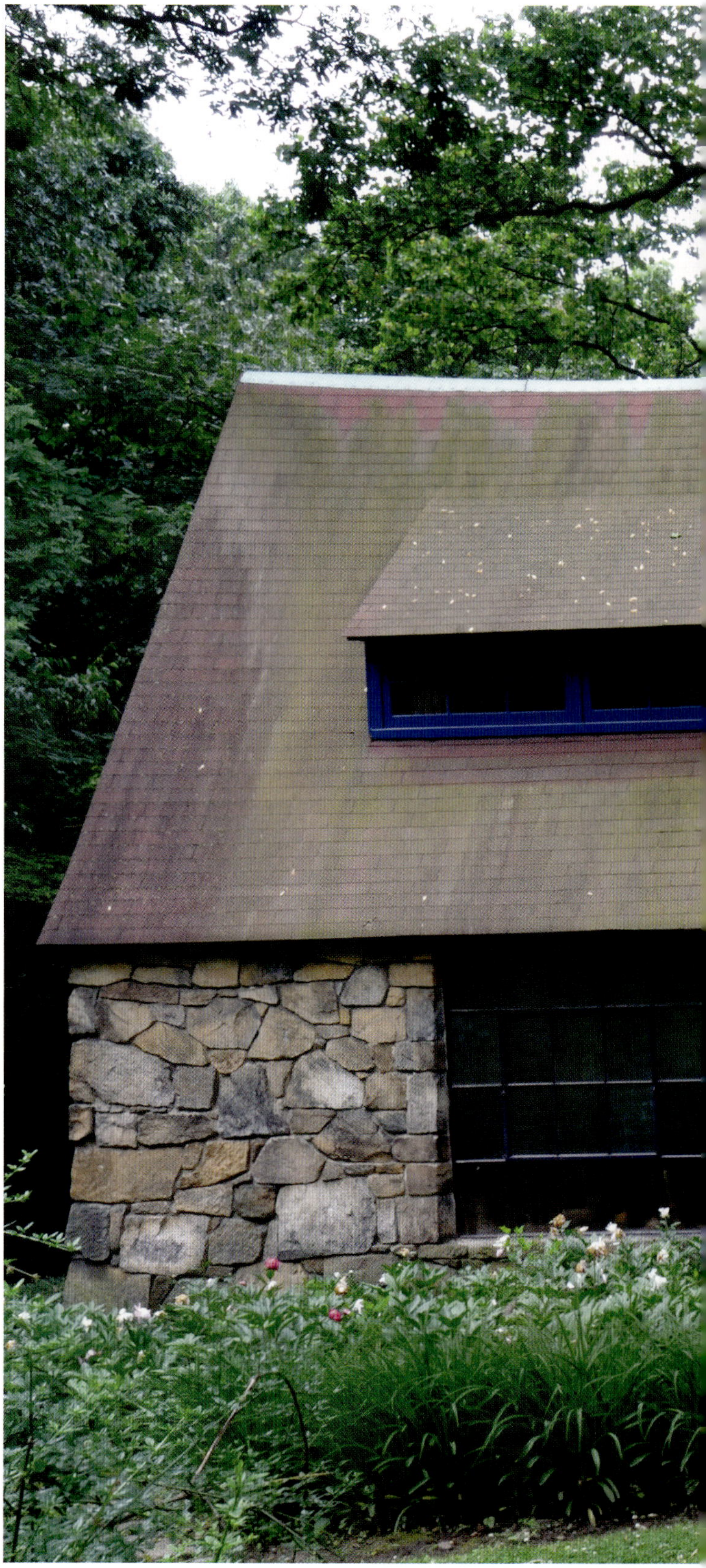

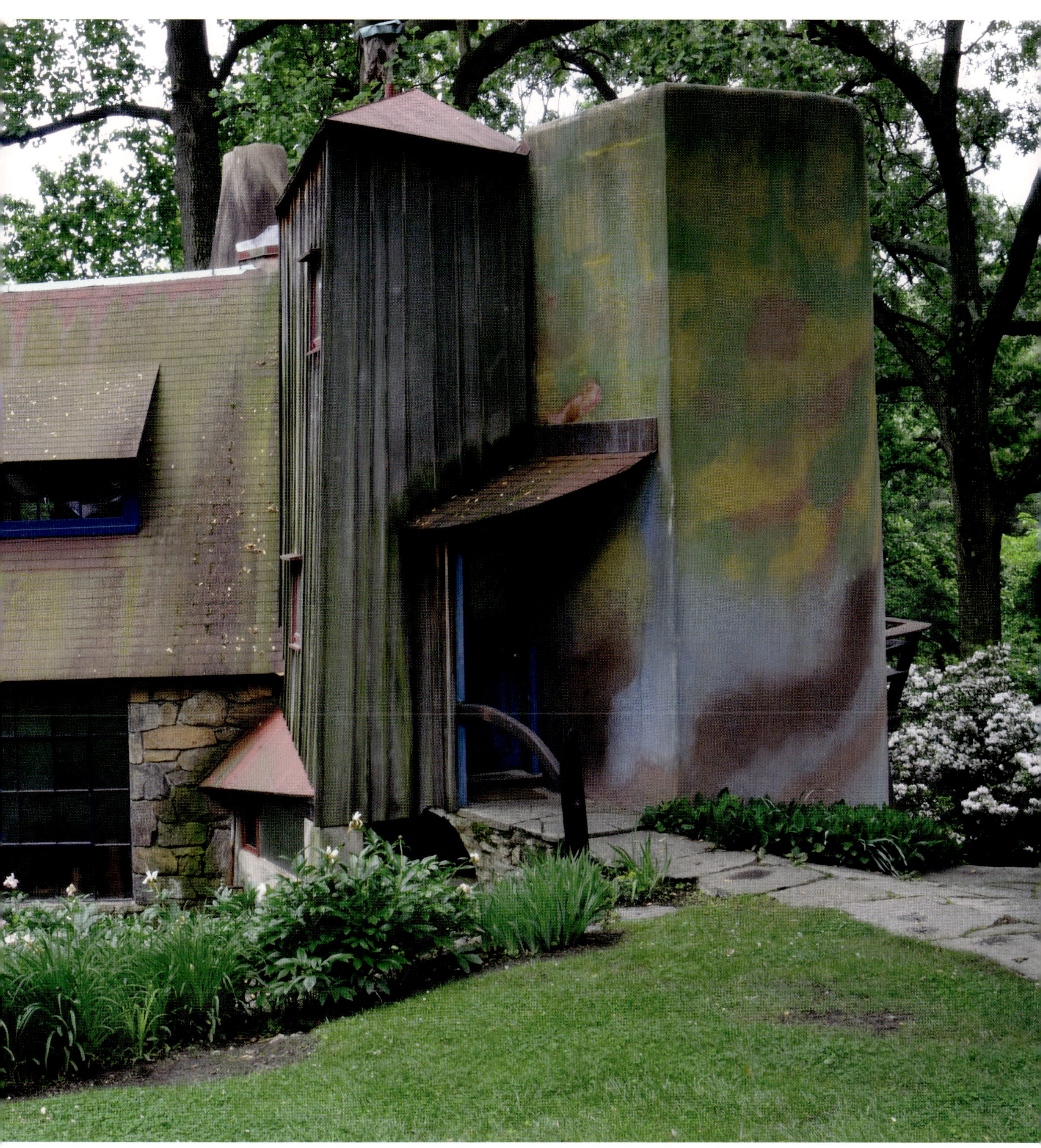

The Studio, 1926-1966. The stone portion to the left was the first part, constructed in 1926. A wooden addition was constructed in 1940, a bath in 1947, and the silo added in 1966. *Photo courtesy of James Mario.*

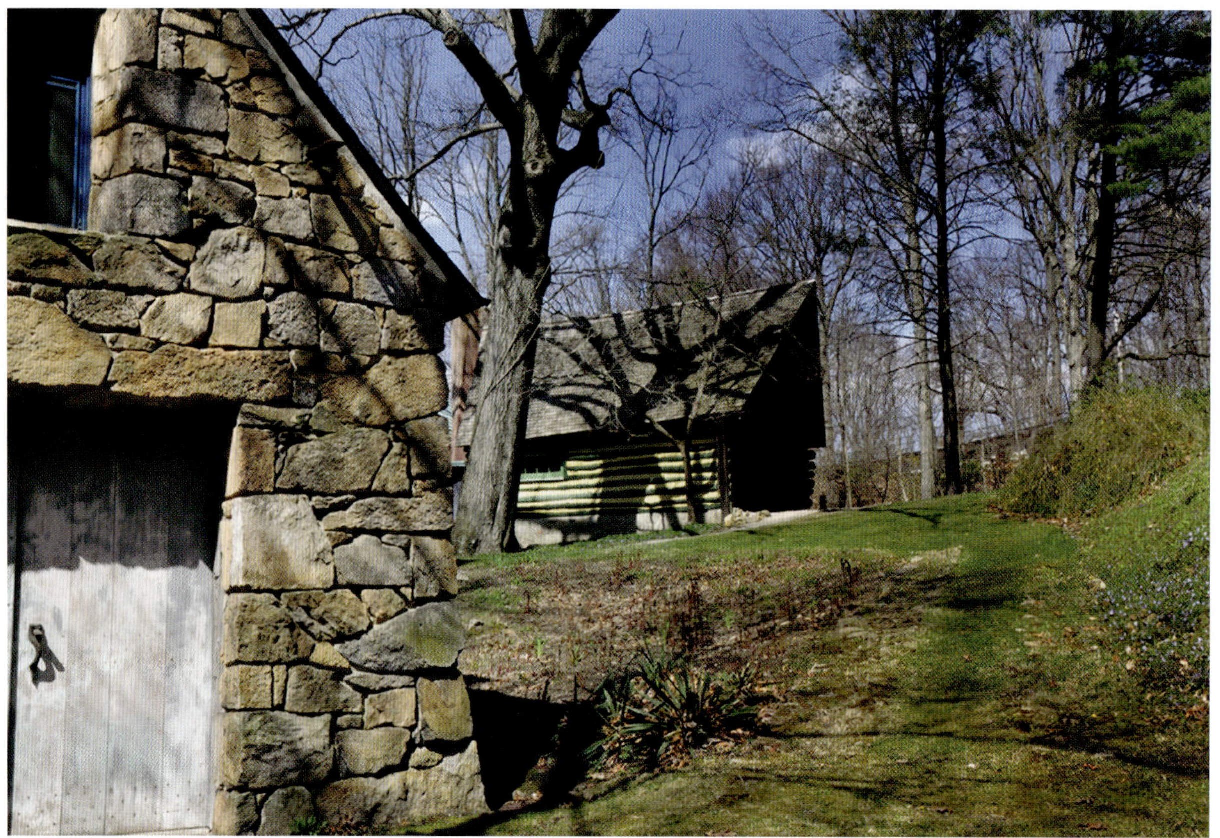

The studio from the east. Note the wall tapering like a tree growing from the ground. In the background is Esherick's 1928 garage. *Photo courtesy of James Mario.*

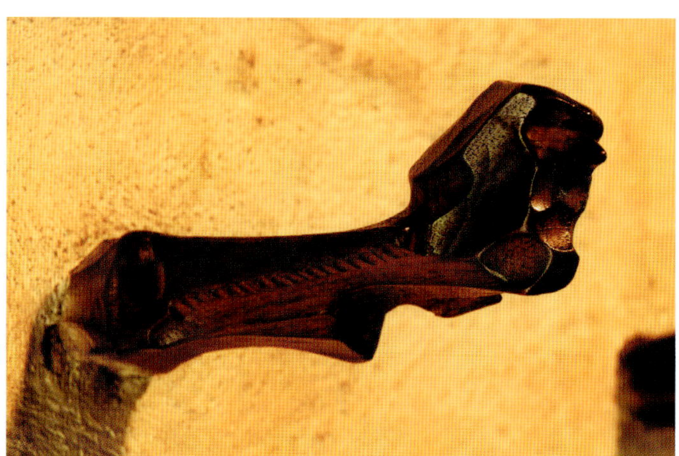

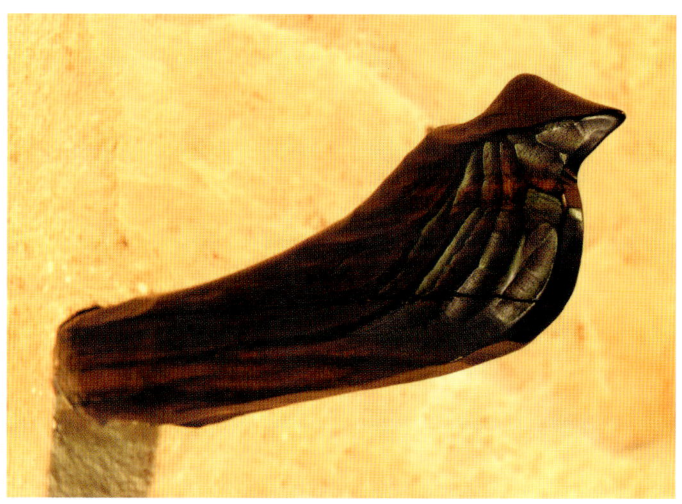

Coat hooks, 1926. Caricaturing the men who helped Wharton build the studio – cabinet maker John Schmidt, the bird that sang to them while they worked, stone mason Albert Kulp, hod carrier Aaron Coleman, laborer Larry Hand, and Wharton, himself, overseeing them all with his hammer and chisel. *Photos courtesy of Mark Sfirri.*

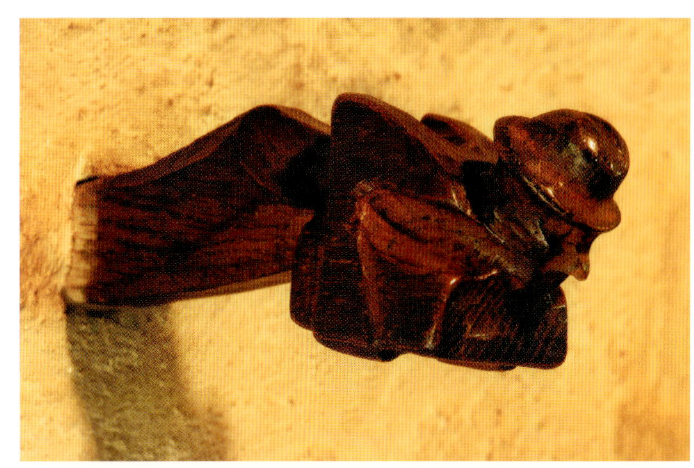

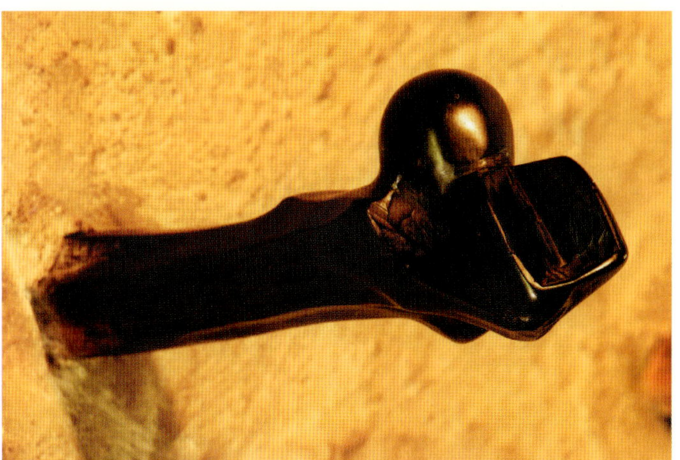

The uphill half of his new studio had a packed earth floor to support large, heavy logs and provide good footing for swinging the broad-axe, which would become his favorite sculpting tool. The downhill half had a basement for a kitchen, shower, coal furnace, and coal bin, with a wood floor above, strong enough for his heavy cast-iron printing press and carving bench. At one end was a large loading door and in the corner a stair to a loft with an outside loading door for storing lumber. He sculpted the door latches and carved outlines of birds on the loading doors. Next to the front door, at the corner nearest the farmhouse, he sculpted coat pegs into caricatures of the workmen who built the studio, including himself cutting stone, and the bird that had cheered them on as they worked. His mind was always busy with his work, even letting his subconscious resolve problems in his sleep. He converted the loft to a summer bedroom so he could be with his work day and night, while Letty and the children went off to rhythmic dance camp.

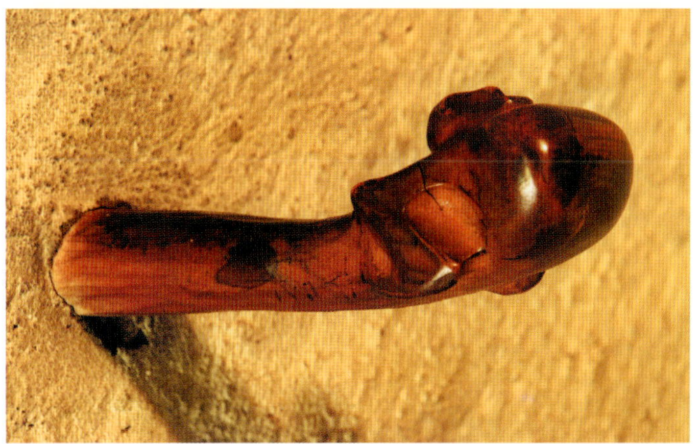

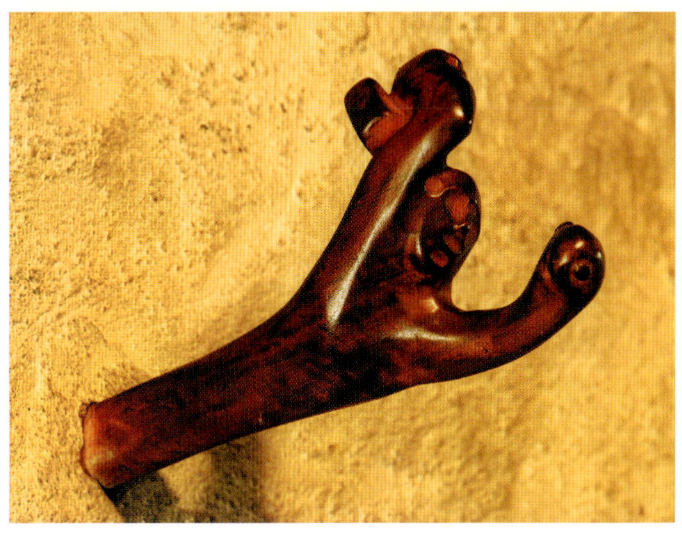

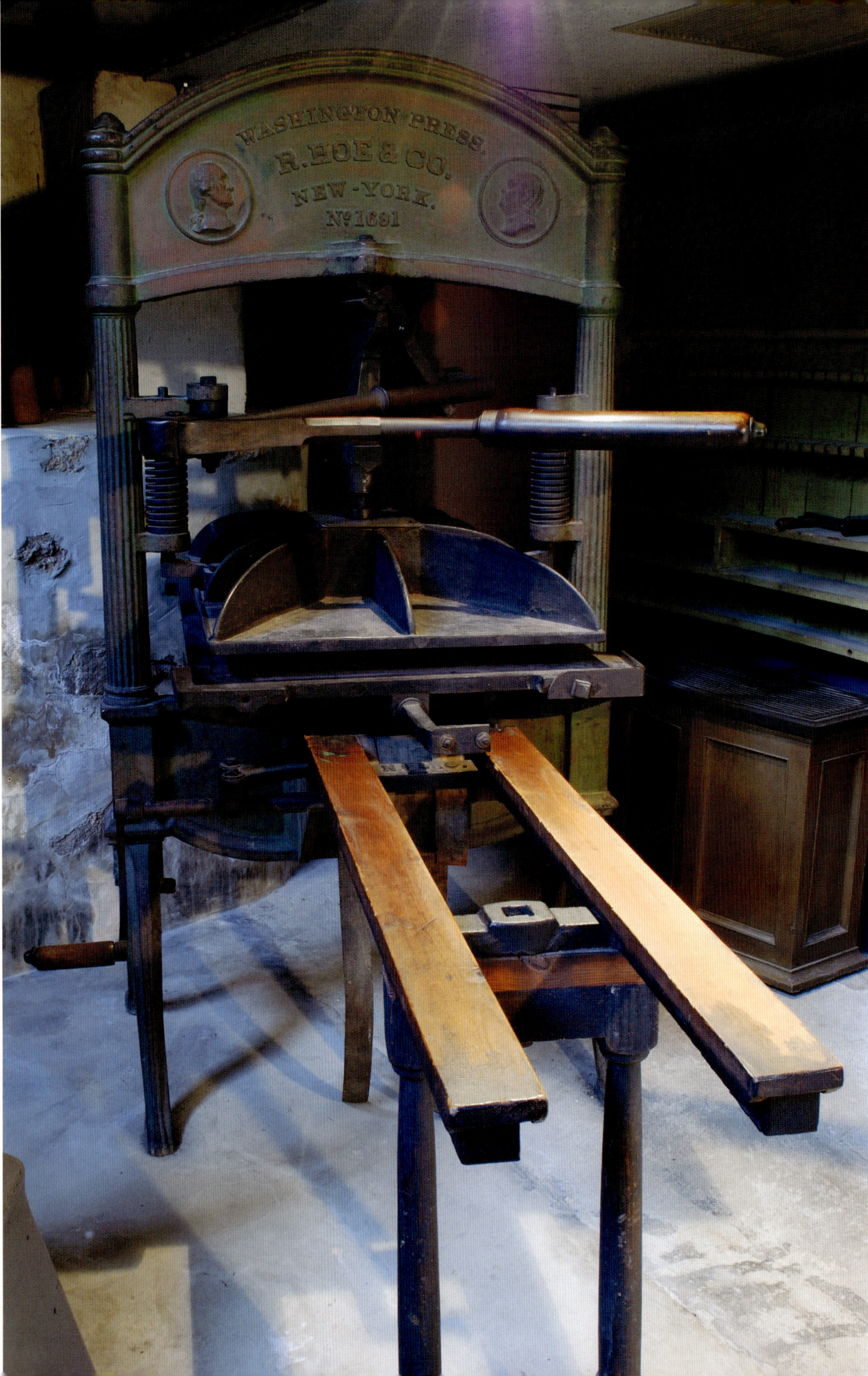
WASHINGTON PRESS.
R. HOE & CO.
NEW-YORK.
No 1691

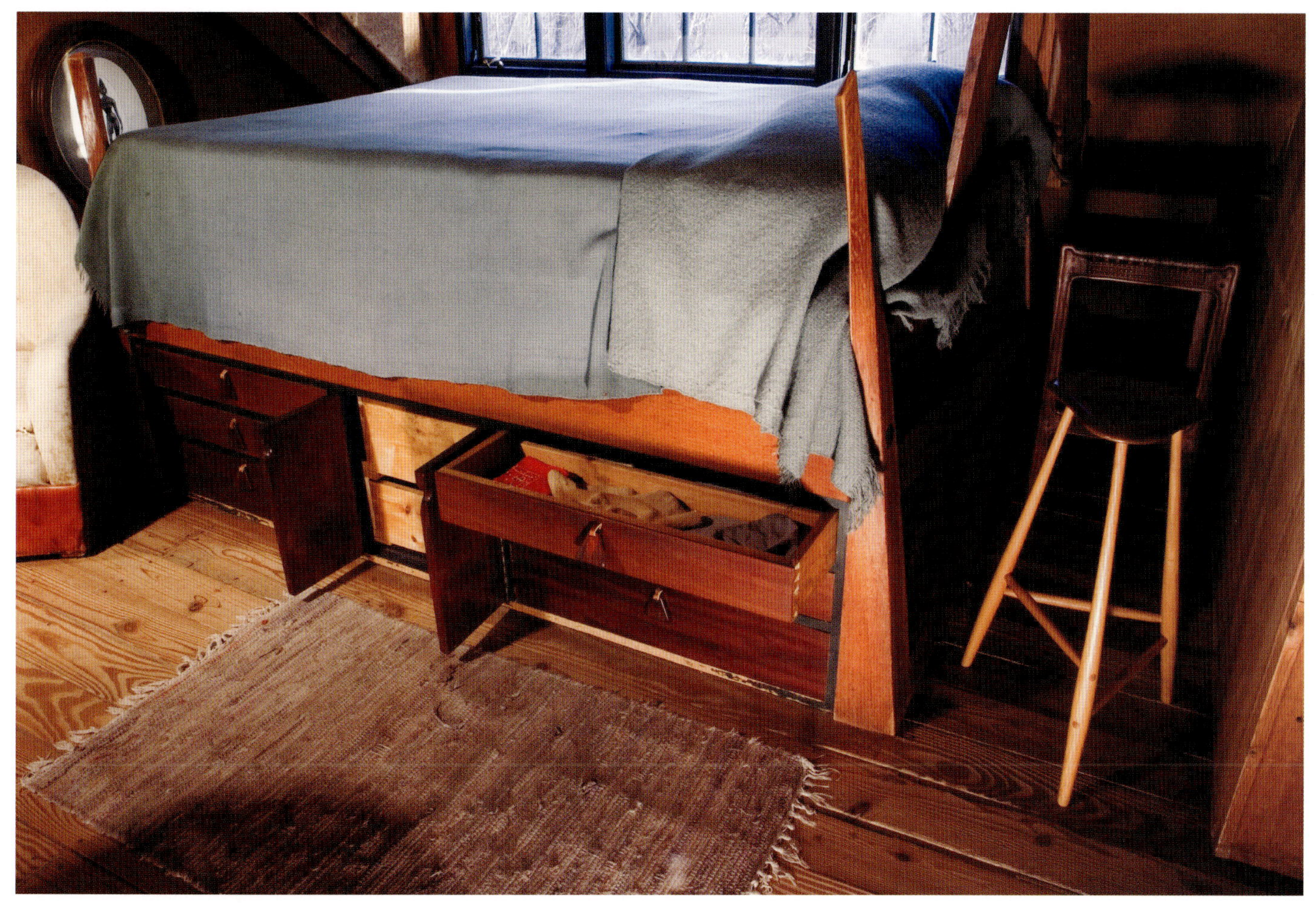

Two Poster Bed, c. 1928. Oak, mahogany, and padouk, 44.5 in. X 85.7 in. X 58.7 in.
Photo courtesy of James Mario.

[opposite]
Washington Press, c.1836. Esherick acquired this press from the Pottstown Mercury and used it to make his wood cut prints. *Photo courtesy of Mark Sfirri.*

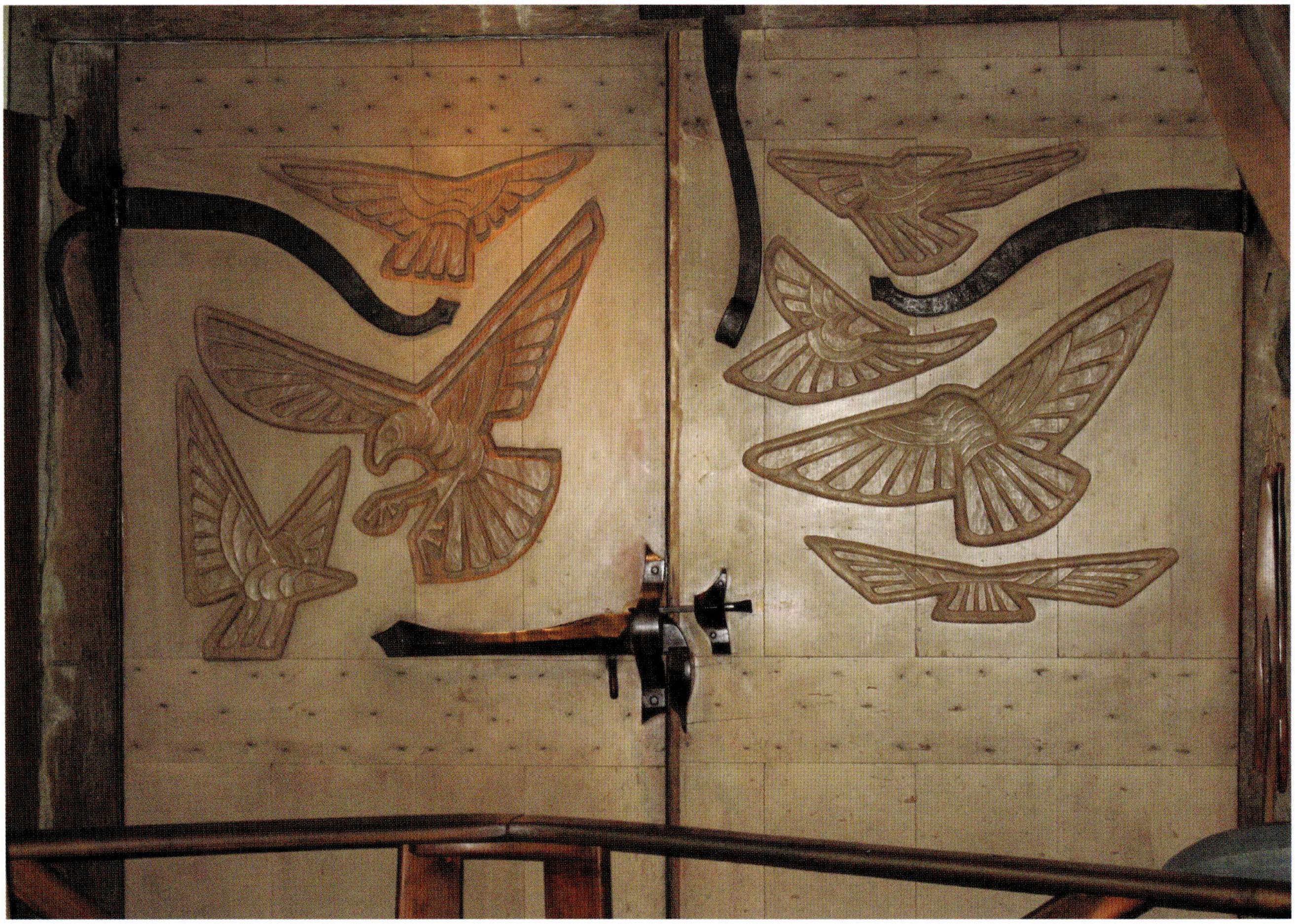

Loading Doors, 1926. Hand forged hinges and macassar ebony latch.

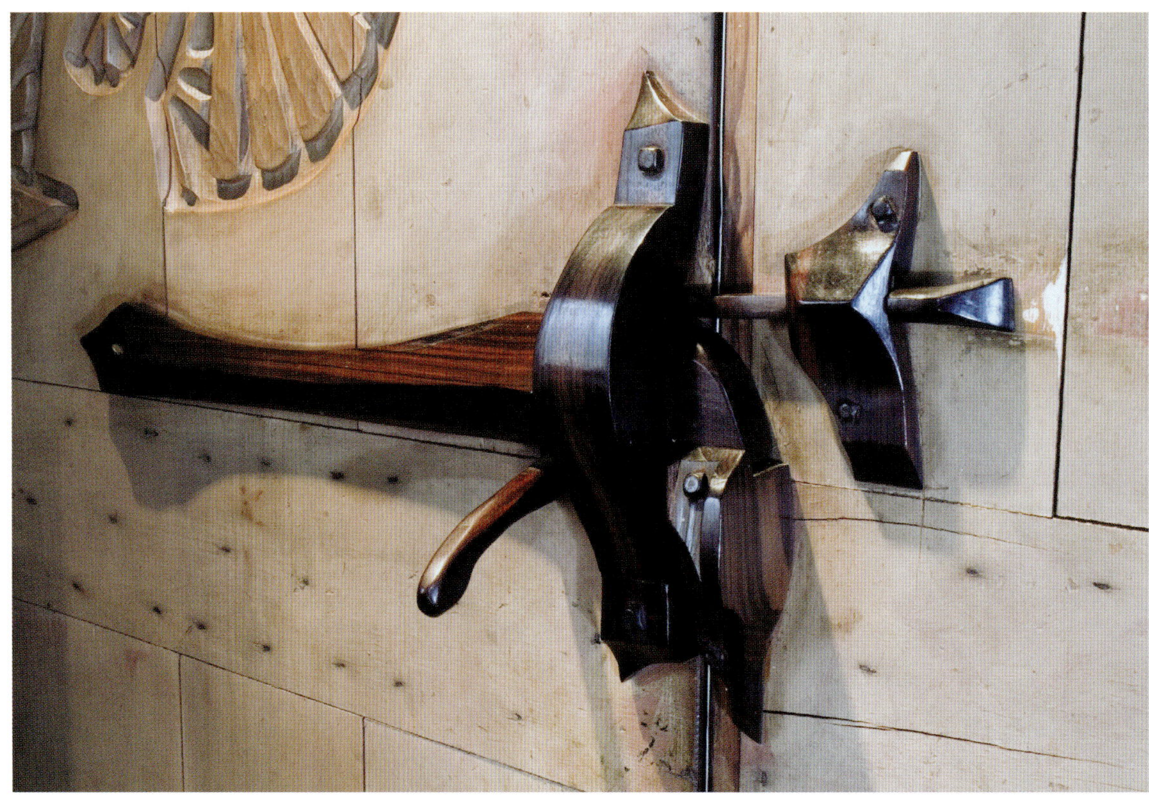

Loading door handle, 1926. Macassar ebony. *Photo courtesy of James Mario.*

By the time he finished the studio he had abandoned the romantic Arts and Crafts style for the more intellectual Expressionism with its asymmetric, prismatic forms. He tried these forms first on a new outhouse – a truncated, three-sided pyramid reminiscent of the 1919 German Expressionist film *The Cabinet of Dr. Caligari* – and next on a two-car garage, offsetting the roof's peak to the right at the front and the left at the rear so the ridge ran diagonally and each rafter was on a different slope. The result was a pair of warped roof surfaces – hyperbolic parabaloids – one appearing concave, the other convex. He repeated these curves in the walls, fanning them higher at the front. Having more trees than money, he built it of readily available oak and chestnut logs, expressing a modern design through a primitive building material.

The new studio was fine for sculpting, but he would need the skills and tools of a cabinet-maker to construct the larger, more complex furniture pieces he envisioned. Fortuitously, John Schmidt, a competent craftsman, had just set-up shop in a small barn over the hill on Jug Hollow Road. The two men began a thirty-year friendship. Though there were often disagreements on the size and shape of a joint, John's skills proved up to every challenge Wharton's designs presented. One of the first such challenges was a dining set unlike anything anyone had done before. The five-sided, three-legged table was made of fanning walnut boards separated by narrow ebony strips. The slender prismatic legs were as awkward as those of a young knock-kneed colt. The tabletop and leg designs were repeated in a backless bench and three chairs, one of them having only three legs. Though cubist in concept, the edges were softly rounded.

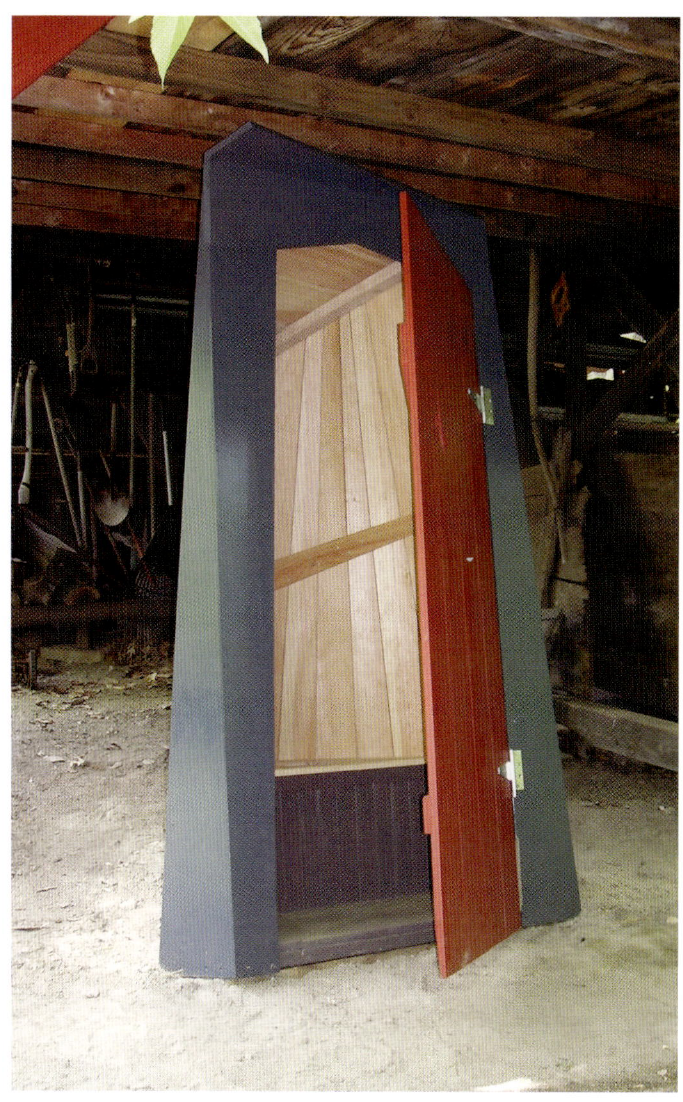

Outhouse, designed c. 1927, reconstructed 2008

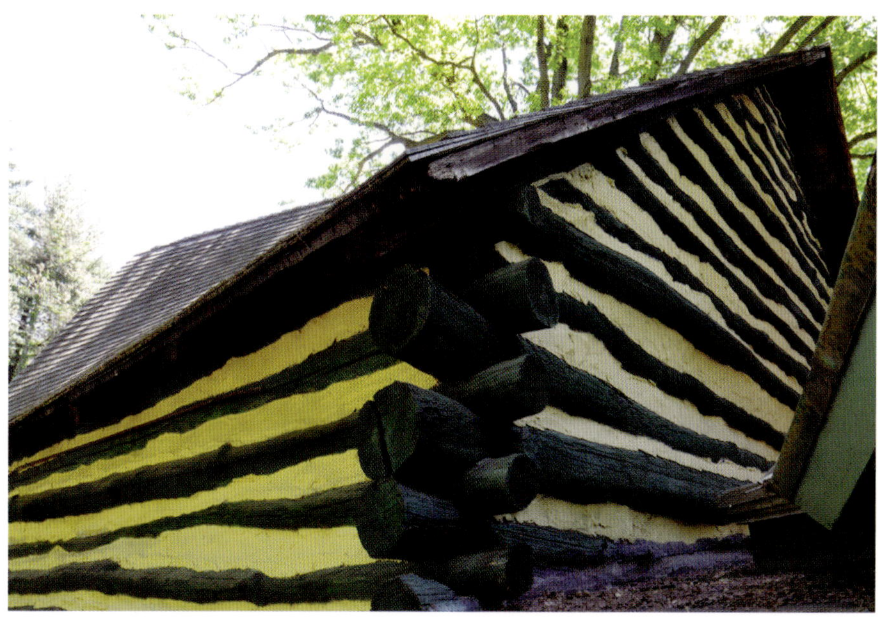

Log Garage, 1928. *Photo courtesy of James Mario.*

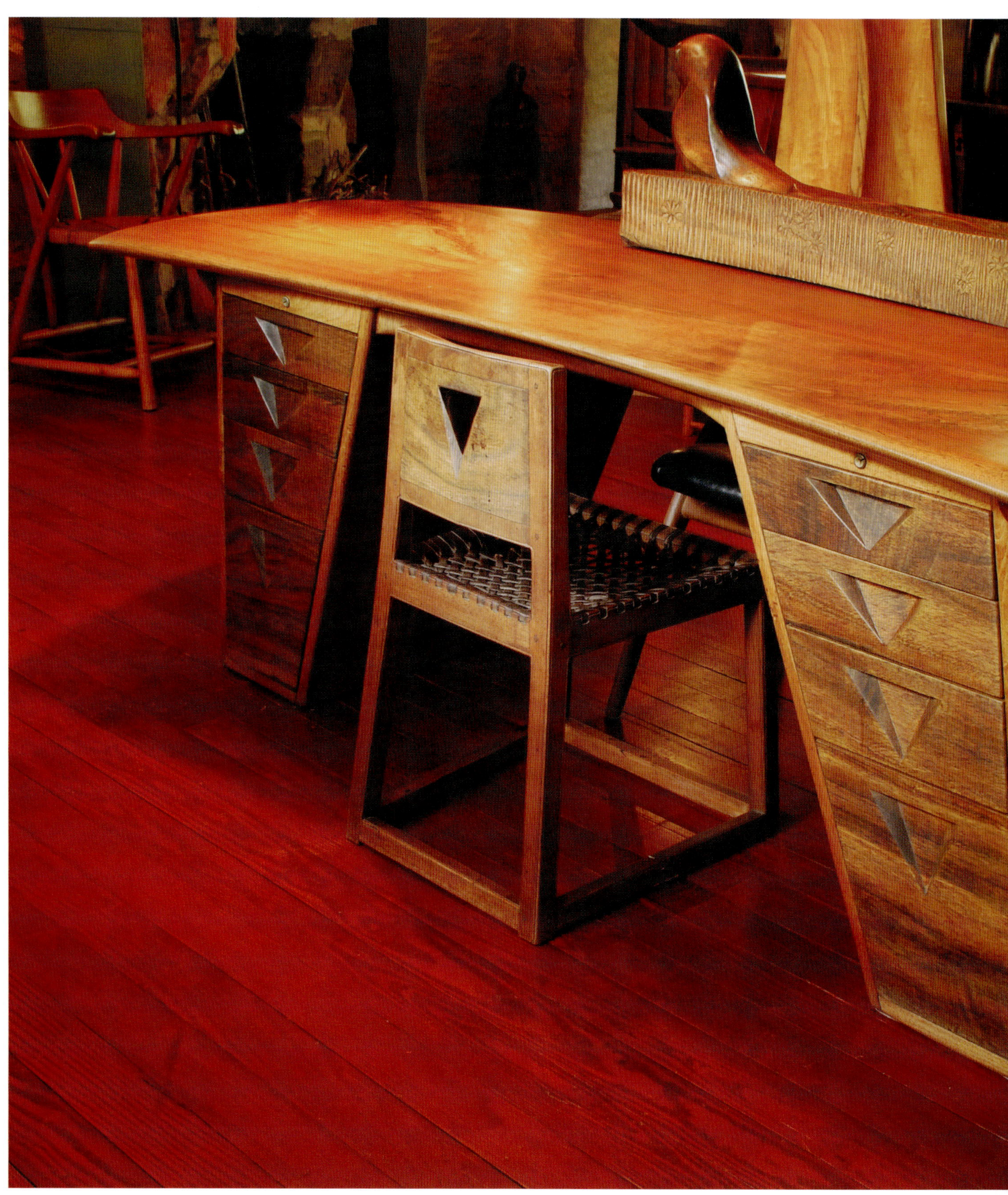

Flat-Top Desk, 1929 (pedestal) and 1962 (top). Walnut and padouk, 28.3 in. X 82.3 in. X 36.4 in. Signed "W.E. 1929 + 1962." The original top was made of 3/16-inch aluminum, the present top made in 1962. *Photo courtesy of Mark Sfirri.*

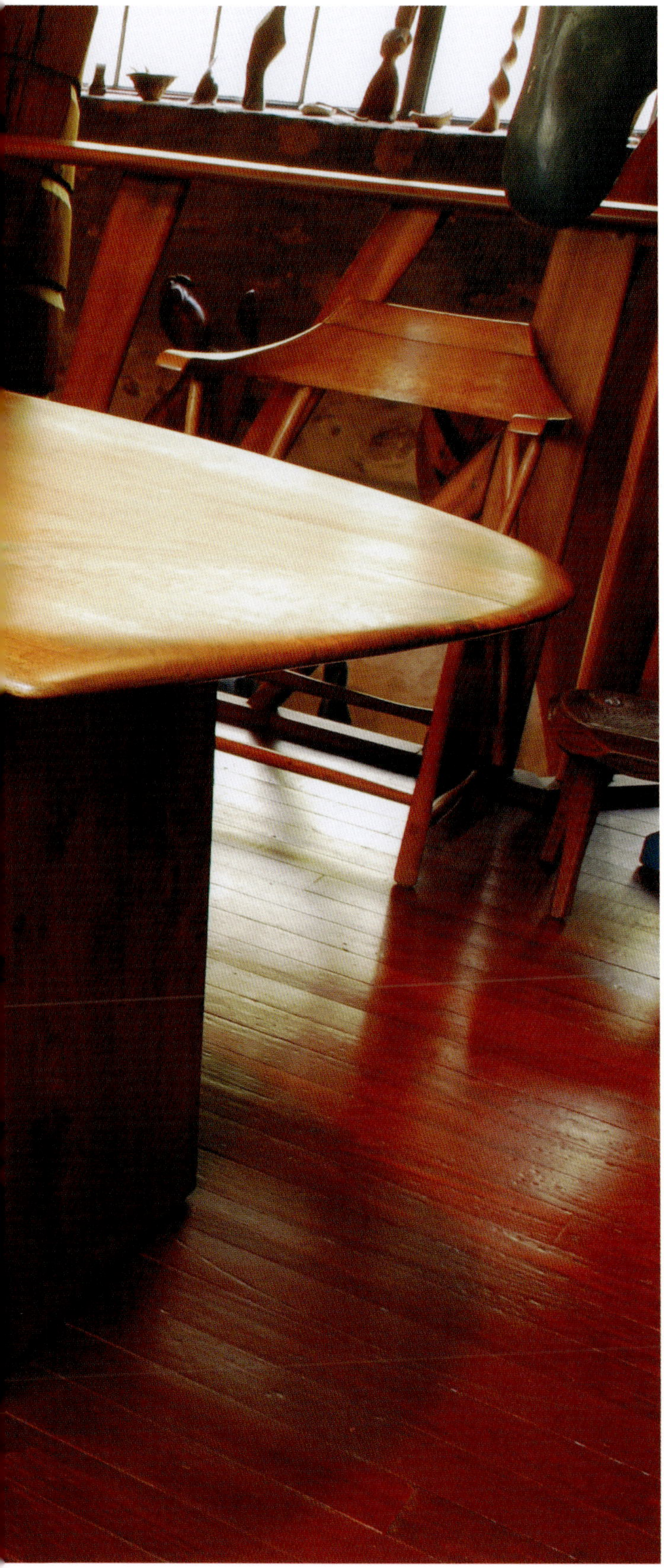

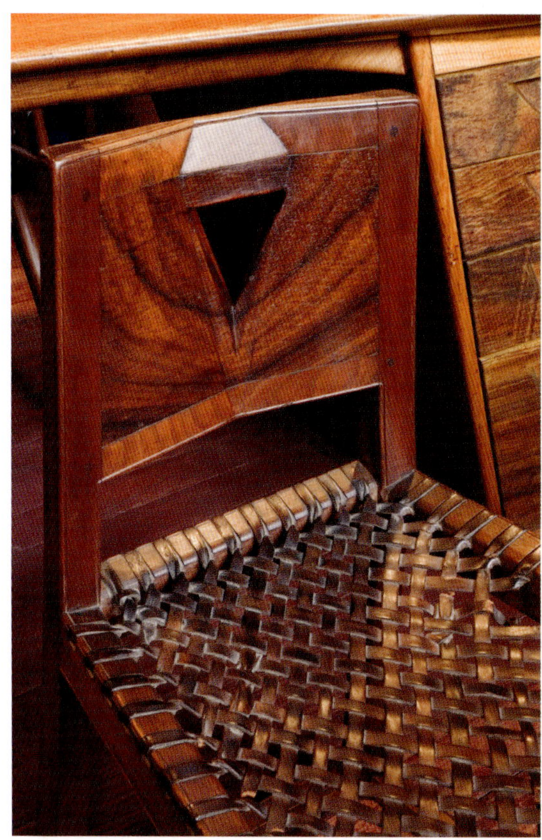

Desk Chair, 1929. Padouk and walnut, laced leather seat, 27.8 in. X 18 in. X 18 in. Signed "WHARTON ESHERICK 1929 J.S." Made for the Flat-Top Desk with the help of the cabinet maker John Schmidt *Photo courtesy of James Mario.*

This was quickly followed by an Expressionist flat-top pedestal desk combining metal and wood in the Bauhaus manner. Wharton had made temporary tables by placing boards on sawhorses, inverting the sawhorses just for fun. He adapted the resulting V design for the pedestals with drawers, and made it even more dynamic by tilting the V. Aluminum had just become commercially available and he used a rectangular 3/16" plate for the top, supporting it above the wood pedestals just enough to accommodate slide-out extensions at each end. In the big carved oak drop-leaf desk, the pulls were concealed within the design; here they became the design, repeating the triangular shapes of the pedestals. Wharton sketched his design for a matching desk chair, leaving the details to John. Those details were sufficiently significant that both men signed the chair.

Letty had taught rhythmic dancing at Sunekrest and had hoped to open a school there. She had taken their daughters Mary and Ruth, and infant son Peter to Croton-on-Hudson, New York, to start a school with friends from the dance camp, until a permanently debilitating attack of encephalitis ended all of Letty's dreams. Wharton had made a set of chairs for the school, one for the teacher and one for each of the five students. The chairs were cubes, with laced leather seats and backs assembled of identical legs, stretchers, and rails that flowed continuously, similar in concept to Marcel Breuer's chairs of plastic- laced, chrome-plated tubing of the same year.

Hessian Hills Chair, 1924. Red oak, laced leather seat and back, 26.3 in. X 15 in. X 15 in. Signed "W.E. 1924." Design made for the Hessian Hills School in Croton, NY. Six chairs were exchanged for daughter Mary's tuition. *Photo courtesy of Mark Sfirri.*

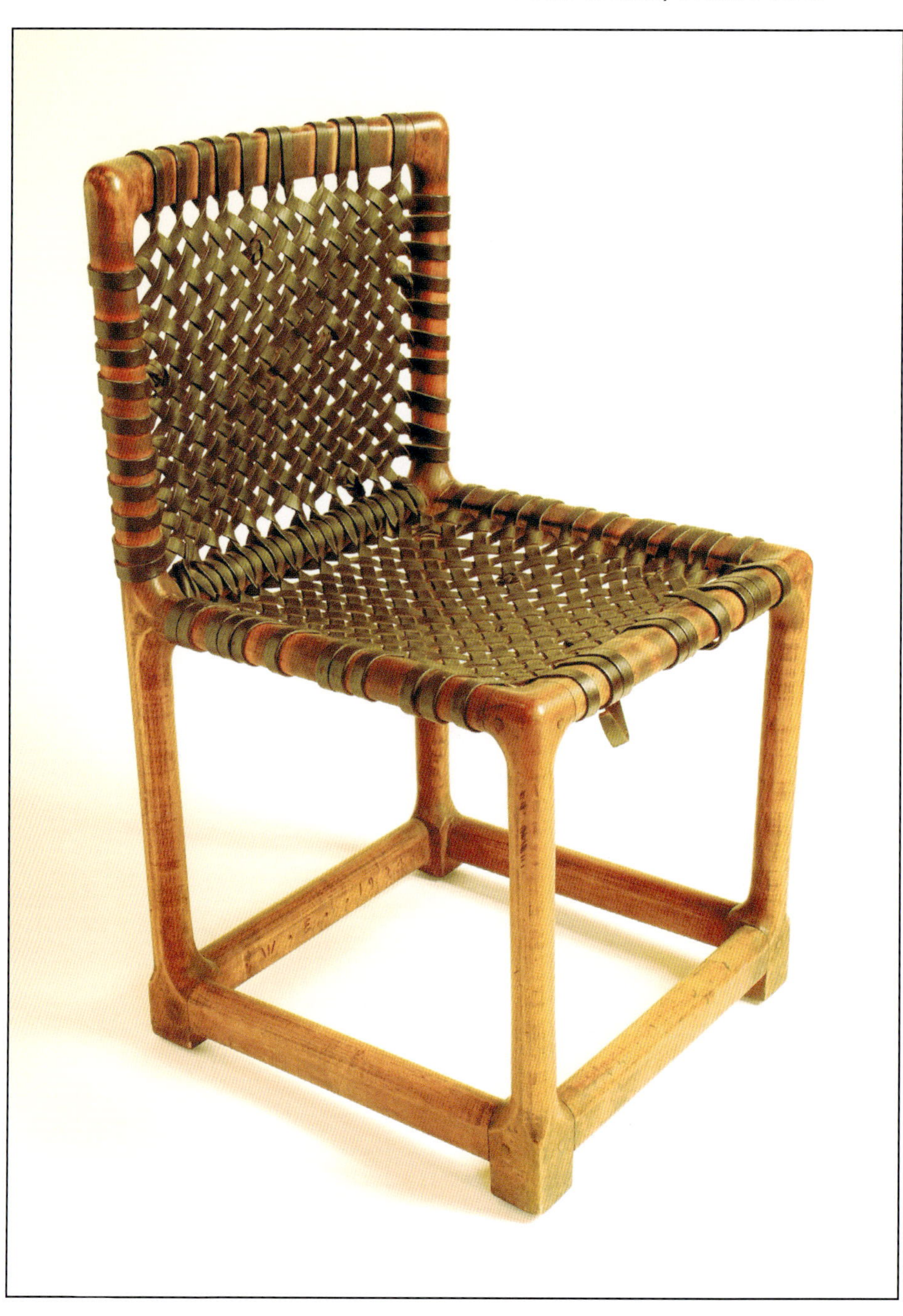

Unable to find a gallery willing to accept and show their work, a group of New York area artists working in craft media, including Henry Varnum Poor and Ruth Reeves, organized The American Artists Gallery, and invited Wharton to exhibit with them. The aluminum-topped desk may well have been made for that purpose, but the stock market failure of 1929 eliminated potential buyers and the gallery closed. With time on his hands, he began work on a new stair for the studio, close to the front door – a stair hewn of oak with treads cantilevered from a common surface of the spiraling central post, like the teeth of some gigantic gear. Realizing that a true spiral stair would require raising the roof, he projected a branch paralleling the roof slope, thus creating a tree form. Though the concept is expressionist, the rough-hewn members give the stair an organic feeling.

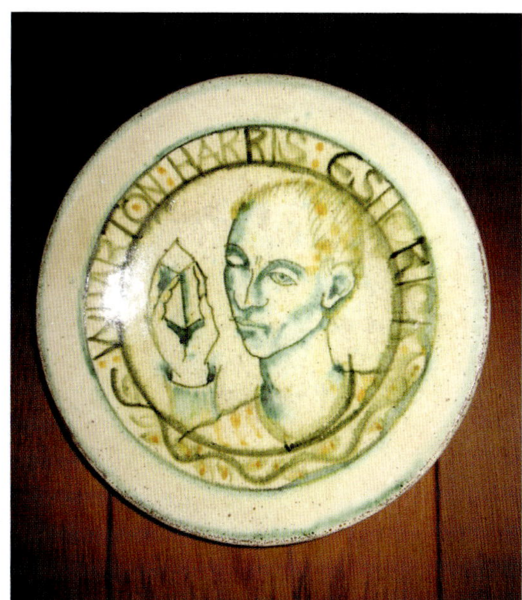

Wharton Esherick Plate, c. 1926, by Henry Varnum Poor.

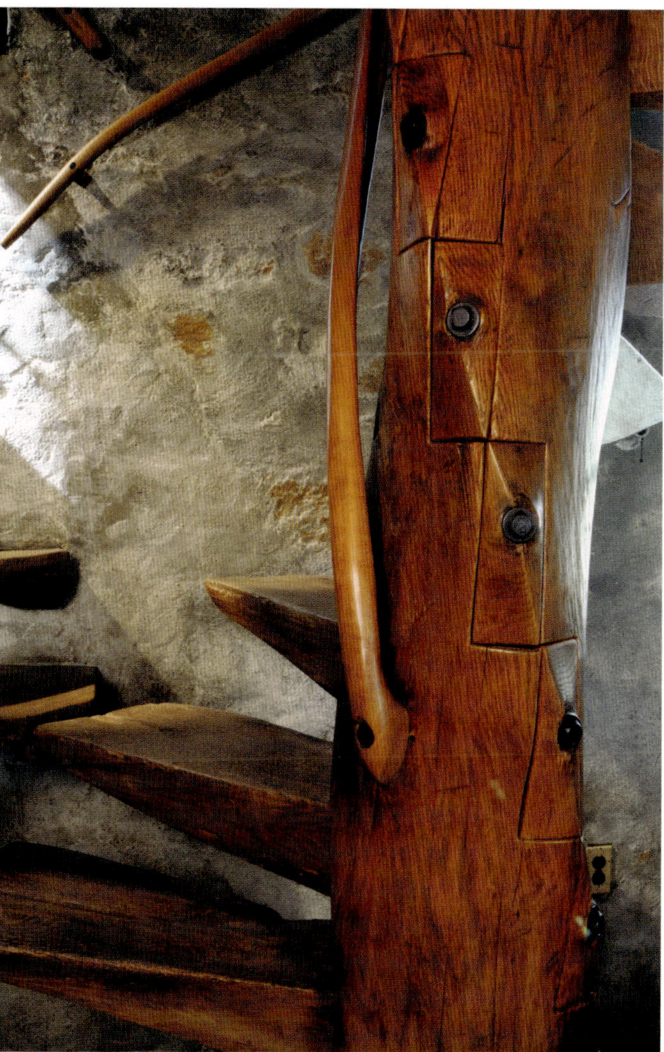

Spiral Stair, detail showing the furniture bolts and rectangular oak end washers that hold the steps tight into the spiraling center post. *Photo courtesy of James Mario.*

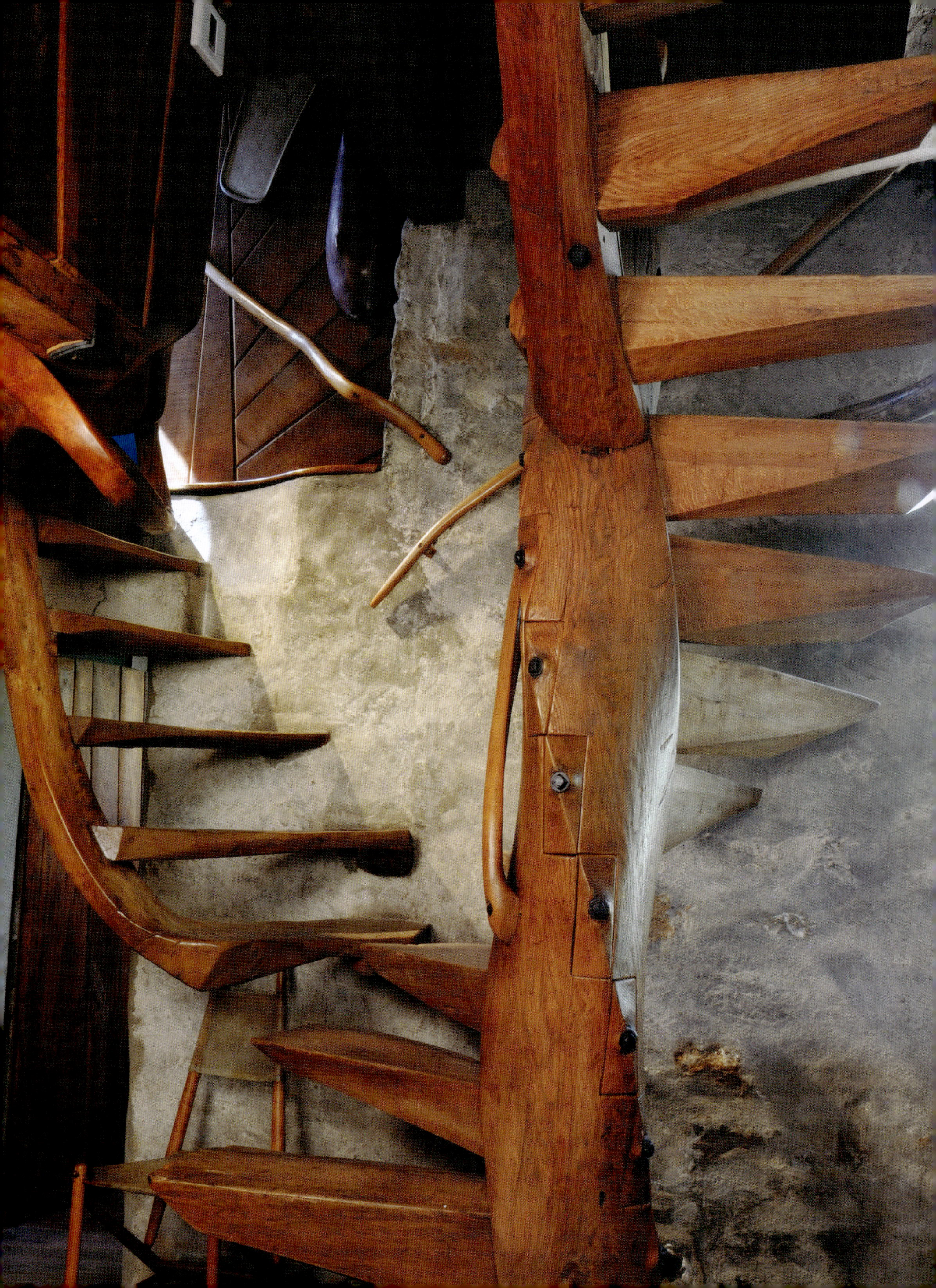

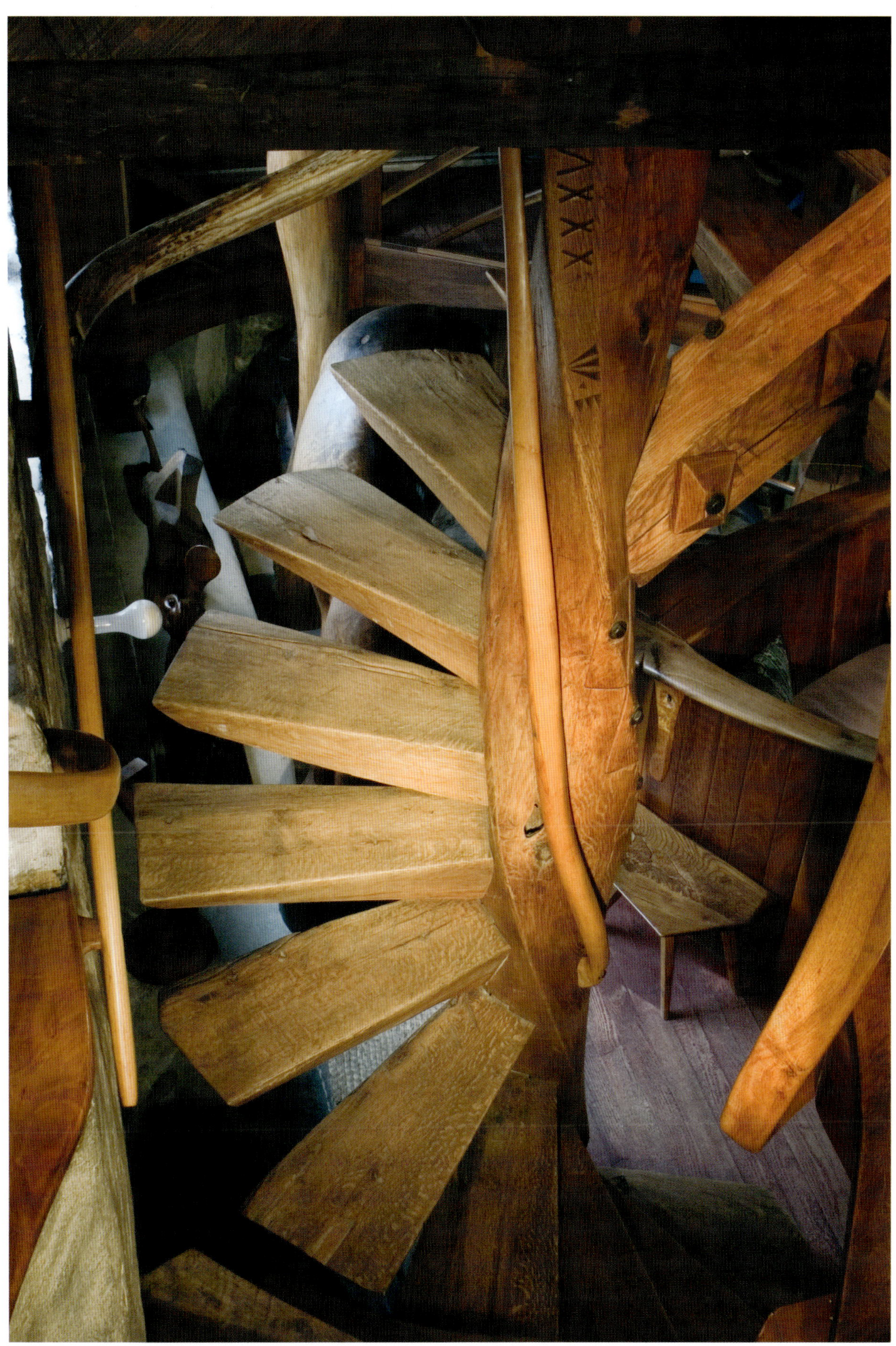

Spiral Stair, from dining room. *Photo courtesy of James Mario.*

[opposite]
Spiral Stair, 1930. Red Oak, 124.2 in. high. *Photo courtesy of James Mario.*

Stretching Out

Wharton's only hope now lay in the selling of his sculpture and in commissions for furniture. At the dance camp he had sketched a dancer reclining on the lawn, one knee raised, allowing the folds of her long gown to drape in a fanning, expressionist design. He exhibited *Finale*, the resulting sculpture in walnut, at Hedgerow Theatre, where it was bought by Mrs. Helene Koerting Fischer. She immediately commissioned him to make a stage for it to recline on, one that would also house her new electronic record player and records. Then she funded his trip to Europe to see the works of contemporary European sculptors, particularly the fountains of Carl Milles. On his return he carved the woodcut *Holzhausen*, the view from her son's porch in Bavaria.

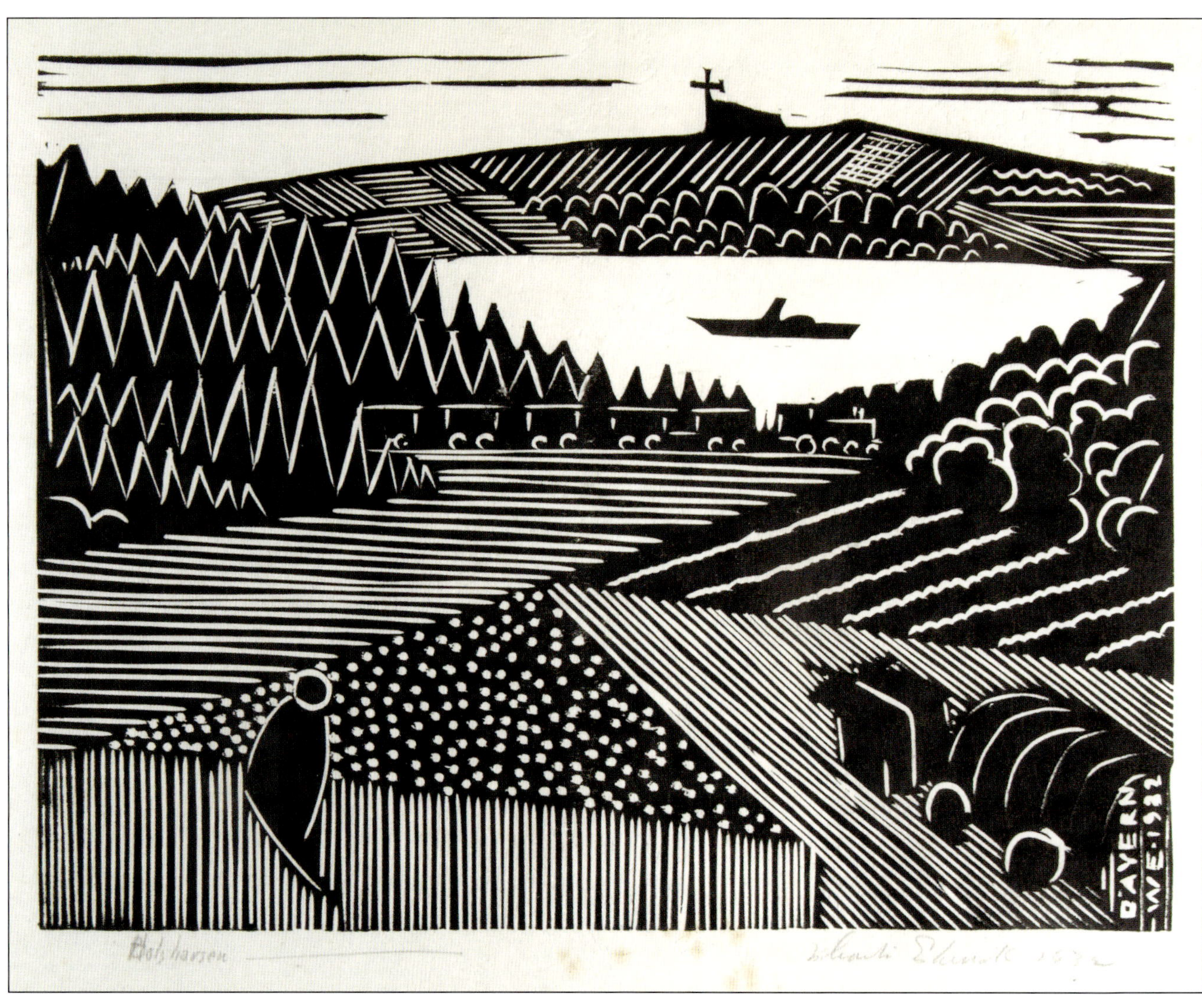

Holzhausen, 1932. Woodcut print, 9 in. X 12 in.

Helene Fischer was delighted to find someone who could design innovative, expressionist furniture rather than the mindless reproductions of antiques so popular at the time; and Wharton to find a patron so encouraging. For the next few years she kept him busy, first with an intimate, prismatic writing desk for a corner of her bedroom, then a large hall bench with illuminated drawers beneath for storing Victrola records, followed by a crystalline end table and a prismatic sewing cabinet that was equally effective as sculpture and furniture. A decade later she would invite him to make new boardroom furniture for the Shutte-Koerting Company, now in the collection of the Philadelphia Museum of Art. Many years later, the American Institute of Architects, awarding him its Gold Medal for Craftsmanship, would consider the *S-K* chair he designed for this room as evidence of his "leading, not following, the Scandinavians."

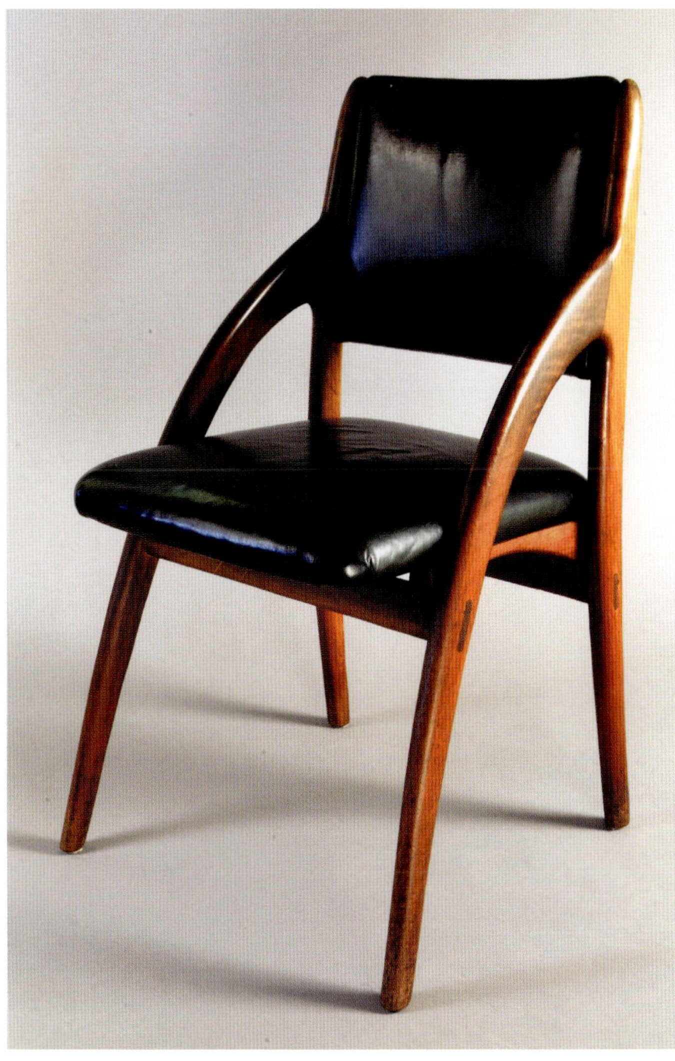

S-K Chair, 1957. Walnut frame, black Naugahide upholstery, 31.8 in. X 20 in. X 17.5 in. Signed "W.E. 1957." Similar design used for ten chairs for Schutte-Koerting boardroom. Popular as a side chair with Esherick tables. *Photo courtesy of James Mario.*

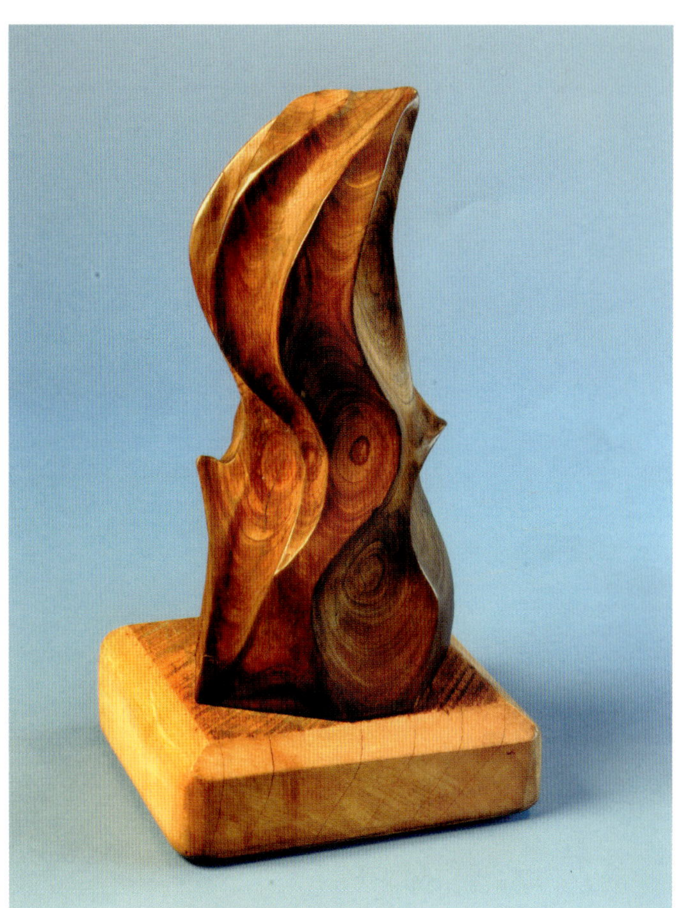

Flame, 1927. Lignum vitae, 13 in. X 7 in. X 6.75 in. *Photo courtesy of James Mario.*

Wharton had become accustomed to working with exotic imported woods, padouk, rosewood, ebony, lignum vitae, but, as he needed larger logs, he turned to local woods, oak, walnut, cherry, yellow poplar, commenting, "If I can't make something beautiful of what grows in my backyard, I should quit." It was not the exoticness of the wood that mattered, but what he did with it. Not only was there an abundant supply of these woods, but Ed Ray who had learned timbering in the Northwest, had set-up a logging business in Valley Forge and was eager to bring Wharton the best of his harvests.

In the early 1930s Marjorie Content, a photographer, commissioned him to produce new furniture for her 10th Street house in New York City. His vanity of two, floor-to-ceiling, narrow, inverted pyramids with in-facing mirrors and out-facing doors to cabinets for cosmetics, was followed by a bed, tucked between a headboard of stacked, arcing drawers for clothing, and a similar footboard housing the telephone and phonebook. These would mark the high point of his interest in expressionism. His large dining table and chairs and high, chest of drawers – which served as a sideboard – were more restrained.

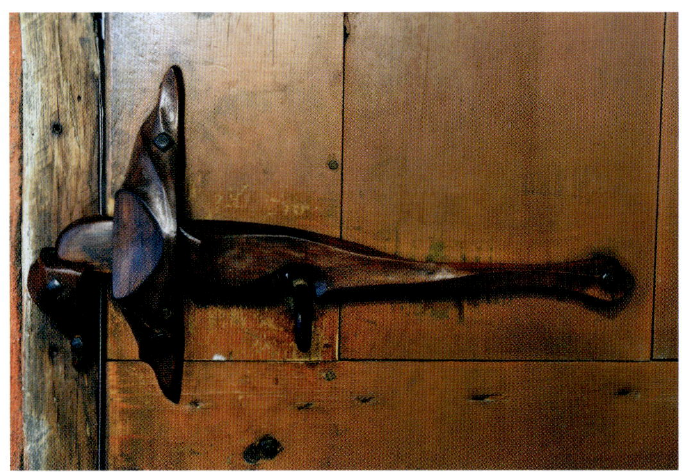

Front Door Handle, 1926. Rosewood. *Photo courtesy of James Mario.*

Wharton had come to accept that he produced furniture for income and sculpture for pleasure. In 1933, with some money in his pocket and time on his hands, he returned to his true love, sculpting. He had admired and absorbed the work of Brancusi exhibited in New York and that summer, at the dance camp, had adapted Brancusi's long, smooth, uninterrupted curves in *Dance Finale,* hoping the camp would buy it. But he had been displeased with the mindless repetition of Brancusi's *Endless Column* and in the spring of 1934, while visiting the writer Sherwood Anderson, another friend from Fairhope, back in the hollows of rural Virginia, he produced *Spiral Pole*, an equally tall reactionary piece combining two opposing, continually changing spirals.

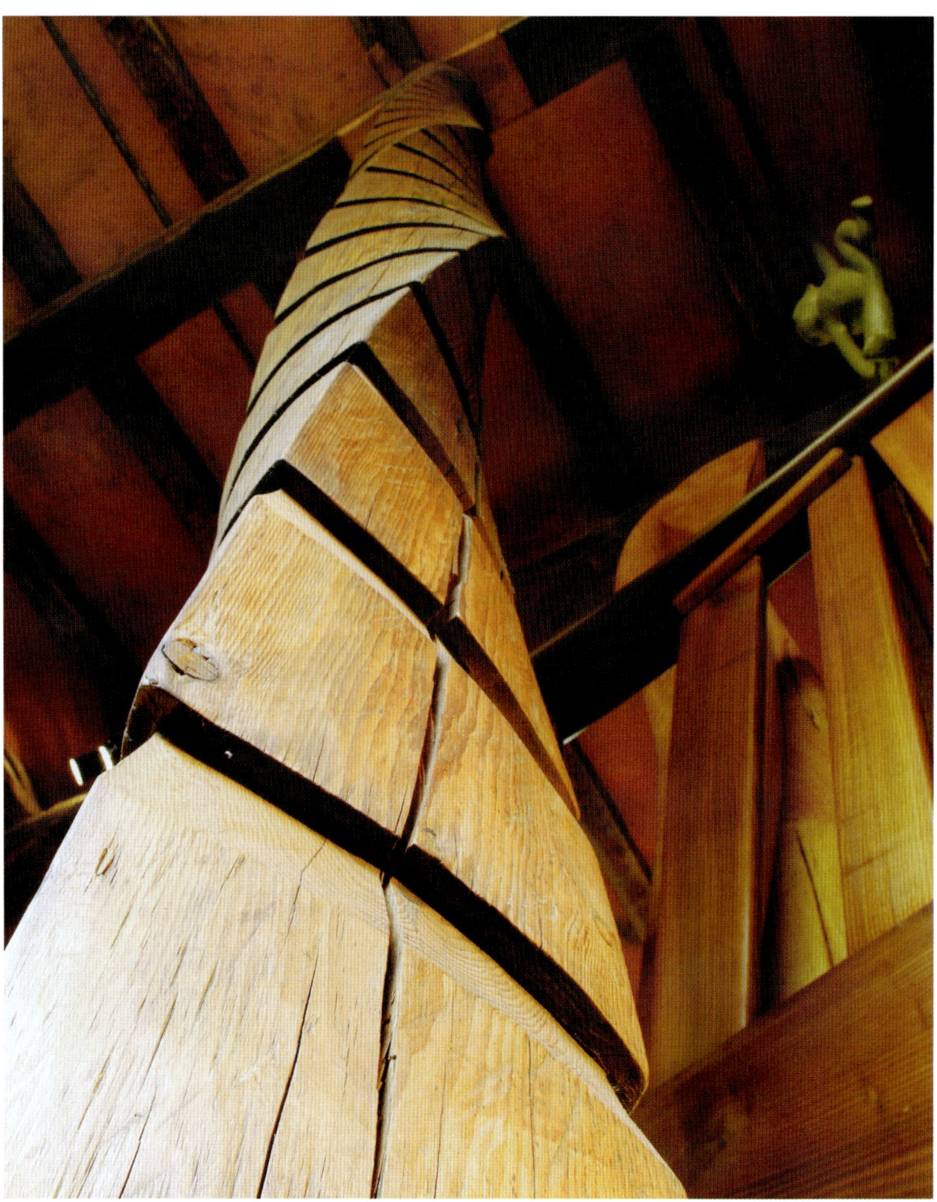

Spiral Pole, 1934. Virginia white pine, 168.1 in. X 10.5 in. diameter. Carved at "Ripshin," Sherwood Anderson's farm in Troutdale, Virginia. Spiral pole is believed to be Wharton's response to Brancusi's *Endless Column*. *Photo courtesy of Mark Sfirri.*

Anderson, known for his collections of short stories, including "Winesburg, Ohio," had acquired two local weekly newspapers, one Republican, the other Democratic, requiring him to write opposing editorials, which he did with the help of a backwoods, mountain-man correspondent Buck Fever, Anderson's alter ego. Wharton's *Buck* caricatured him in the act, covering one ear while cupping the other, interchangeably. Back at the studio, he produced *Oblivion*, embracing lovers, inspired by a scene from a play at Hedgerow, and *Jeeter* and *Cheeter,* a pair of life-size horses to stand guard at the theater.

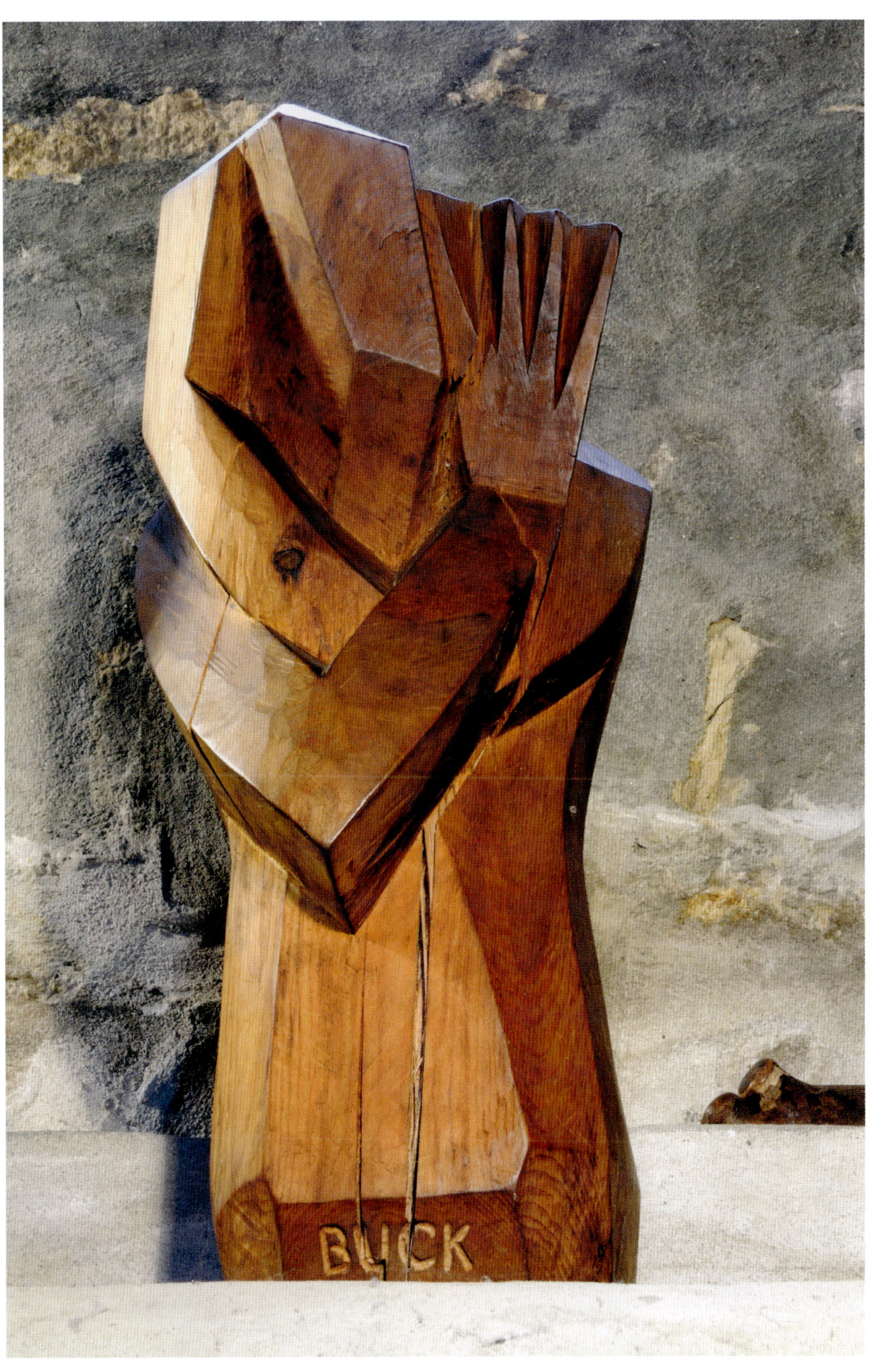

Buck, 1934. Virginia white pine, 30.3 in. X 13 in. X 11.4 in. Signed "WHARTON ESHERICK MCMXXXIV RIPSHIN." Caricature of Sherwood Anderson's alter ego 'Buck Fever,' carved at Anderson's farm. *Photo courtesy of James Mario.*

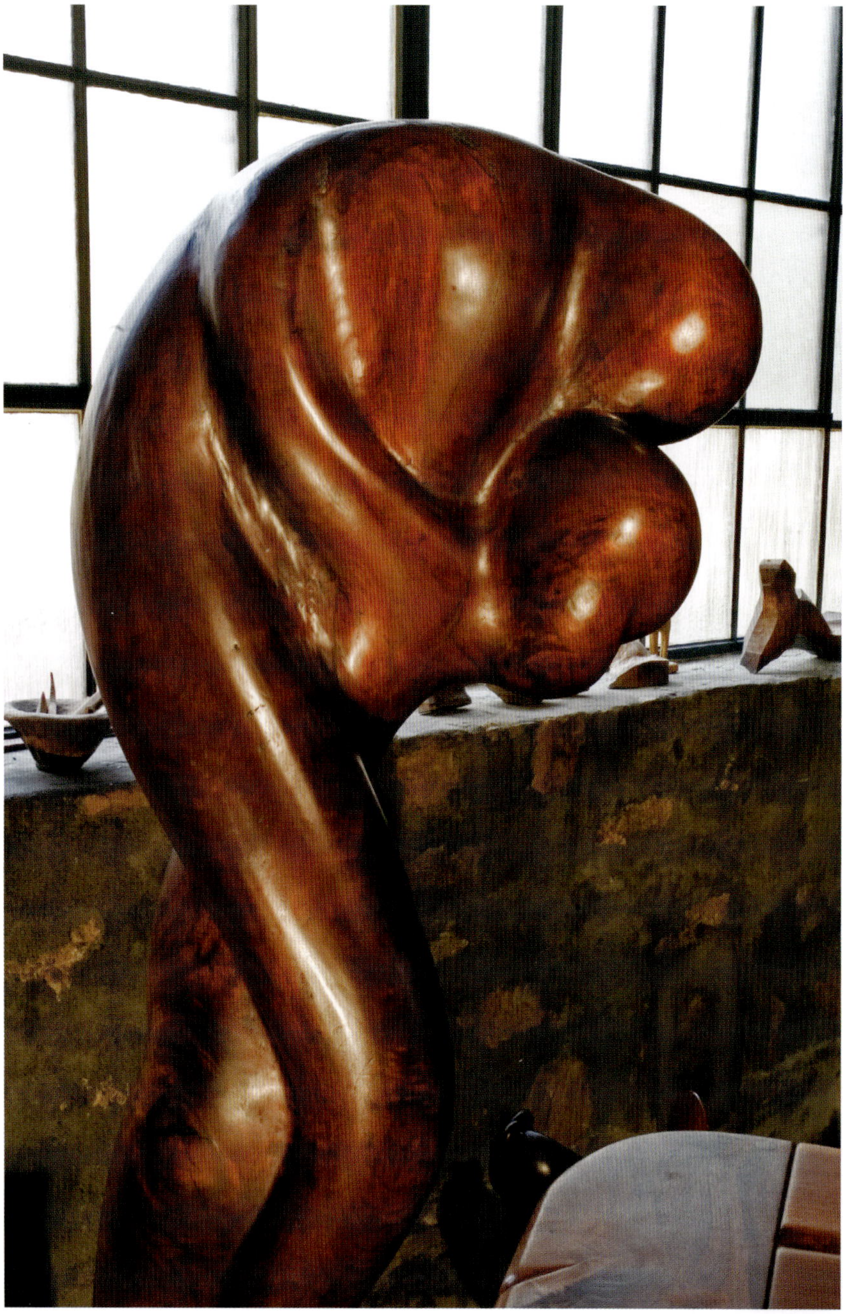

Oblivion, 1934. Walnut, 76.4 in. X 23.6 in.. Signed "WHARTON ESHERICK MCMXXXIV." Created after sketches made by Wharton of the climactic scene of Hedgerow Theatre's production of James Gould Cousin and Lynn Riggs' "Son of Perdition." *Photo courtesy of James Mario.*

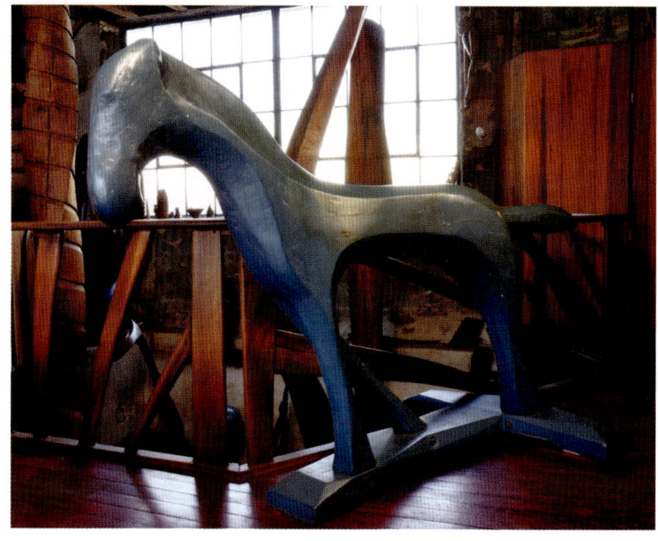

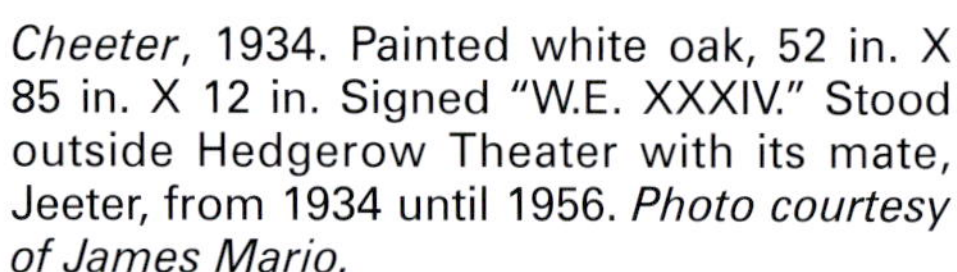

Cheeter, 1934. Painted white oak, 52 in. X 85 in. X 12 in. Signed "W.E. XXXIV." Stood outside Hedgerow Theater with its mate, Jeeter, from 1934 until 1956. *Photo courtesy of James Mario.*

In 1935, as Wharton's finances were becoming drained and the Great Depression was showing no signs of waning, his friend Alexander Hillsberg, First Violinist of the Philadelphia Orchestra, was asked by the orchestra's wealthy president, Curtis Bok, if he new a good carpenter who could build some bookshelves for a house he had bought. After Bok saw the studio and photographs of Wharton's imaginative work, he realized his house needed more than bookshelves. For the next three years he kept Wharton busy converting the parlor into a library with floor to ceiling, wall to wall bookcases in a Mondrian design to fit his sets of books, a new fireplace surround for the dining room, another for the library, an intimate alcove with sofa and desk for Mrs. Bok, new hall steps hewn from a large oak log, a spiral stair sculpted from used bridge timbers, a portal from the hall to the dining room, and a large music room with fireplace, a 4 ft. X 16 ft. single-pane window surrounded by a massive sculpted oak frame, paneled walls, a record player that could be rolled about the room, and a record storage cabinet. At one time Wharton employed eleven workers – wood carvers, cabinetmakers, masons, plasterers, metalworkers, electricians, and plumbers. On completion of the work, Bok wrote, "Never in my wildest dreams did I think it would be so beautiful, or cost so much." The house has been torn-down, but Wharton's interiors are safely in museums and private collections.

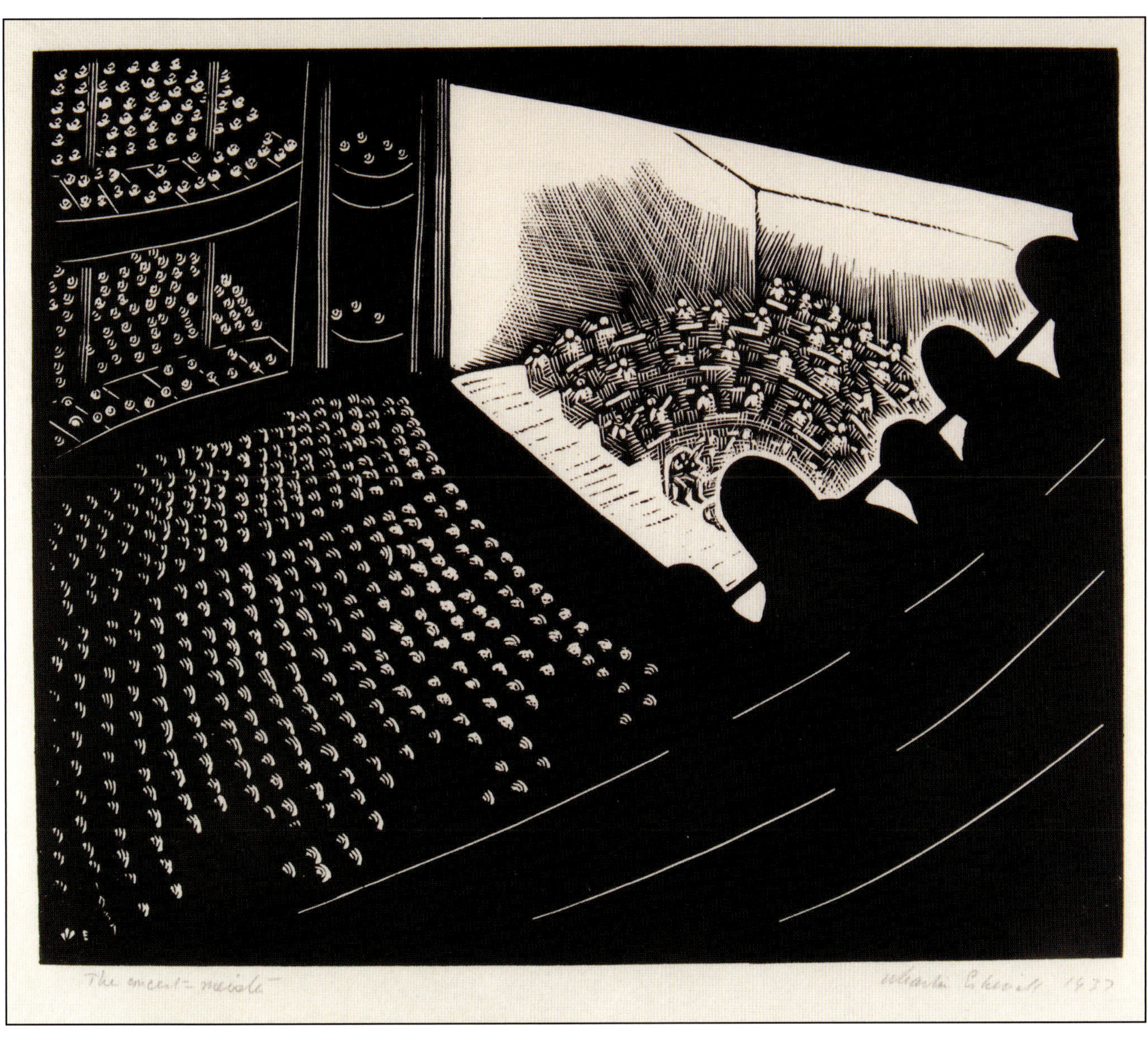

The Concert Meister, 1937. Wood engraving 9.1 in. X 11.1 in. Print of and for Wharton's friend Alexander Hilsberg, the concert meister of the Philadelphia Orchestra.

By the end of the 1930s, Letty and their daughters had become resident members of the Hedgerow Theatre company, leaving Wharton and teenage Peter in the farmhouse. Just as Wharton had paid Mary's tuition at the Hessian Hills school with chairs, he now paid for Ruth's apprenticeship at Hedgerow with thirty-six chairs for the rehearsal room. This time he used hammer handles obtained at an auction. Making the chairs in small batches, he changed the design incrementally from stiff, disciplined vertical lines to relaxed, splayed, more comfortable forms.

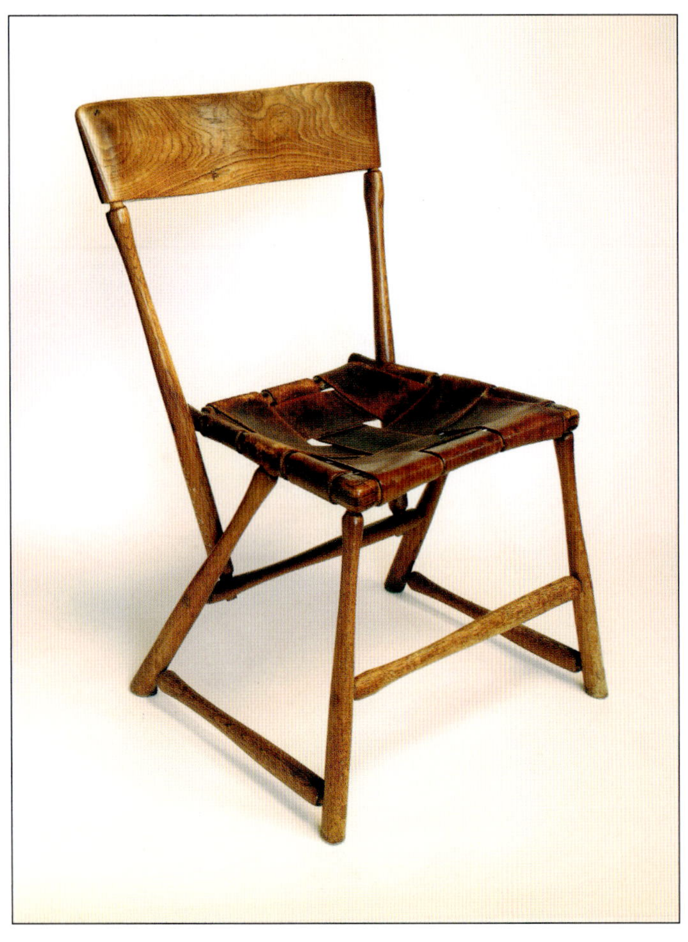

Hammer Handle Chair, 1938. Hickory and oak, laced leather seat, 32x21 in. X 17.8 in. *Photo courtesy of Mark Sfirri.*

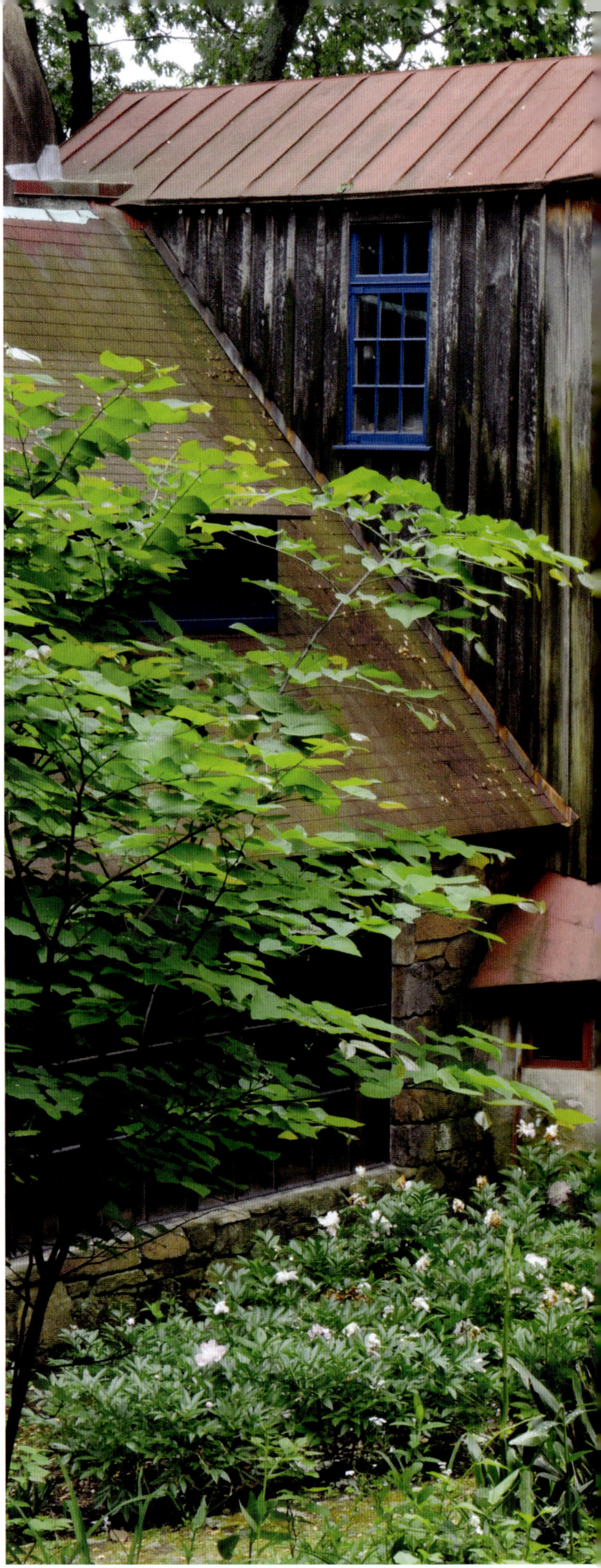

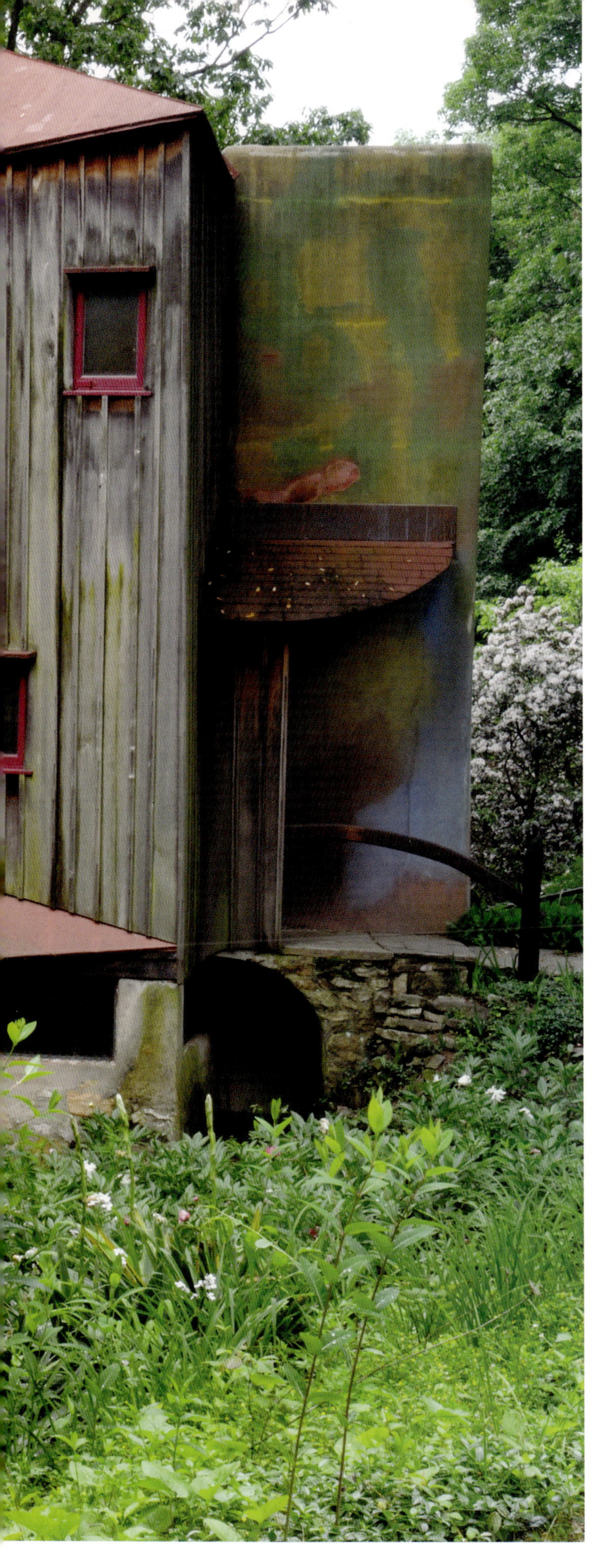

To make a sitting-bedroom, he insulated the studio loft and lined it with Celotex, a naturally tan board of compressed, chopped sugar cane fiber. In 1940 he constructed a two-story frame addition with a dining room and bedroom for Peter, and rented the farmhouse for needed income. The kitchen was still in the basement, accessible only from the outside, in all weather, as was the outhouse.

The New York World's Fair had opened in 1939 under the banner, "The World of Tomorrow," with displays of the technical marvels of the time. For the second year, the fair added a new pavilion, "America at Home," and engaged leading architects to design its dozen rooms. One of those was Wharton's friend George Howe, who, with the French designer William Lescaze, had just built America's most modern skyscraper for the Philadelphia Savings Fund Society. Howe designed a room incorporating works from the studio, including the oak spiral stair and uninstalled wall paneling for the new dining room. But, the publicity and fame it brought Wharton was for naught; the world of tomorrow was World War II and the nation had more on its mind than furniture and interiors.

Studio, from the east, showing the two story wooden addition that Esherick built in 1940 (and extended in 1966.) The bathroom, added in 1947, is located beneath the lower red prismatic roof. *Photo courtesy of James Mario.*

Success

Wharton returned to sculpting, producing *Twin Twist* a sixteen-foot tall oak piece, and *Darling,* a life-size deer – both later bought by the Pennsylvania Academy of the Fine Arts – followed by *Reverence* a twelve-foot tall walnut figure intended as a grave marker for his friend Sherwood Anderson. When Anderson's widow rejected it for being subject to rot and vandalism, he designed a squatter abstract form in black granite. *Reverence* was exhibited in "Sculpture of the Twentieth Century" at the Museum of Modern Art, the Chicago Art Institute, and the Philadelphia Museum of Art, and then purchased by the Fairmount Park Art Association. Rather than wait for another large commission, Wharton turned to producing more universally marketable small items – cutting boards, trays, bowls, spoons, and three-legged stools – each a unique design. Initially, he shaped the slender legs with a spoke-shave, smoothly enlarging them at the stretchers, which he spaced at different heights to avoid weakening the legs. The stool seats, each shaped by the grain figures, were a good way of using interesting scraps. Ultimately he would produce more than 250 stools, each seat a different shape.

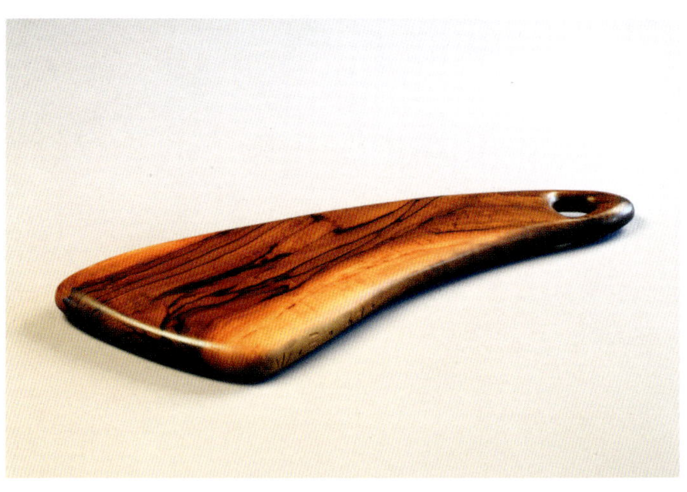

Cutting Board, 1964. Kentucky coffeewood, 10.5 in. X 5 in. *Photo courtesy of James Mario.*

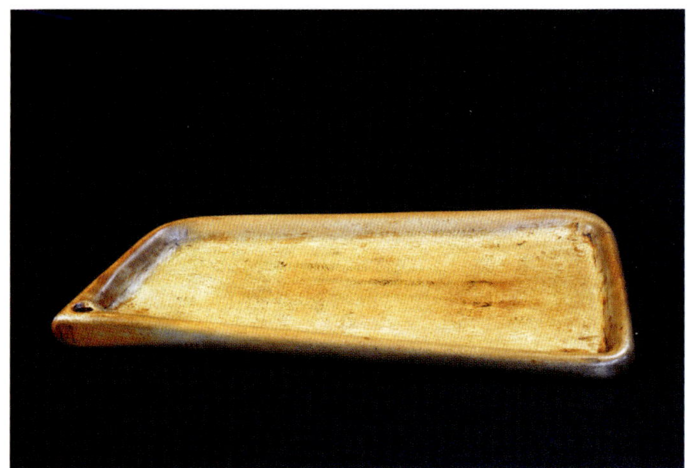

Make-up Tray, 1945. Satinwood, inscribed "Miryasha 1945 Hedgerow Theatre in New York." Made for Miriam Phillips. *Photo courtesy of James Mario.*

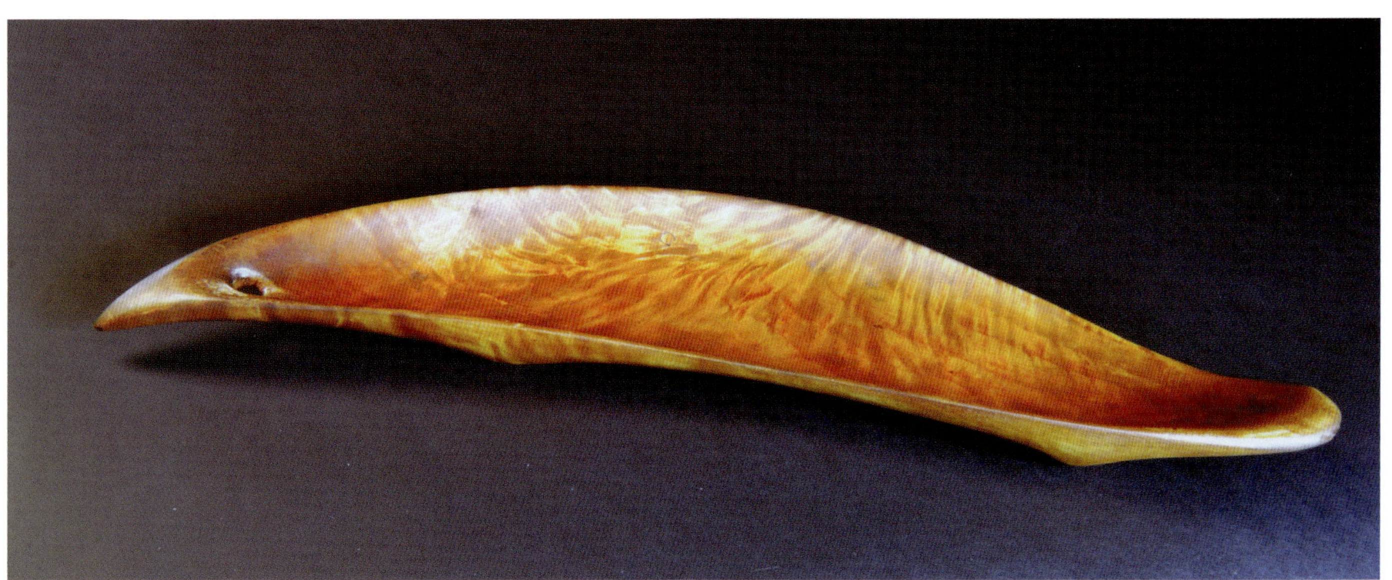

Bowl, 1968. Cottonwood, 1.62 in. X 22 in. X 6 in. *Photo courtesy of James Mario.*

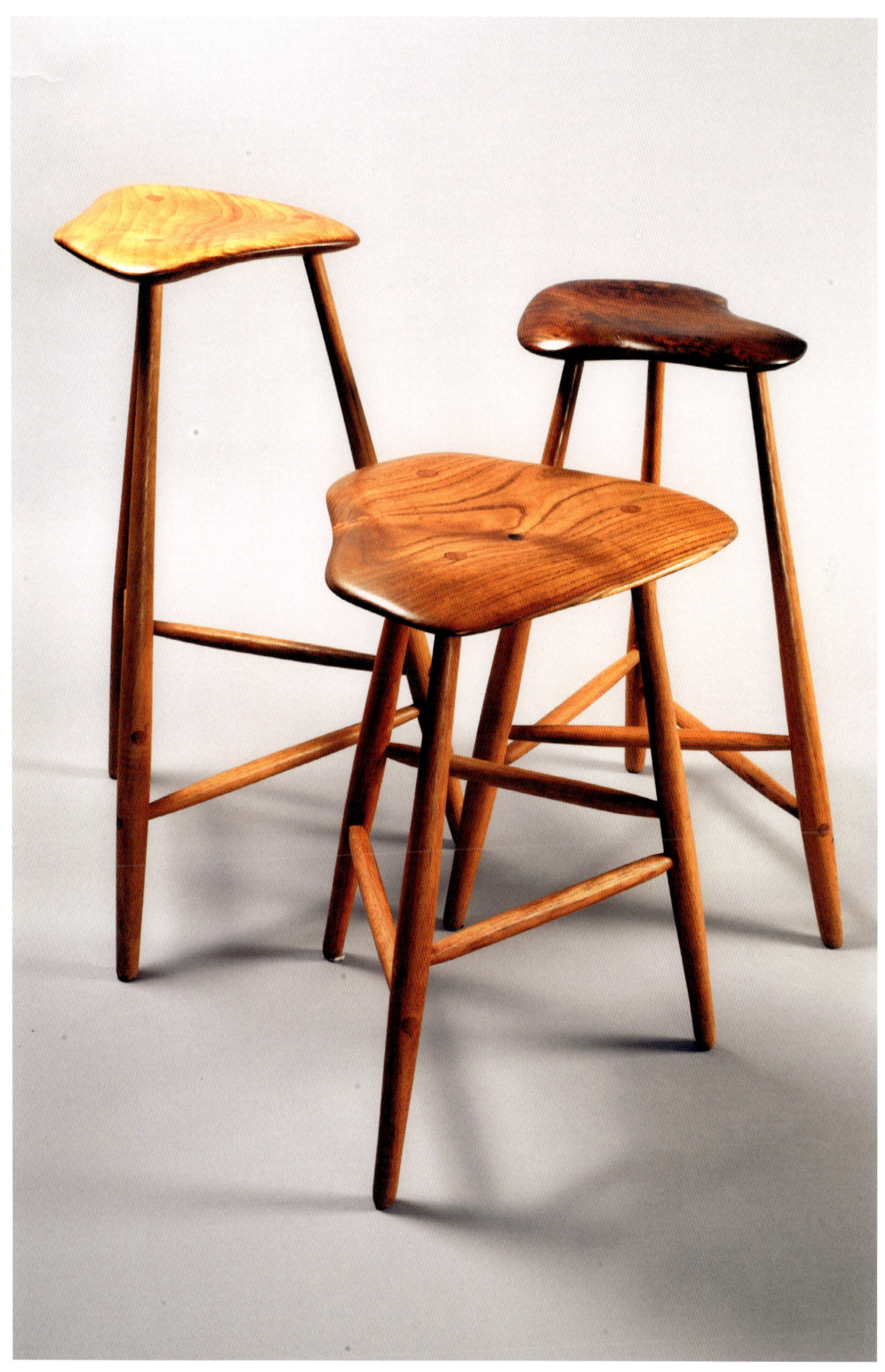

Three stools: *High Stool*, 1966. Hickory and cottonwood, 25.39 in. high. *Medium Stool*, 1966, Hickory and walnut, 22.25 in. high. Low stool, 1968. Hickory and coffeewood, 20 in. high. *Photo courtesy of James Mario.*

Using corrugated industrial skylight glass and red clay structural tile, he tucked an asymmetric bath onto the studio and perched a small, prismatic, tarpaper-clad shed kitchen above it. Soon, he was creating new kitchens for others. First for Henry Milliken's modern, open plan, solar-heated house, separating the kitchen from the living-dining room with a curvilinear oak fence that also served as backsplash and cupboards. With similar kitchens he converted a barn into an enjoyable house for Olaf and Elin Rove, and another for Marjorie Content.

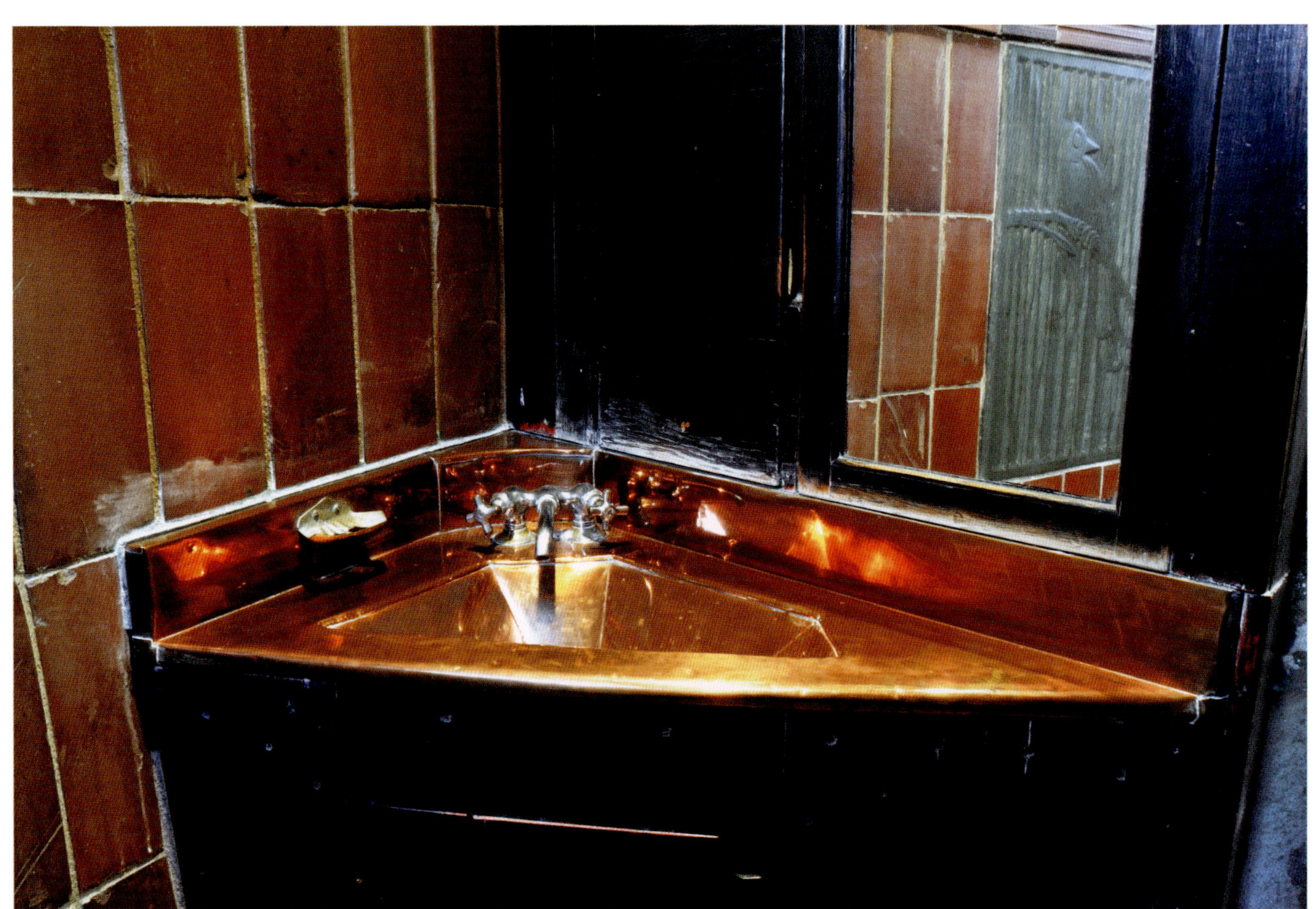

Bathroom sink, 1947. Copper in wood frame. *Photo courtesy of James Mario.*

Captain's Chair, 1951. Walnut and cherry, laced leather seat, 29.5 in. X 20.9 in. X 20.9 in. Signed "W.E. 1951." *Photo courtesy of James Mario.*

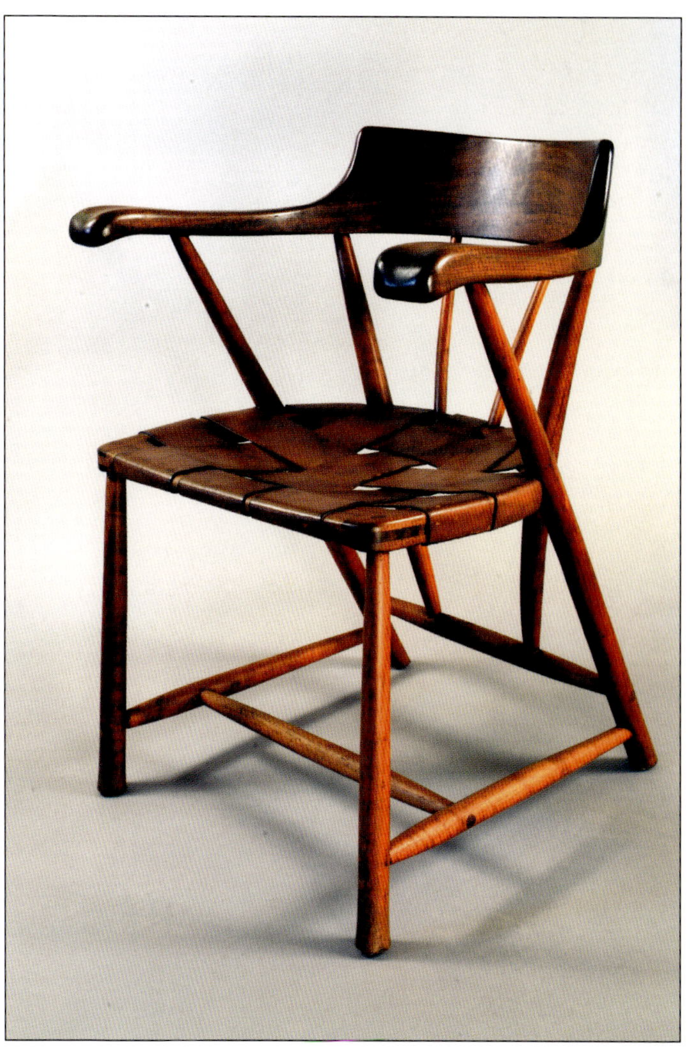

In 1950 he designed a captain's chair with a steam-bent walnut back, something John Schmidt could make in his shop while Wharton shaped the one-of-a-kind pieces in the studio. The chair became his *entrée*, a foot in the door, for a new generation of clients who found his custom-made work so addictive that they kept returning for more. First, was Nathan Rubinson who commissioned a music stand for his cellist wife, Rose. He had wanted a salad bowl until Wharton convinced him he first needed a new dining table on which to put the bowl. Many years later, after the new dining table and chairs, a sideboard, telephone desk, sofa, coffee and end tables, music cabinet, bed, dressers, and study, he got the bowl. Alice and Lawrence Siever began furnishing their new contemporary house with captain's chairs, adding a dining table, followed by a sofa and coffee table, fireplace surround, even a new kitchen. Similarly, Dena and James Dannenberg filled their traditional Tudor with his built-in and free-standing curvilinear work, making the corners disappear.

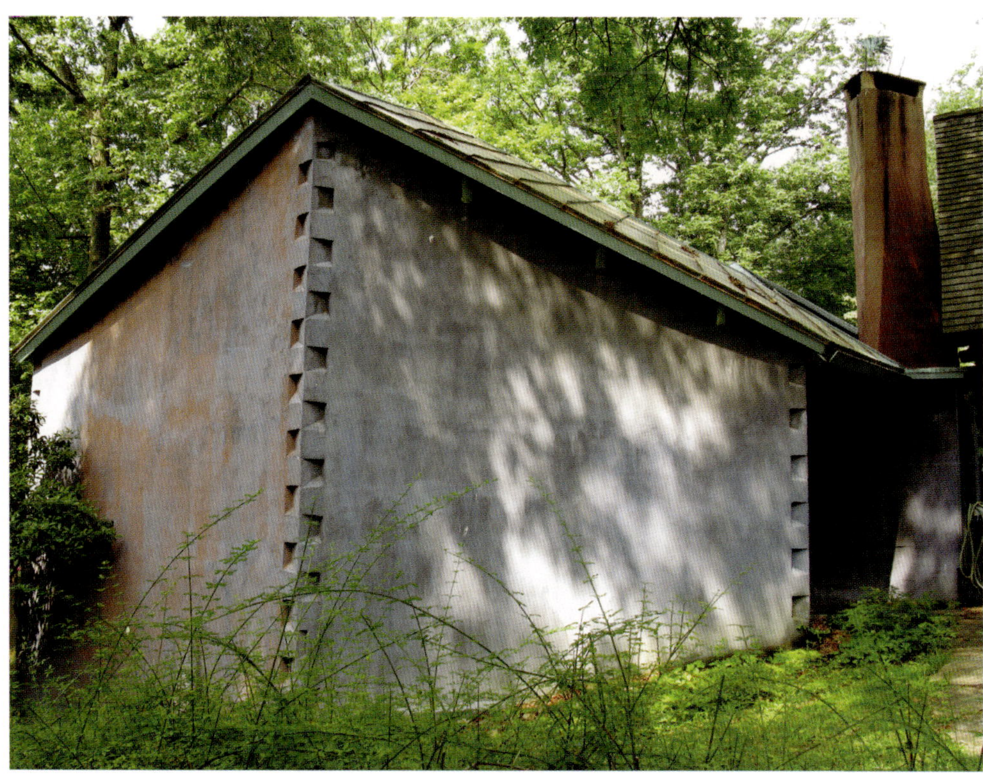

Workshop, 1956. From the east.

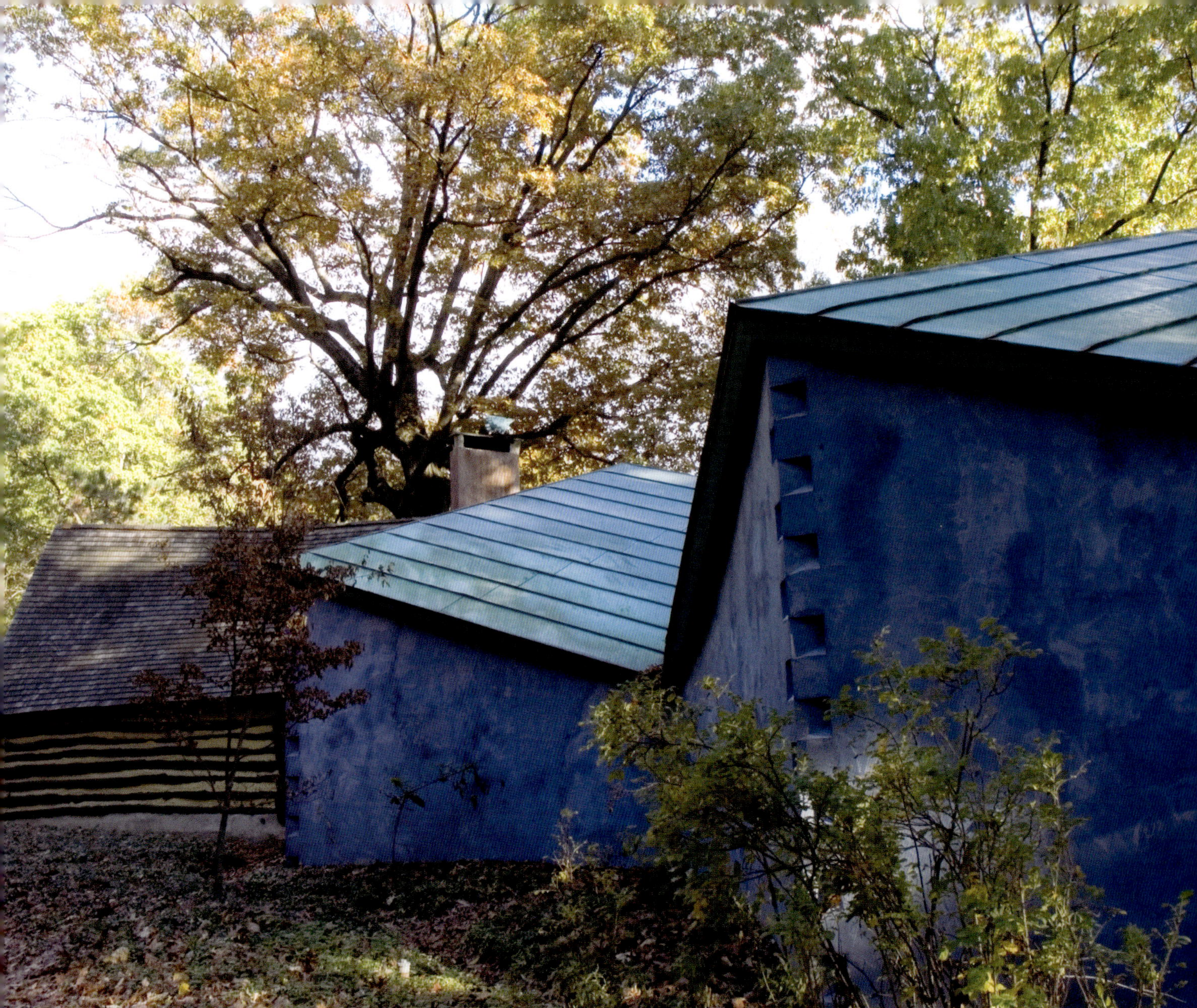

Workshop, 1956. From the west.

In the middle of all this activity, John Schmidt moved, taking his tools and sawmill with him. By chance, an aunt died and Wharton spent his small inheritance on a new workshop adjacent to the studio. Needing an architect to make drawings for a building permit – something he hadn't previously bothered with – he turned to George Howe who recommended Louis I. Kahn. Kahn's penchant for pure geometric forms, repeated, was the antithesis of Wharton's free curves. The product was three hexagons, each having three diamond shaped roof planes with sloping eaves. Partially dug into the hillside it has large windows overlooking the valley. The interlocking of the concrete block walls at the corners created a dovetail design that Wharton insisted the masons retain. Although Kahn's drawings showed straight walls, Wharton managed to slightly curve the eight inch walls over the twelve inch foundation. John's apprentice, William McIntyre, stayed on to help Wharton, and Horace Hartshaw, who had helped build the workshop, joined them.

The war had spawned a new interest in handcrafted furniture, led by the government's offer of educational opportunities to veterans, including training in crafts for those not academically inclined. Mrs. Ailene Vanderbilt Webb formed the American Crafts Council, which opened the Museum of Contemporary Crafts in New York. One of the museum's early shows, in the winter of 1958-59, was a retrospective of Wharton's work, recognizing him for his pioneering accomplishments and contributions to modern furniture design. This was followed by a show at the Brooklyn Museum of Art. New clients and new design challenges evolved. In each case the clients were willing to let Wharton make multiples of his designs, spreading the development cost. One of these designs was a 1962 *Spiral Library Ladder* for Mr. and Mrs. Isard. It repeats the form of his 1920, Steiner-influenced, sculpture, a dancer, her gown spiraling about her, one arm bent at the waist, the other raised to the sky with the fingers pulling the powers of heaven to Earth.

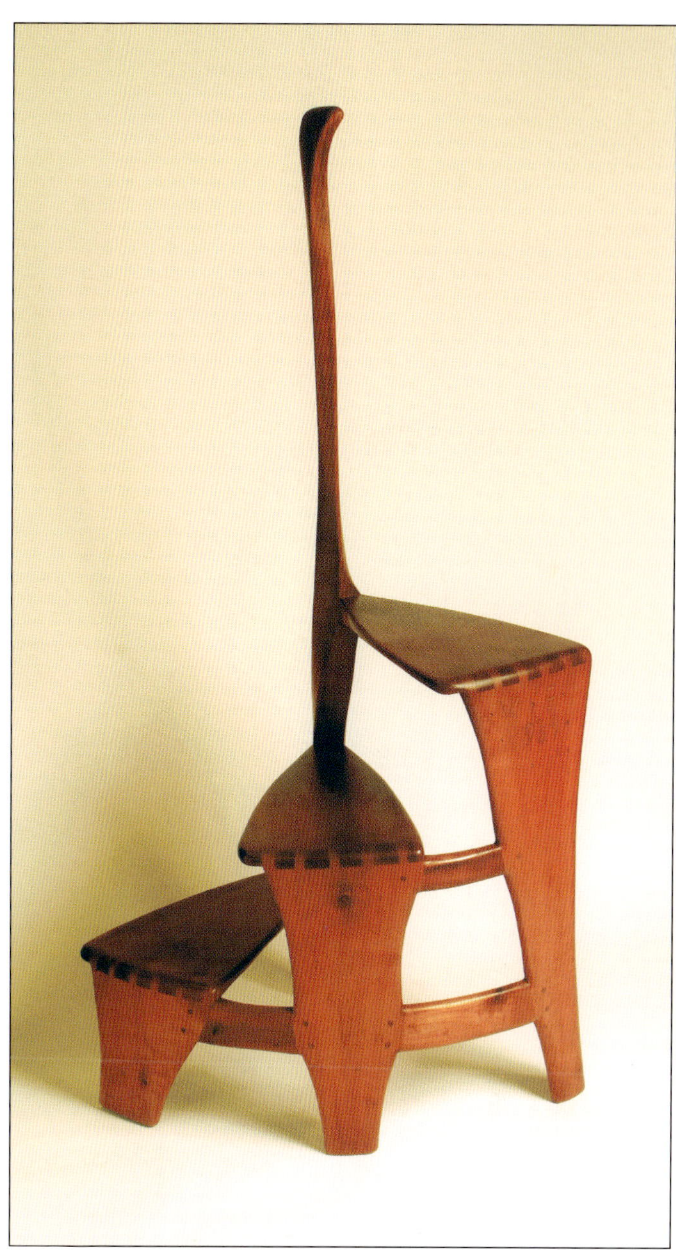

Spiral Library Ladder, 1969. Cherry, 48.4 in. high. Signed "W.E. 1969." *Photo courtesy of Mark Sfirri.*

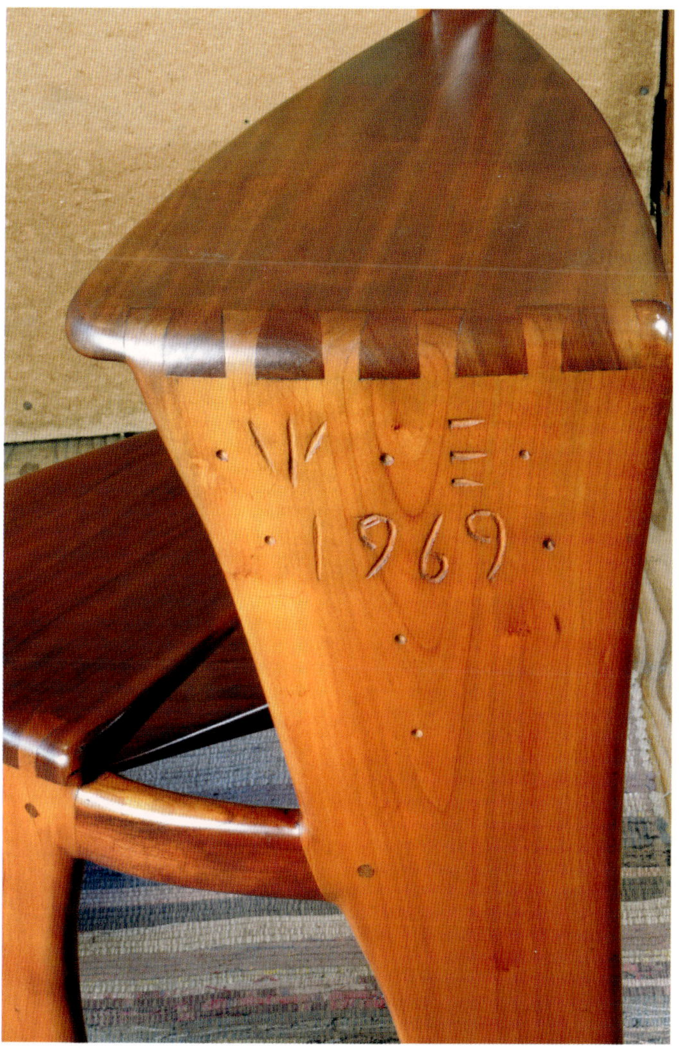

Spiral Library Ladder, joinery detail. *Photo courtesy of James Mario.*

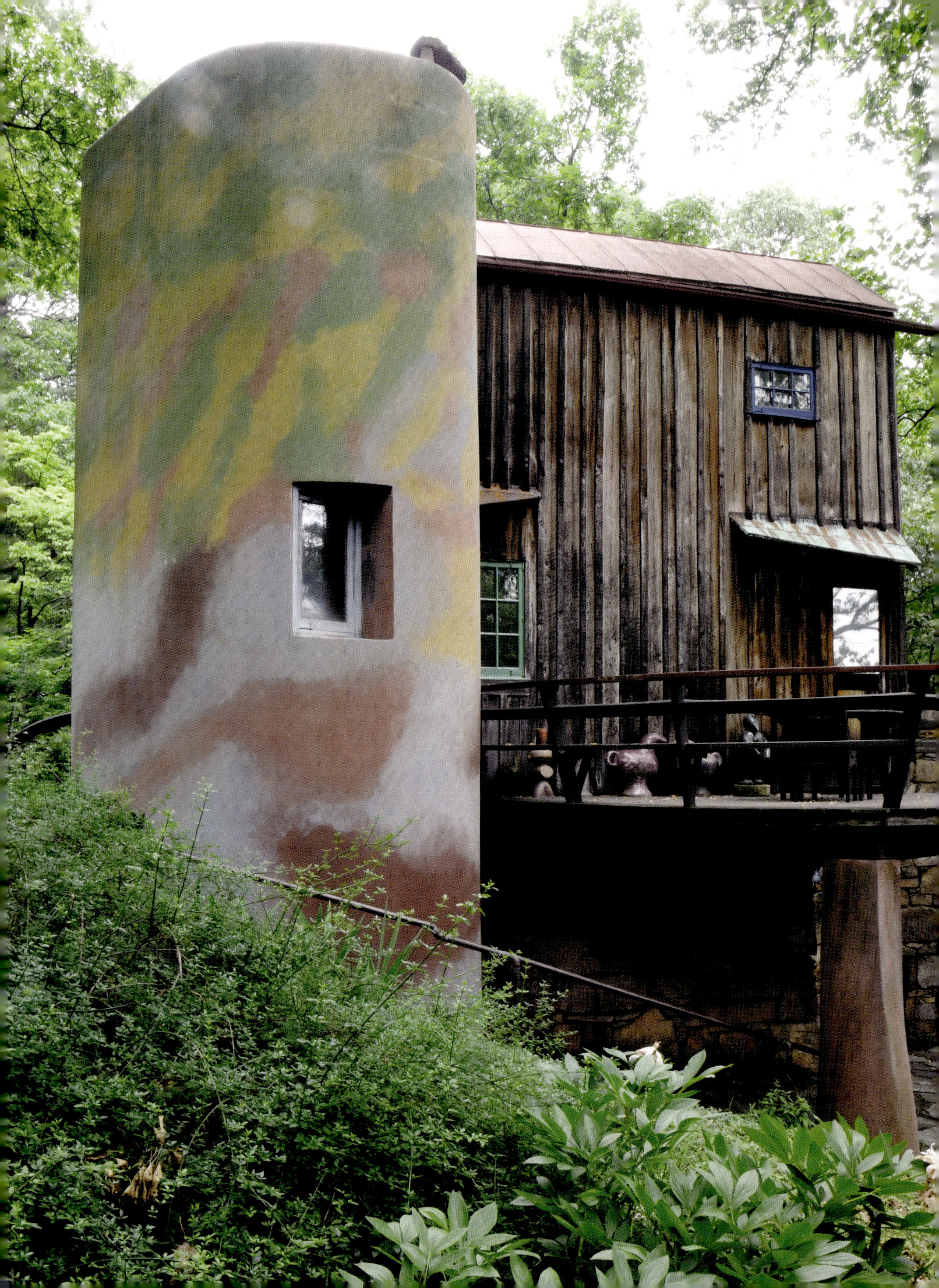

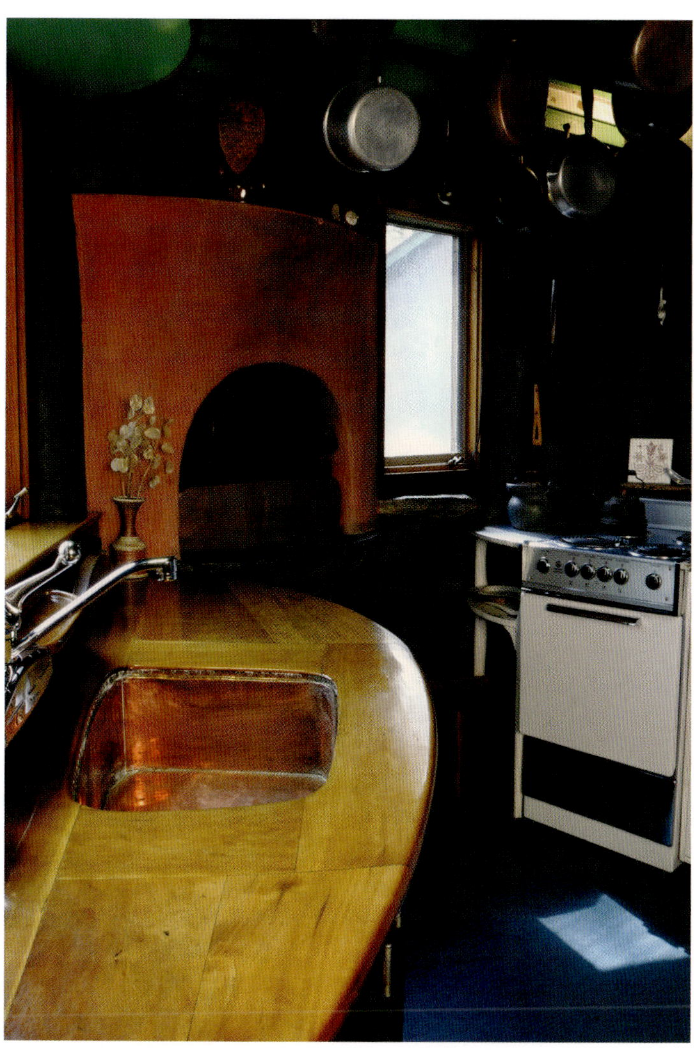

Kitchen in the silo. *Photo courtesy of James Mario.*

In 1965, Wharton added a curving deck off of his dining room for relaxing and catching the summer breezes. The following year he added a curving tower, a silo he called it, to the studio to add a visual anchor to balance the high, narrow wooden wing. He expanded his kitchen into the silo, with a curving cherry countertop, copper sink, and countertop fireplace. Wharton added pigment to the stucco as it was applied to the exterior to create an abstraction of autumn leaves above brown branches against a blue sky. His castle was now complete.

After a stroke in 1967, when Wharton was 79, there were no truly new designs, but variations on earlier models. He died May 6, 1970, prior to being given an American Institute of Architects Gold Medal for Craftsmanship award. In December 1971, the Renwick Gallery of the Smithsonian Institution produced *Wooden Works.* Wharton's work held center stage, surrounded by comparable pieces of the next generation, Wendell Castle, Sam Maloof, Arthur Espinet Carpenter, and George Nakashima.

Wharton's heirs agreed to keep the studio and collection intact, as it was when he lived there, and founded the Wharton Esherick Museum to preserve this gem and make it permanently accessible to the public. The museum opened to visitors in October of 1972 with the mission "to preserve, maintain, and exhibit the artistic creations of the late Wharton Esherick so that the general public, and particularly artists/craftspeople, may gain enjoyment, education, and inspiration from Esherick's life work."

[opposite]
Studio Silo and Deck, 1965-66. *Photo courtesy of James Mario.*

Selected Works from the Collection

Prints

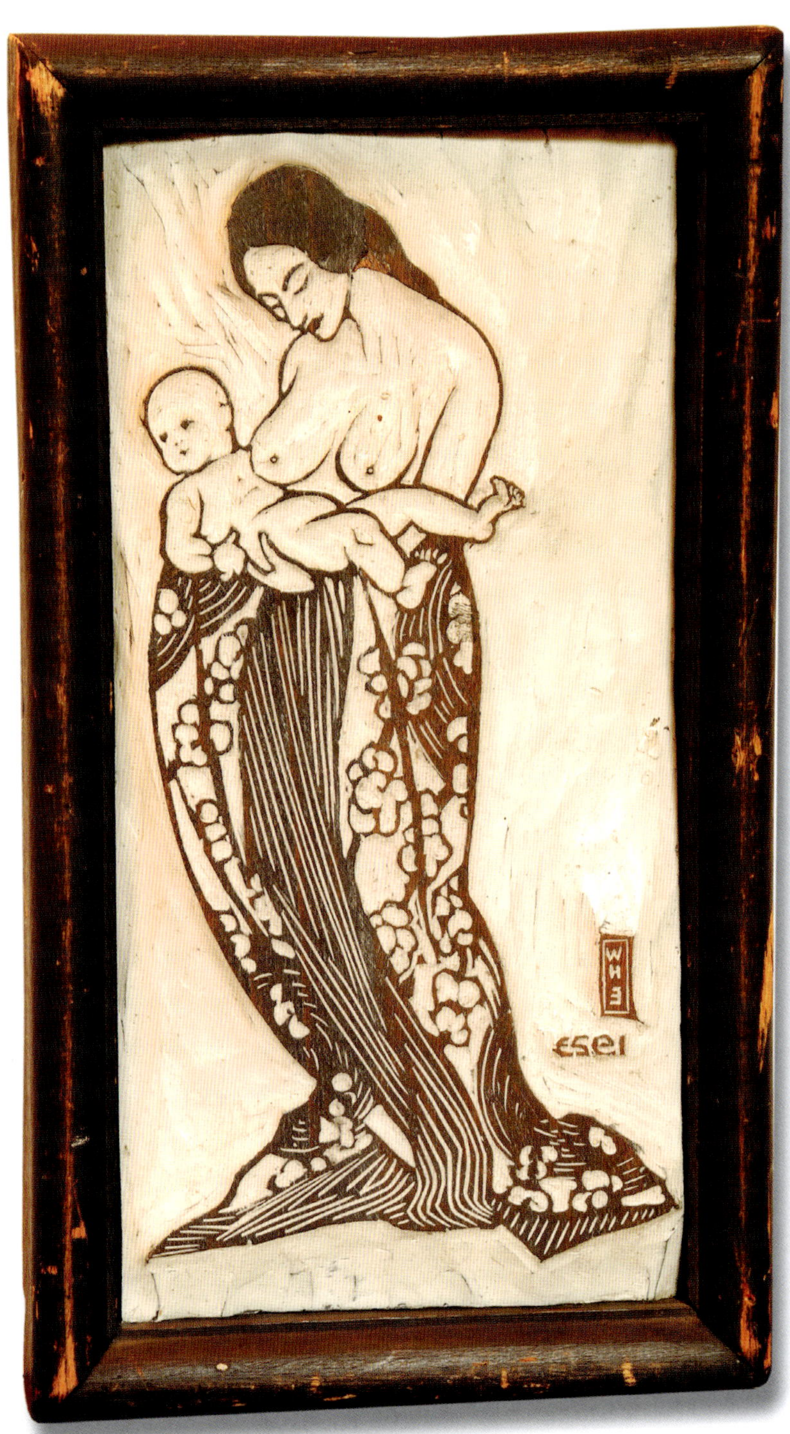

The Bath, 1923. Woodblock. 8.62 in. X 4.25 in. Inscribed in block "WHE." Framed. *Photo courtesy of Mark Sfirri.*

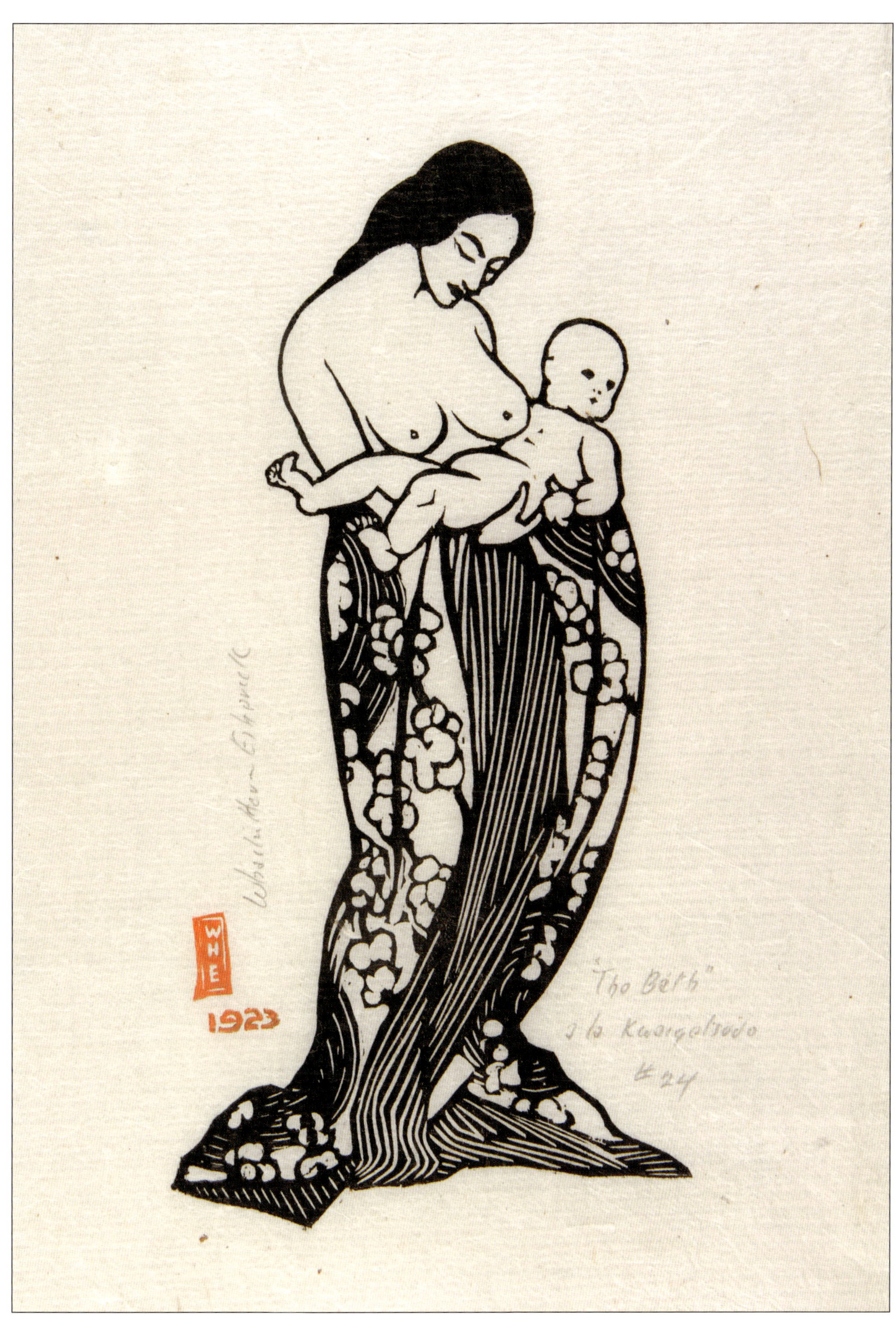

The Bath, 1923. Woodcut print, 9.1 in. X 4.7 in. Signed "Wharton Harris Esherick"

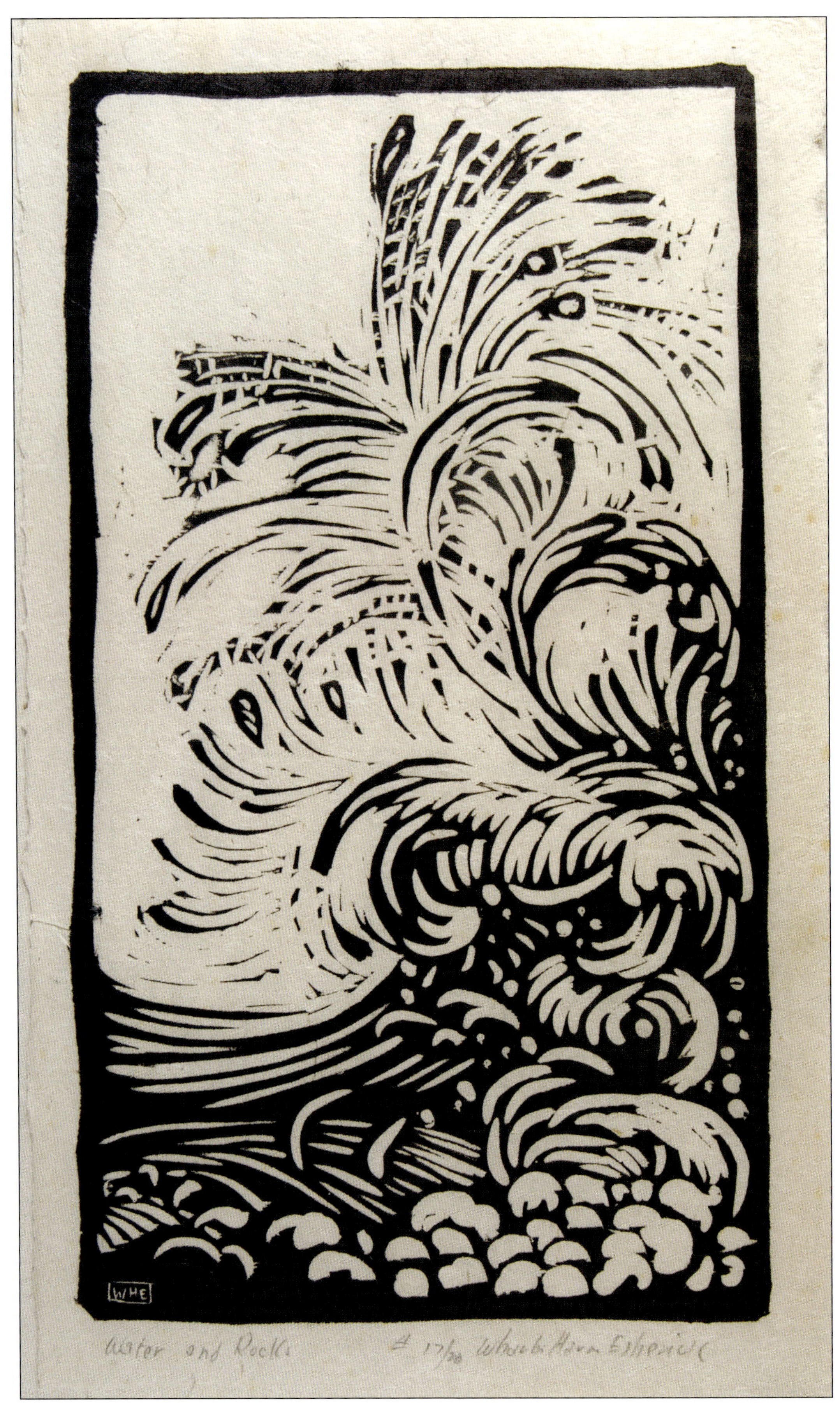

Water and Rocks, 1923. Woodcut print, 11.1 in. X 6.4 in.

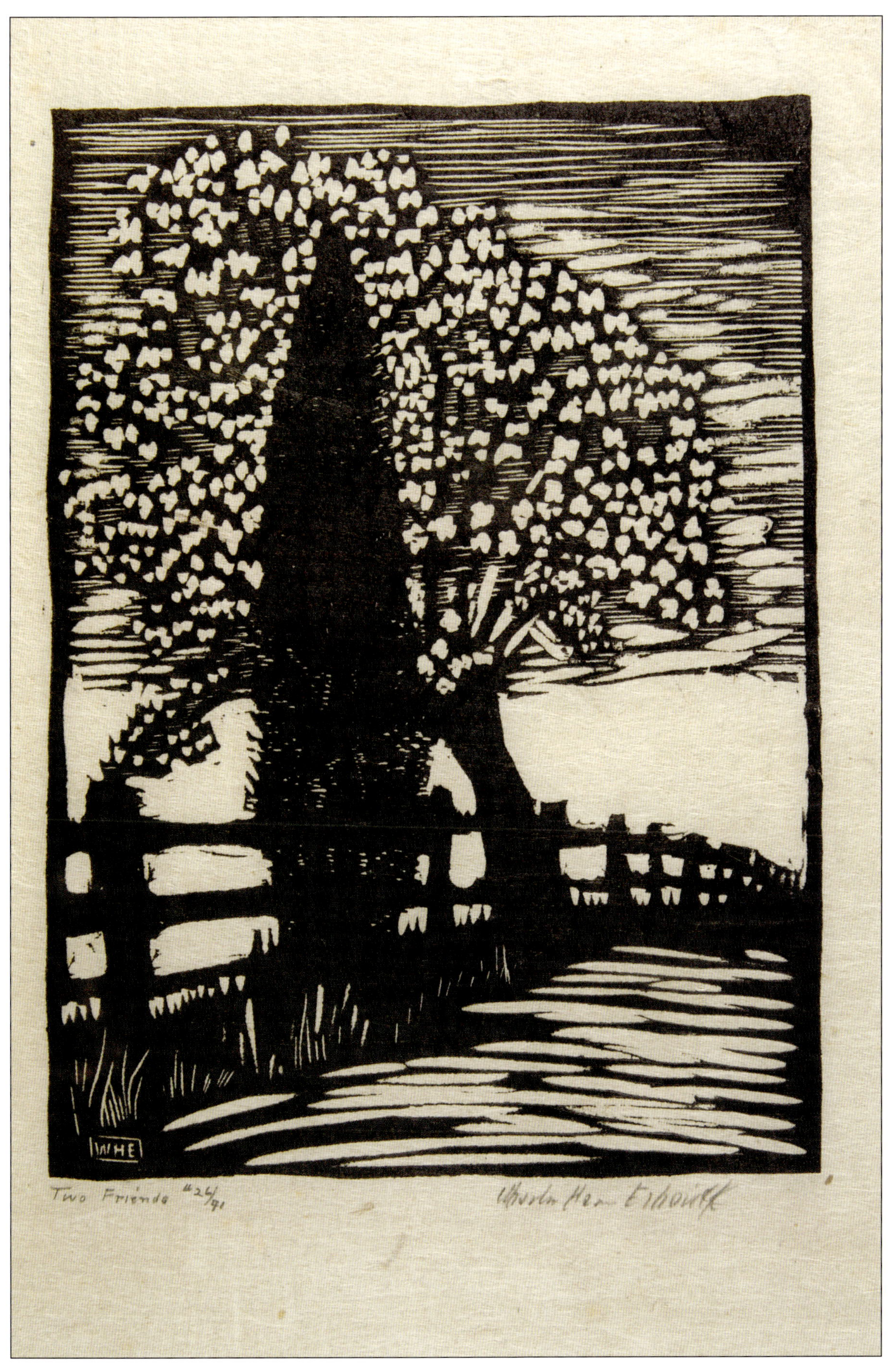

Two Friends, 1923. Woodcut print, 7.87 in. X 5.75 in.

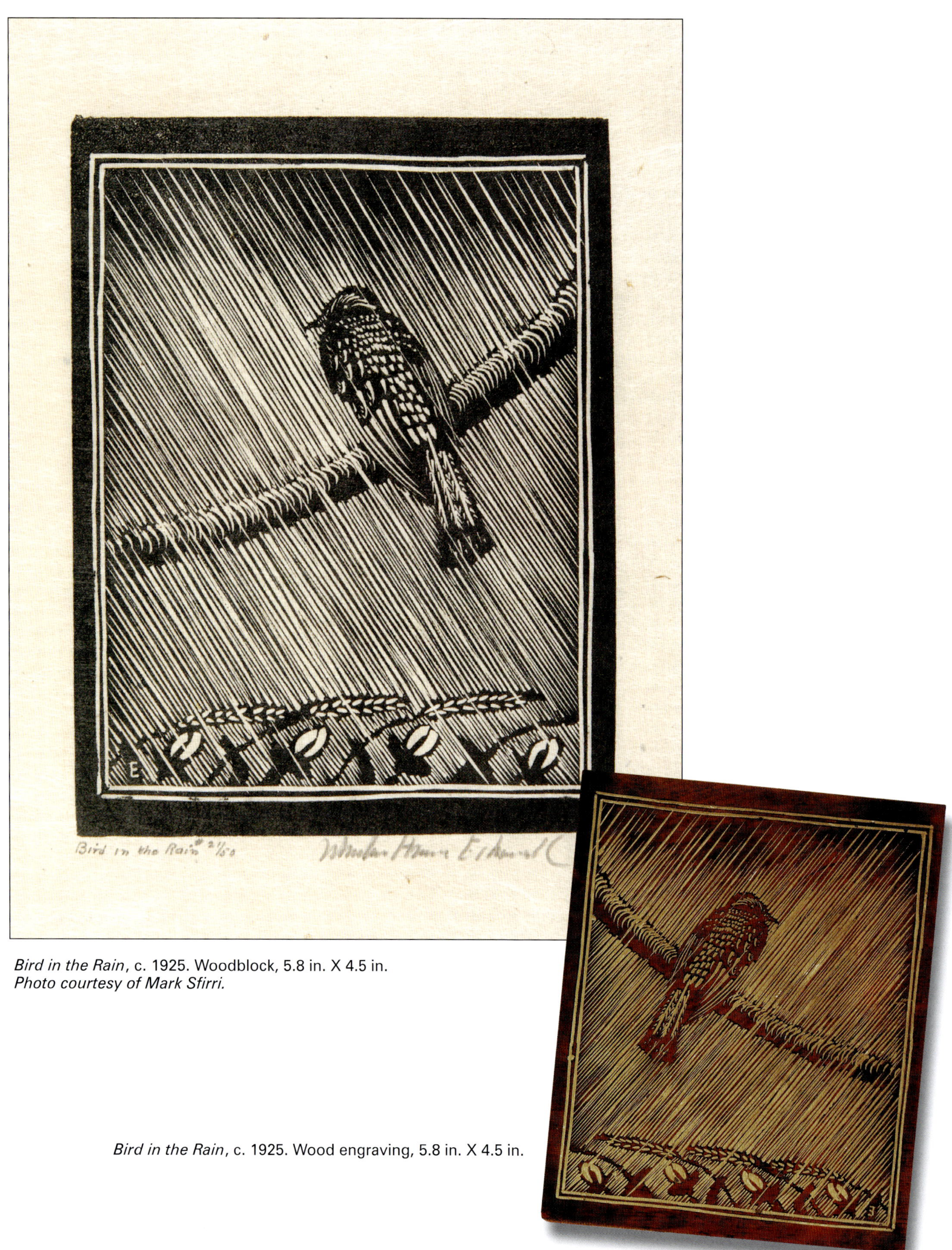

Bird in the Rain, c. 1925. Woodblock, 5.8 in. X 4.5 in.
Photo courtesy of Mark Sfirri.

Bird in the Rain, c. 1925. Wood engraving, 5.8 in. X 4.5 in.

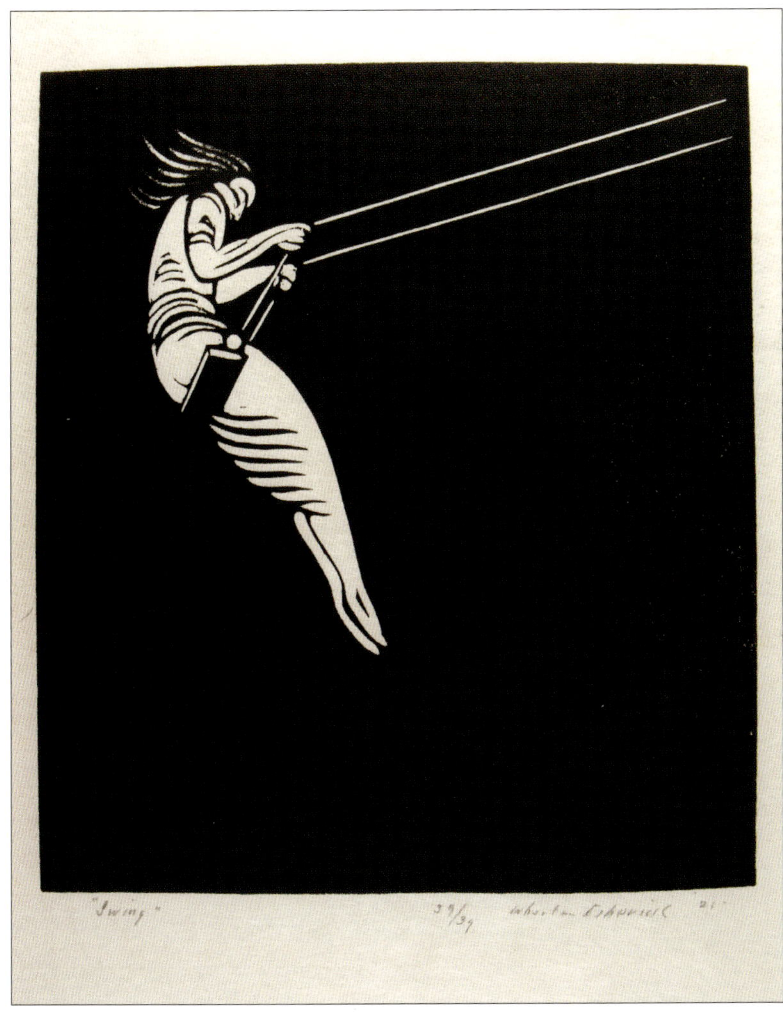

Swing, 1925. Woodcut print, 10.2 in. X 9.1 in.

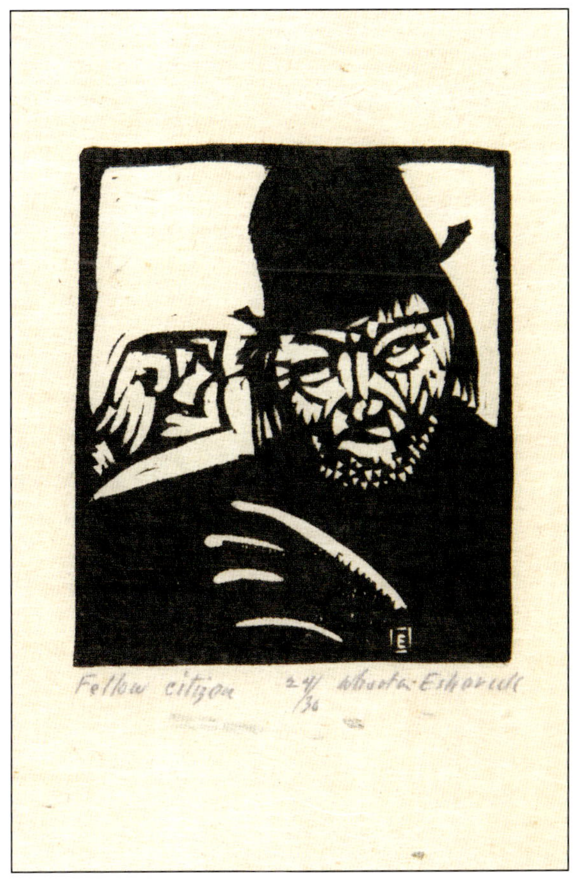

Fellow Citizen, 1925. Wood engraving, 4 in. X 3.5 in.

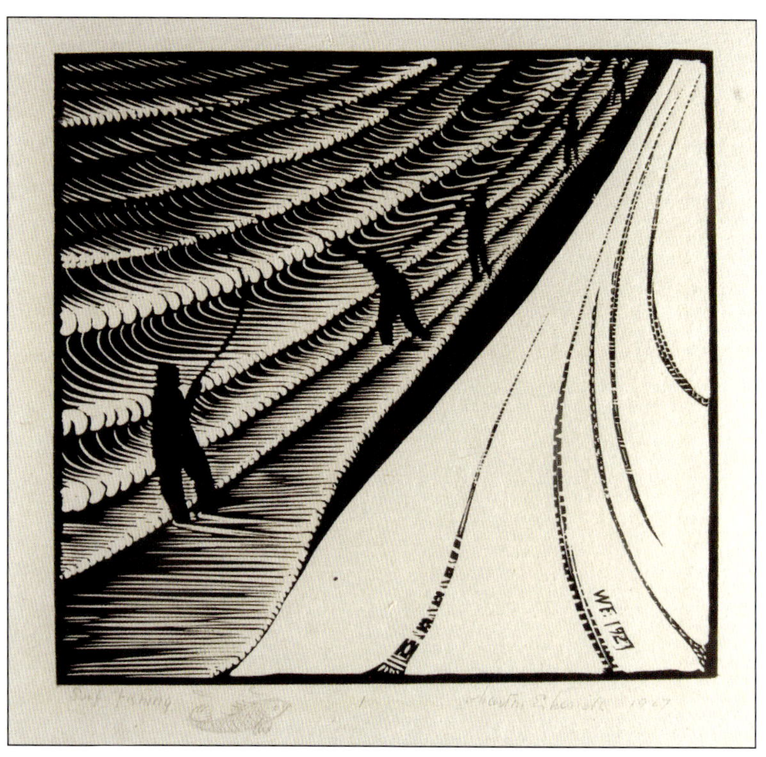

Surf Fishing, 1927. Wood engraving, 7.5 in. X 8.3 in.

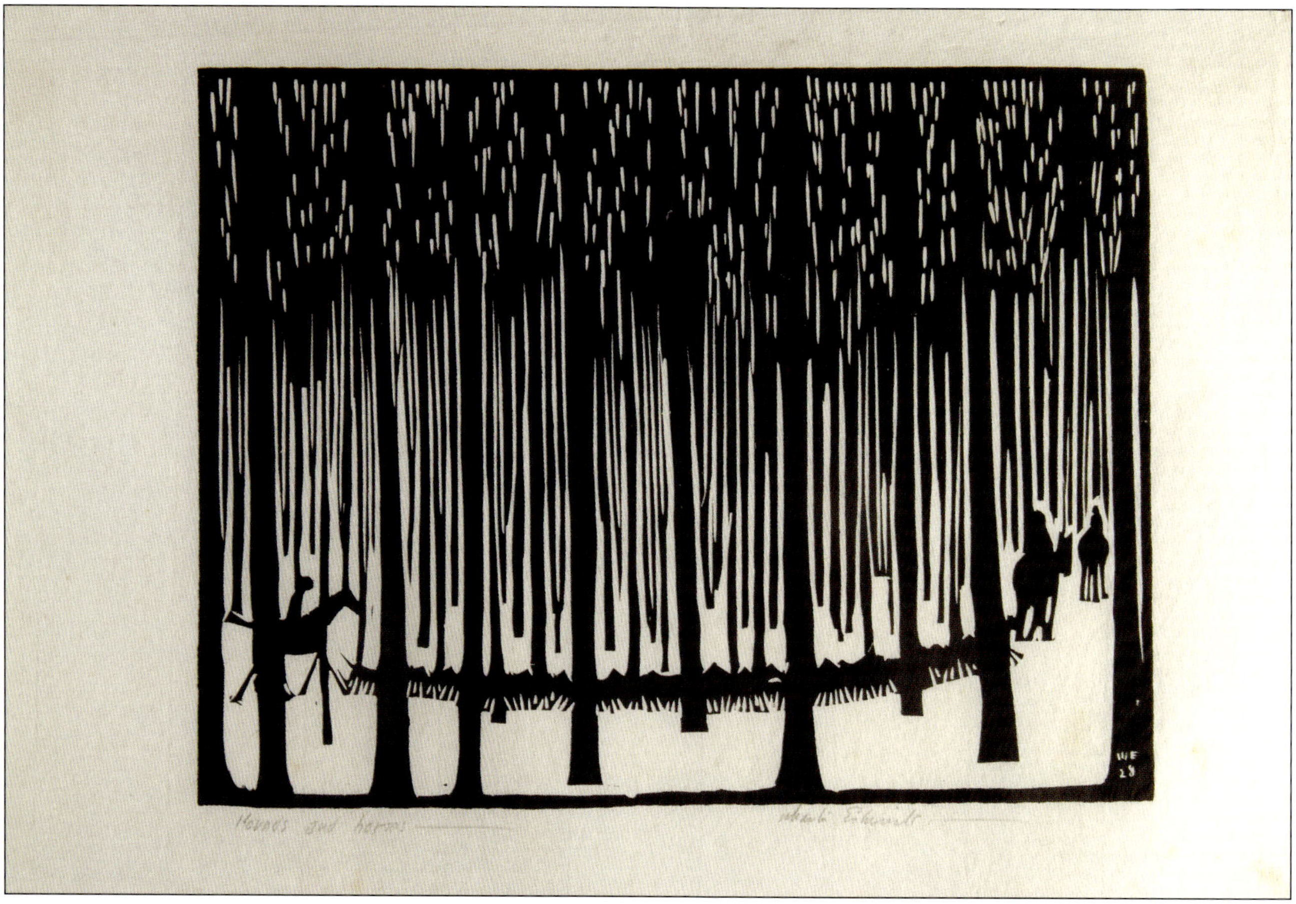

Hounds and Horses, 1928. Woodcut print, 7.7 in. X 10.2 in.

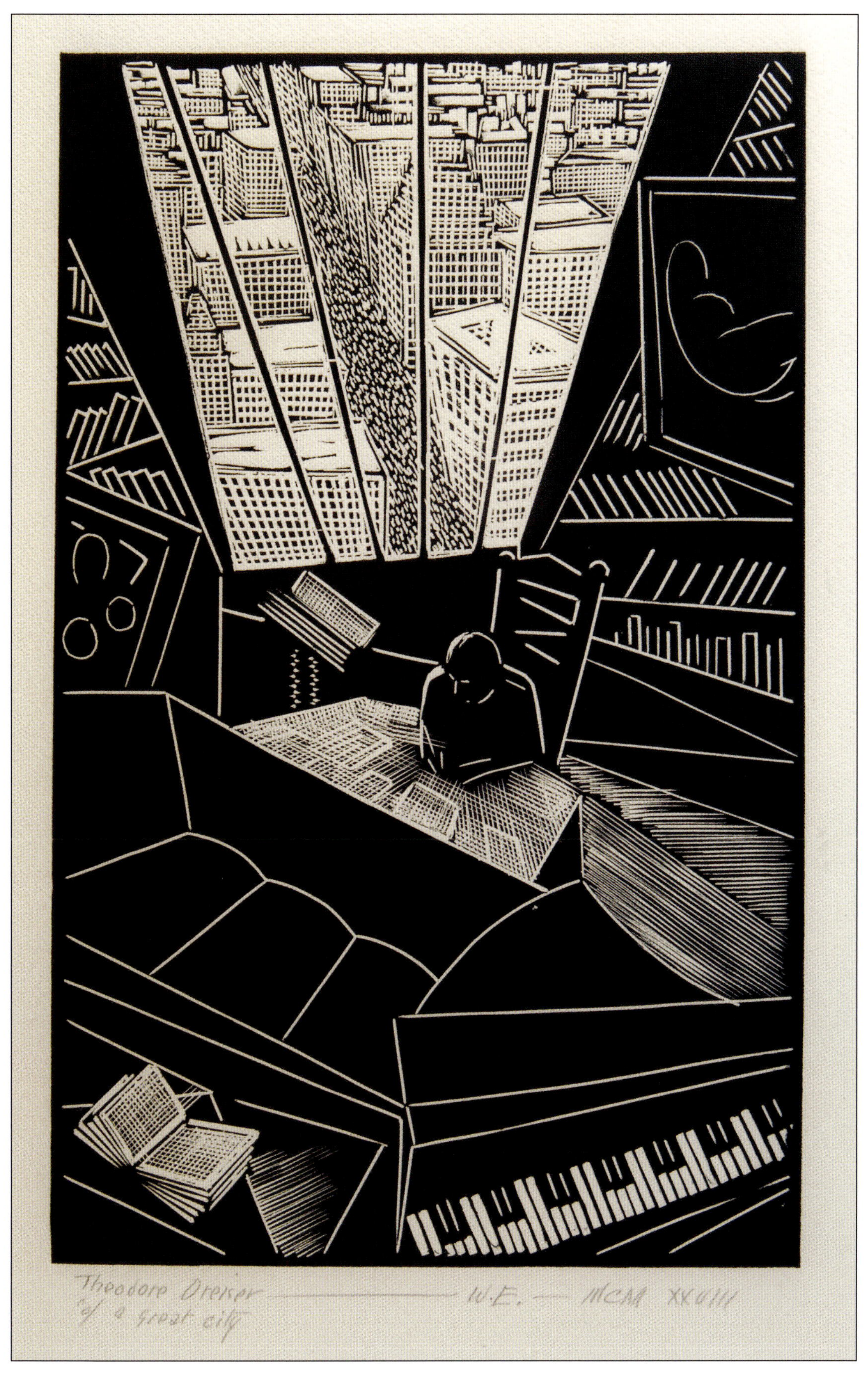

Of A Great City, 1928. Wood engraving, 9.9 in. X 6.3 in. Print of Wharton's friend Theodore Dreiser in his 57th Street apartment in New York City.

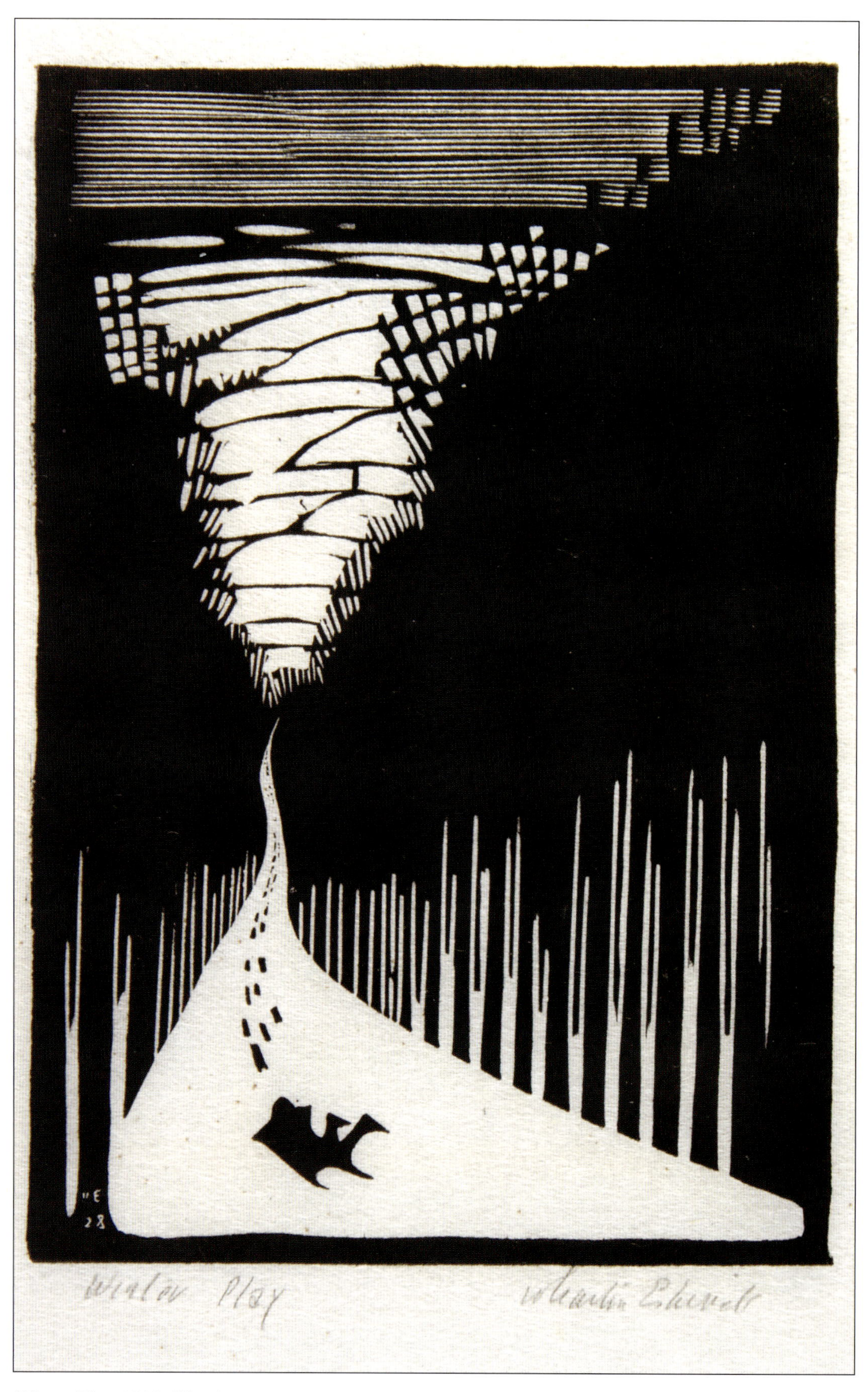

Winter Play, 1928. Wood engraving, 6.6 in. X 4.6 in. Sledding down Diamond Rock Hill.

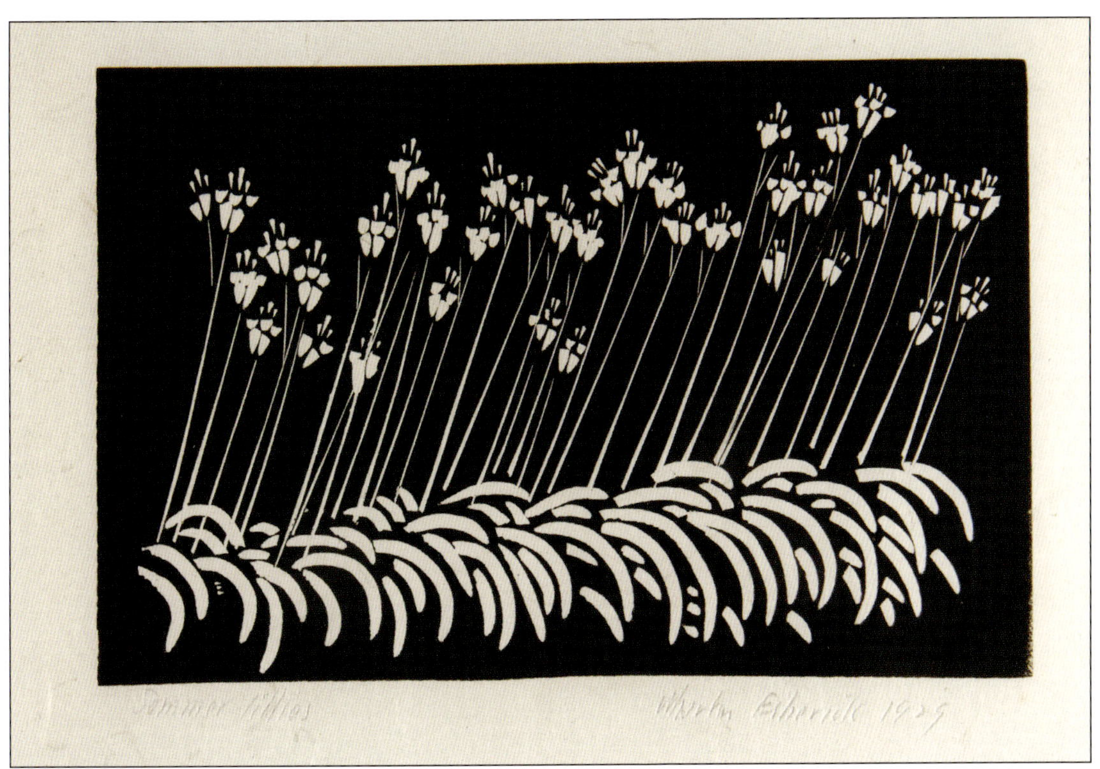

Summer Lillies, 1929. Wood engraving, 4.75 in. X 7.5 in.

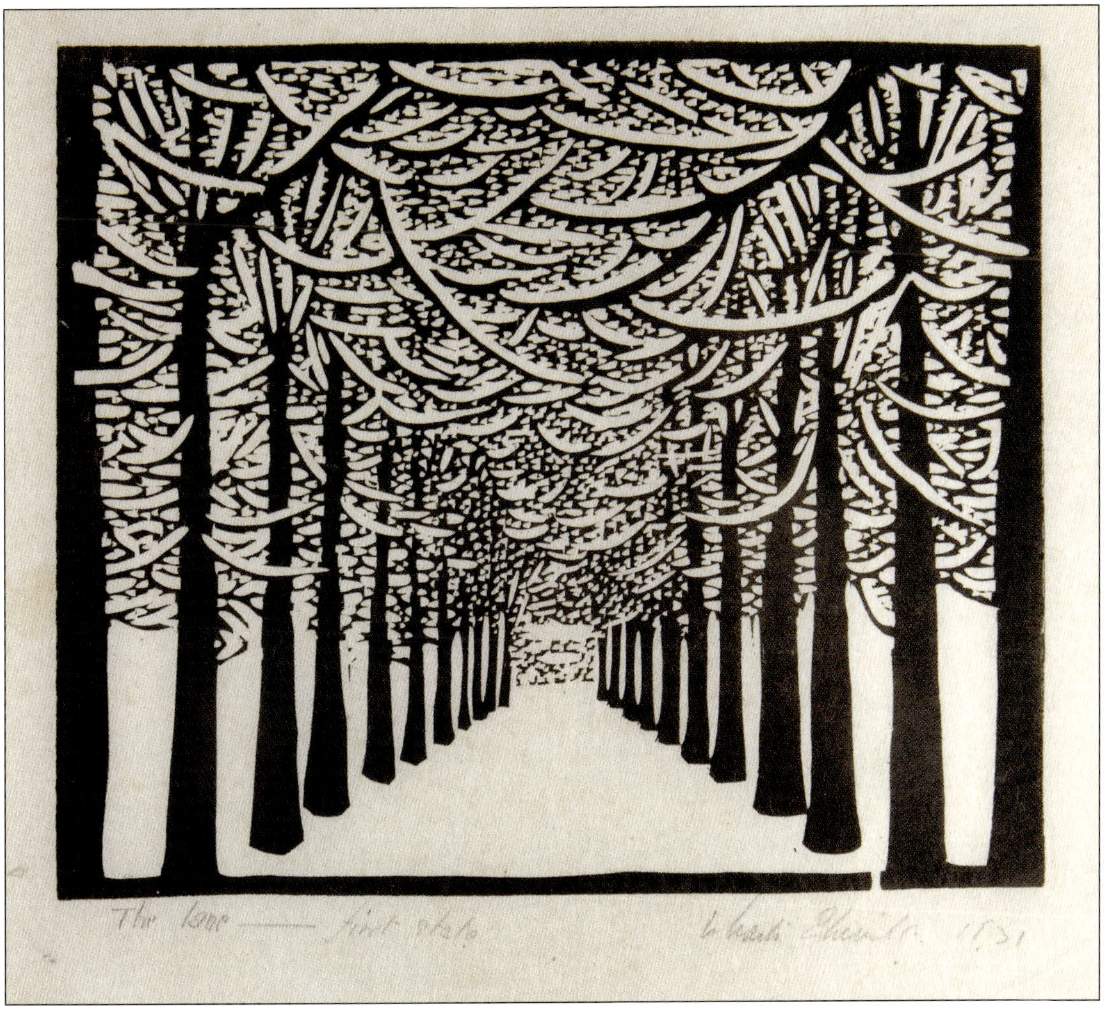

The Lane, 1931. Wood engraving, 7.63 in. X 9.25 in. The driveway to the Fischer's house.

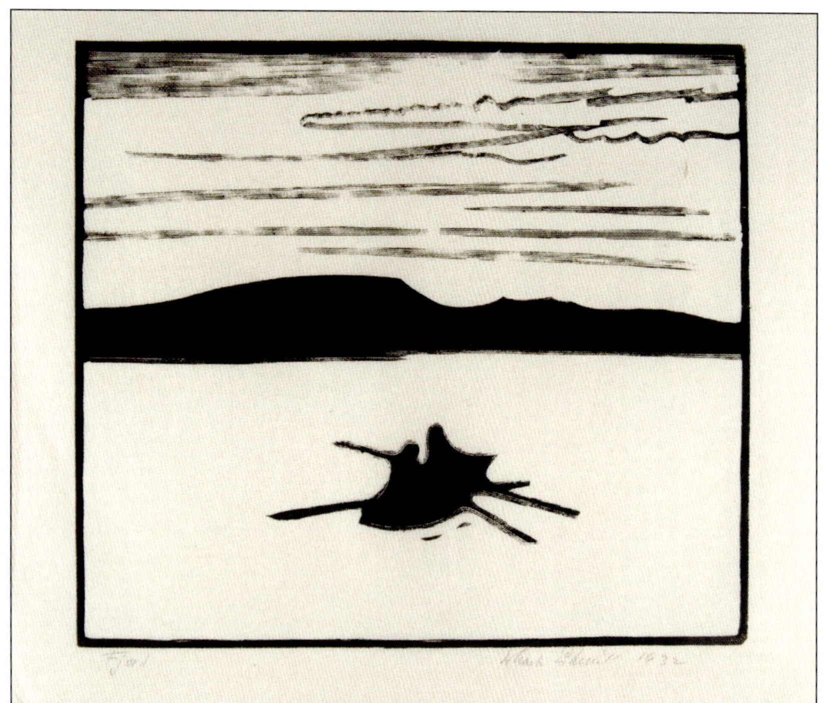

Fjord, 1932. Wood engraving, 8 in. X 9.3 in.

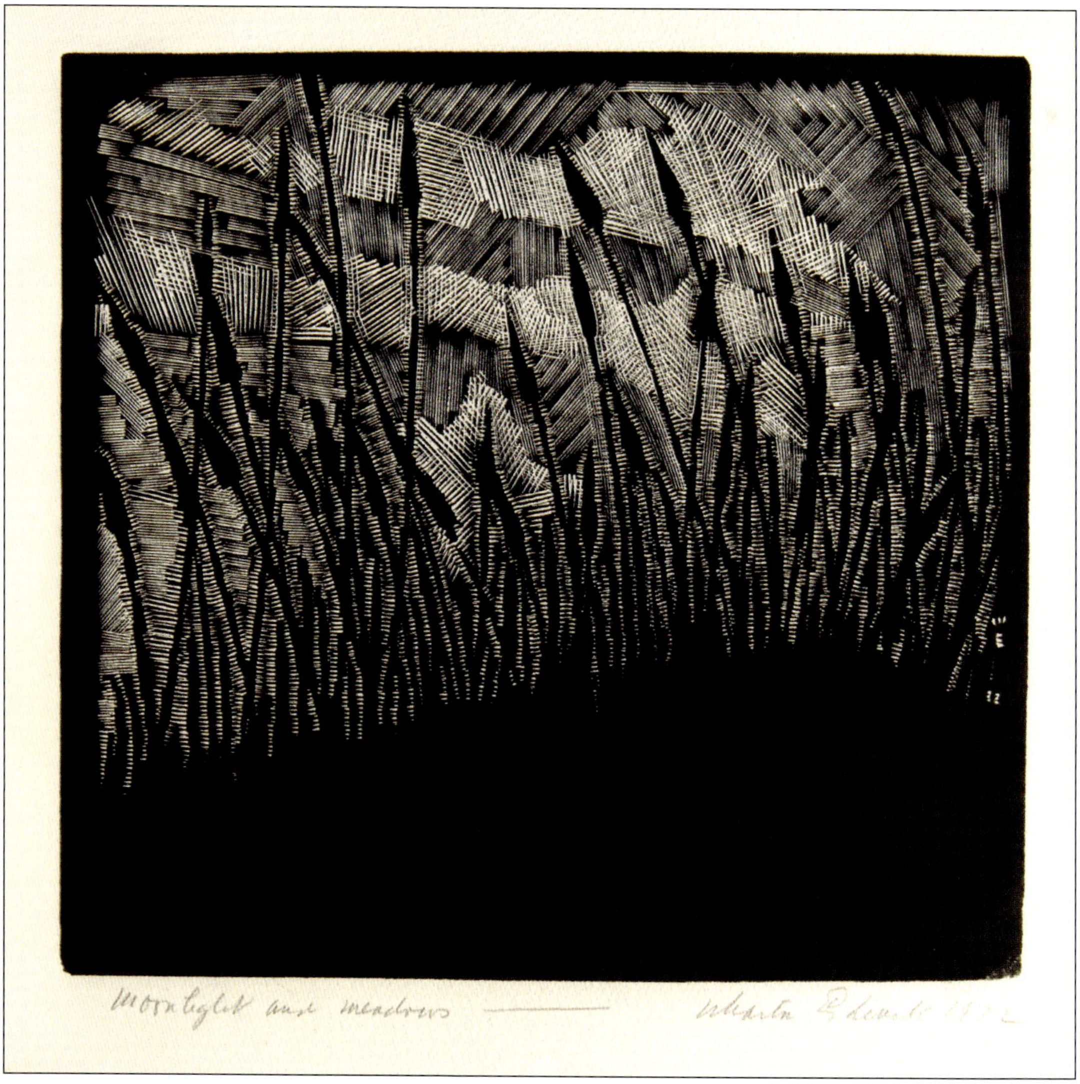

Moonlight and Meadows, 1932. Wood engraving, 7.5 in. X 8.1 in.

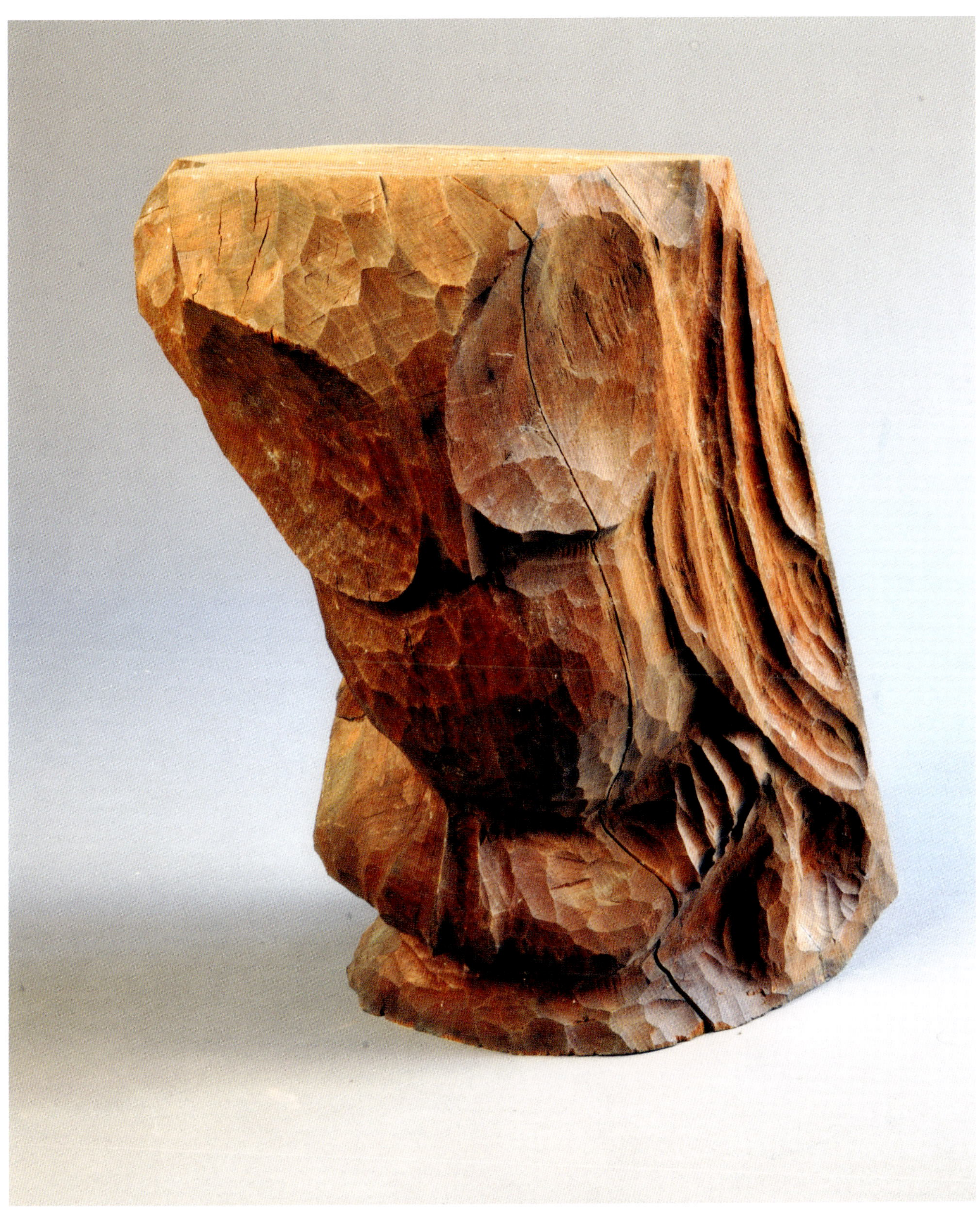

Owl, not dated. Pine, 14 in. X 16 in. X 7.75 in. *Photo courtesy of James Mario.*

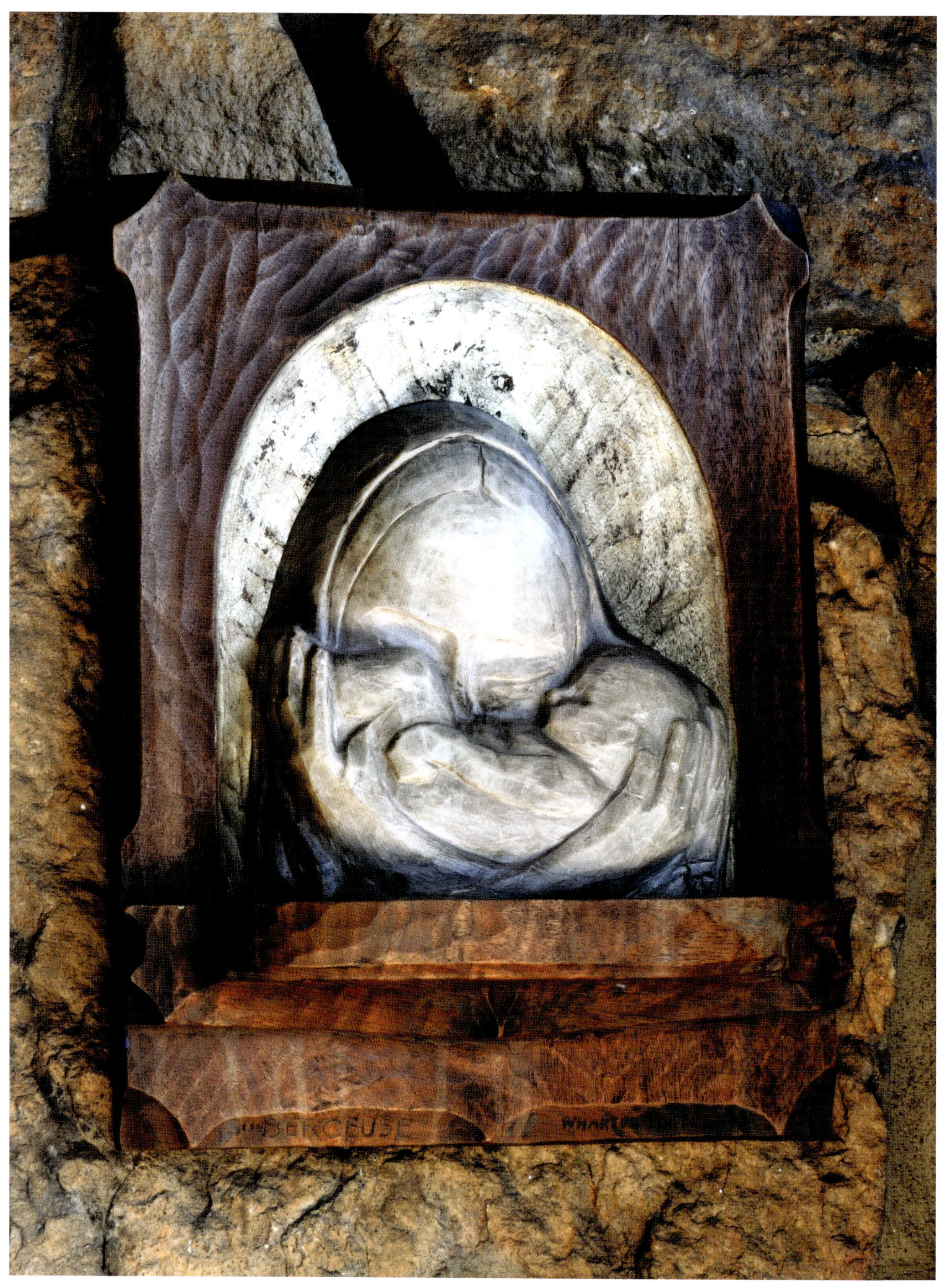

Berceuse, 1923. Soapstone relief in walnut frame, 17 in. X 12.6 in.
Signed "Wharton Esherick 23." *Photo courtesy of James Mario.*

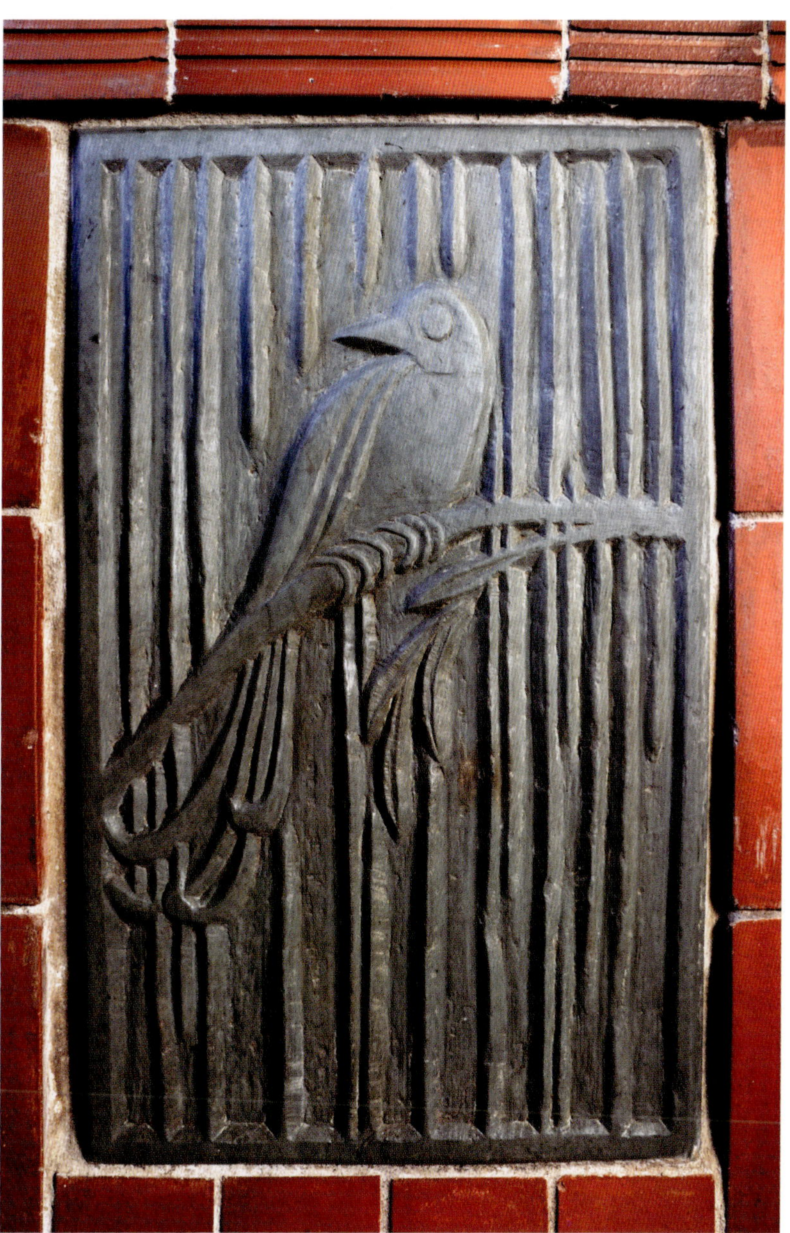

Bird In Rain, c. 1924. Green marble relief, 31.7 in. X 20 in. *Photo courtesy of James Mario.*

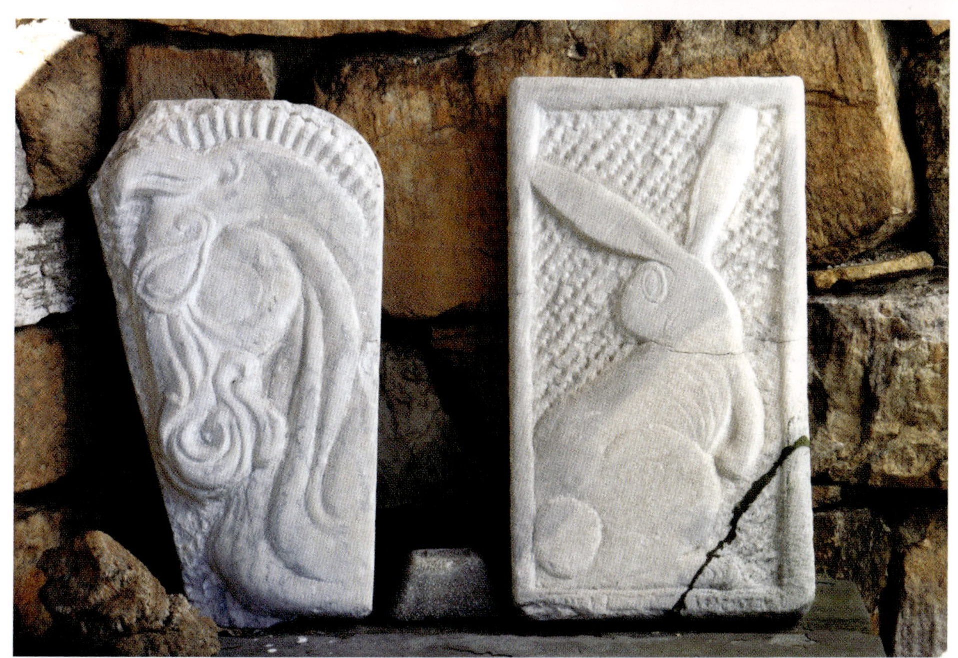

Horse's Head, c. 1924. White marble relief, 25 in. X 14 in. *Rabbit*, 1924. Marble relief, 25.5 in. X 13.3 in. Signed "E. MCXXIV." These two bas-reliefs were displayed on the side of the farmhouse. *Photo courtesy of James Mario.*

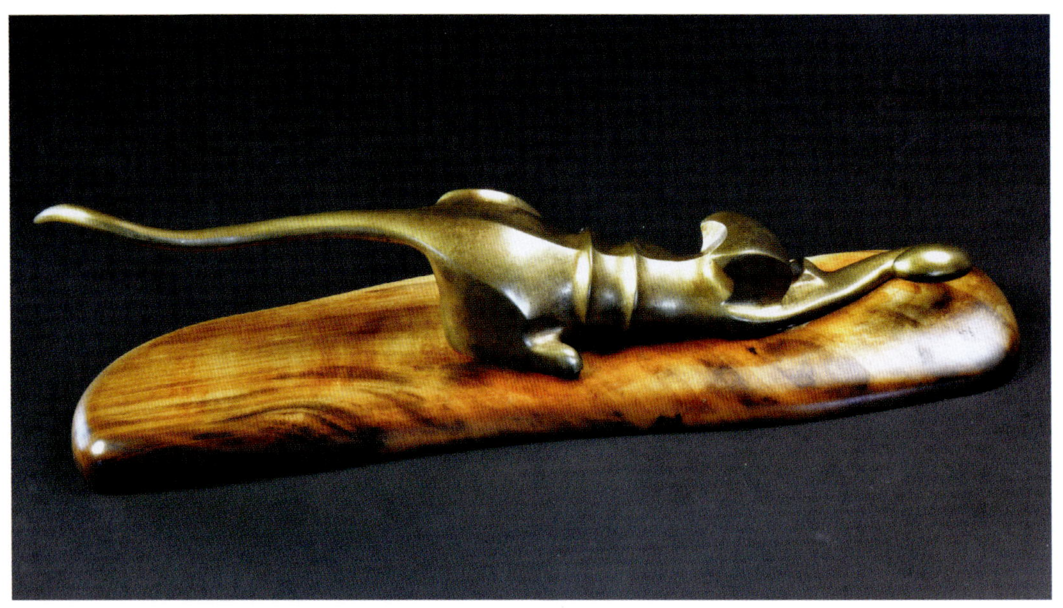

Cat and Snake, 1925. Bronze casting from original snakewood, walnut base, 3.3 in. X 18 in. X 6.7 in. Signed "W.E. 25." *Photo courtesy of James Mario.*

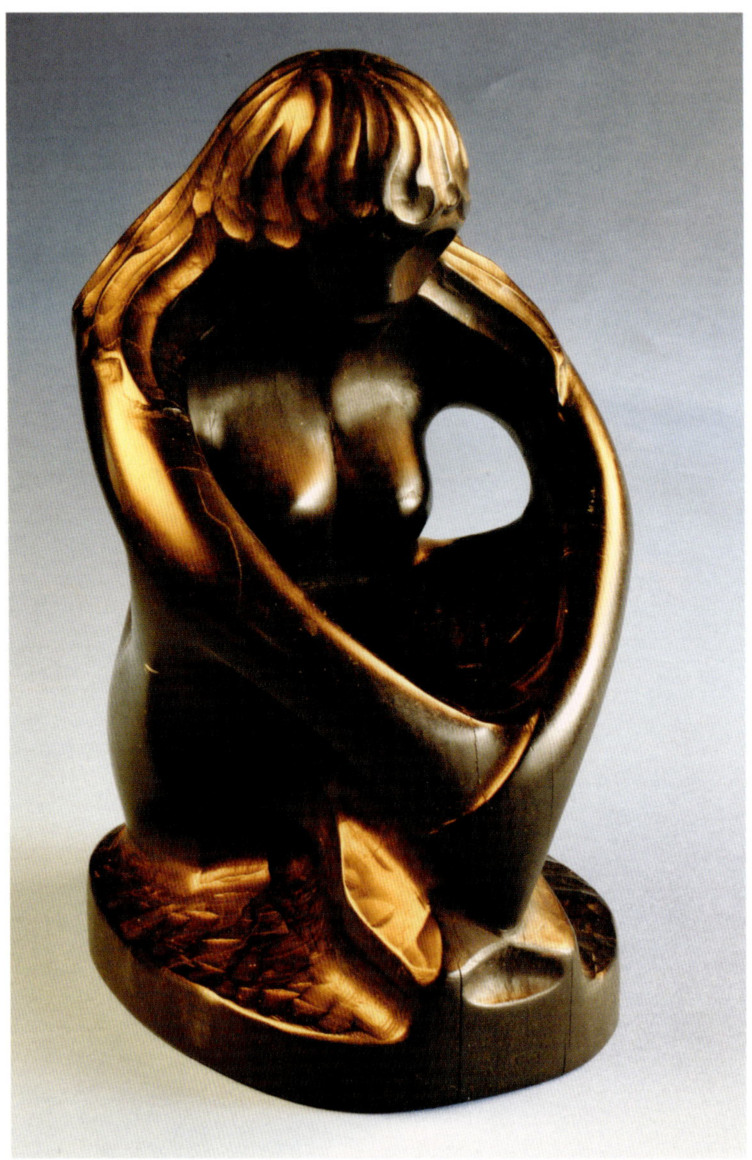

Muse, 1925. Gabon ebony, 10.2 in. X 7 in. X 5.5 in. Signed "Wharton Esherick MCMXXV." *Photo courtesy of James Mario.*

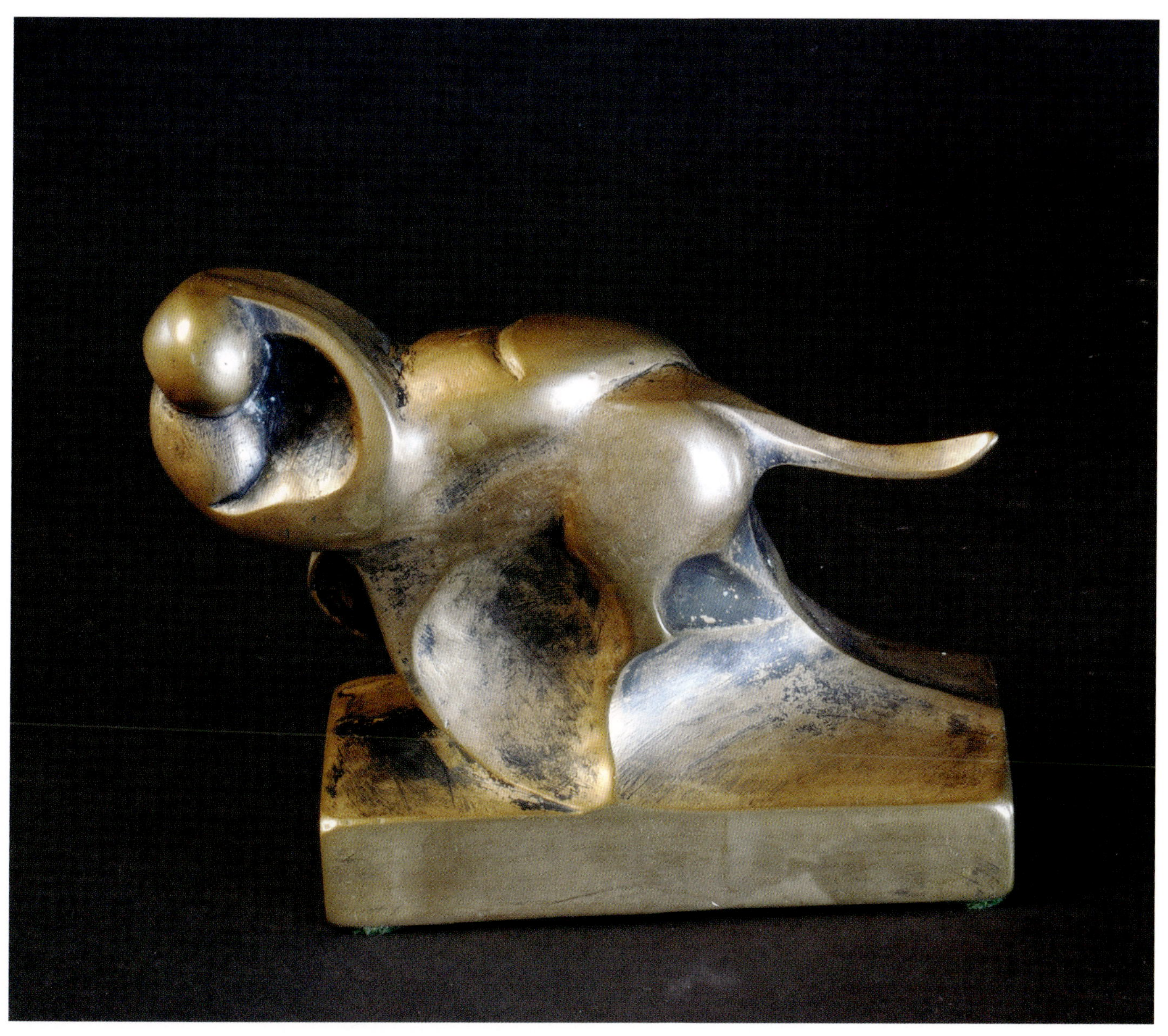

Centaur and Maiden, 1926. Bronze casting from cocobolo original, 4.6 in. X 6 in. X 2.4 in. Signed "W.E. MCMXXVI." *Photo courtesy of James Mario.*

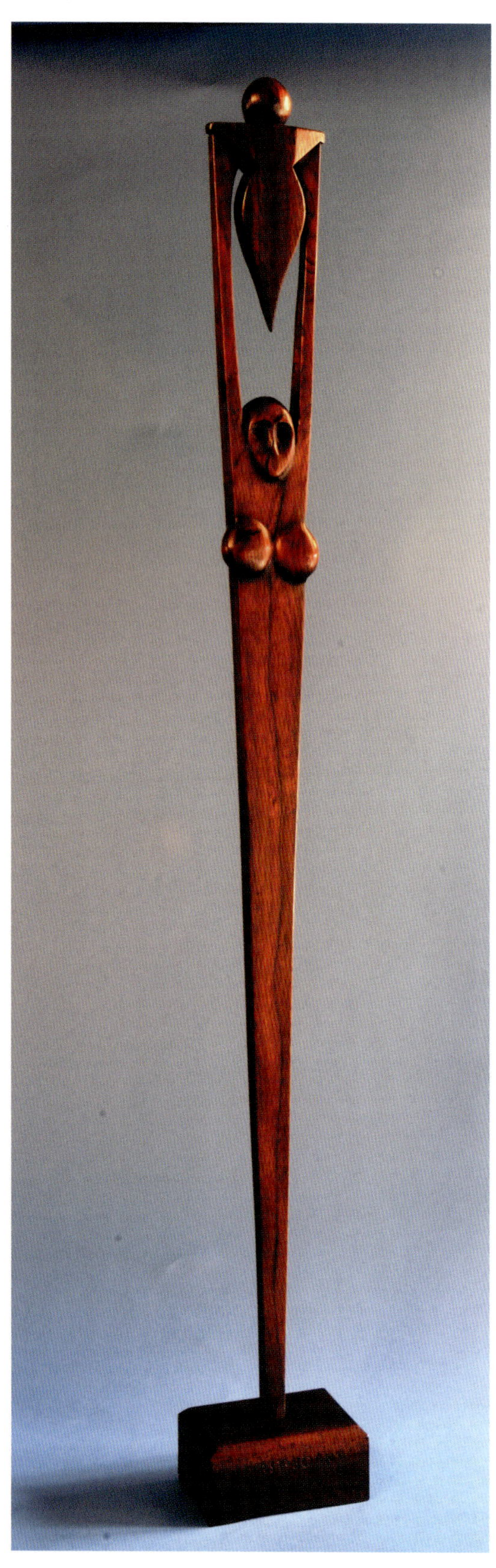

First Born, 1927. Rosewood and padouk, snakewood base, 49.3 in. high. Signed "W.E. 1927." Commemorates the birth of Peter Esherick, artist's only son. *Photo courtesy of James Mario.*

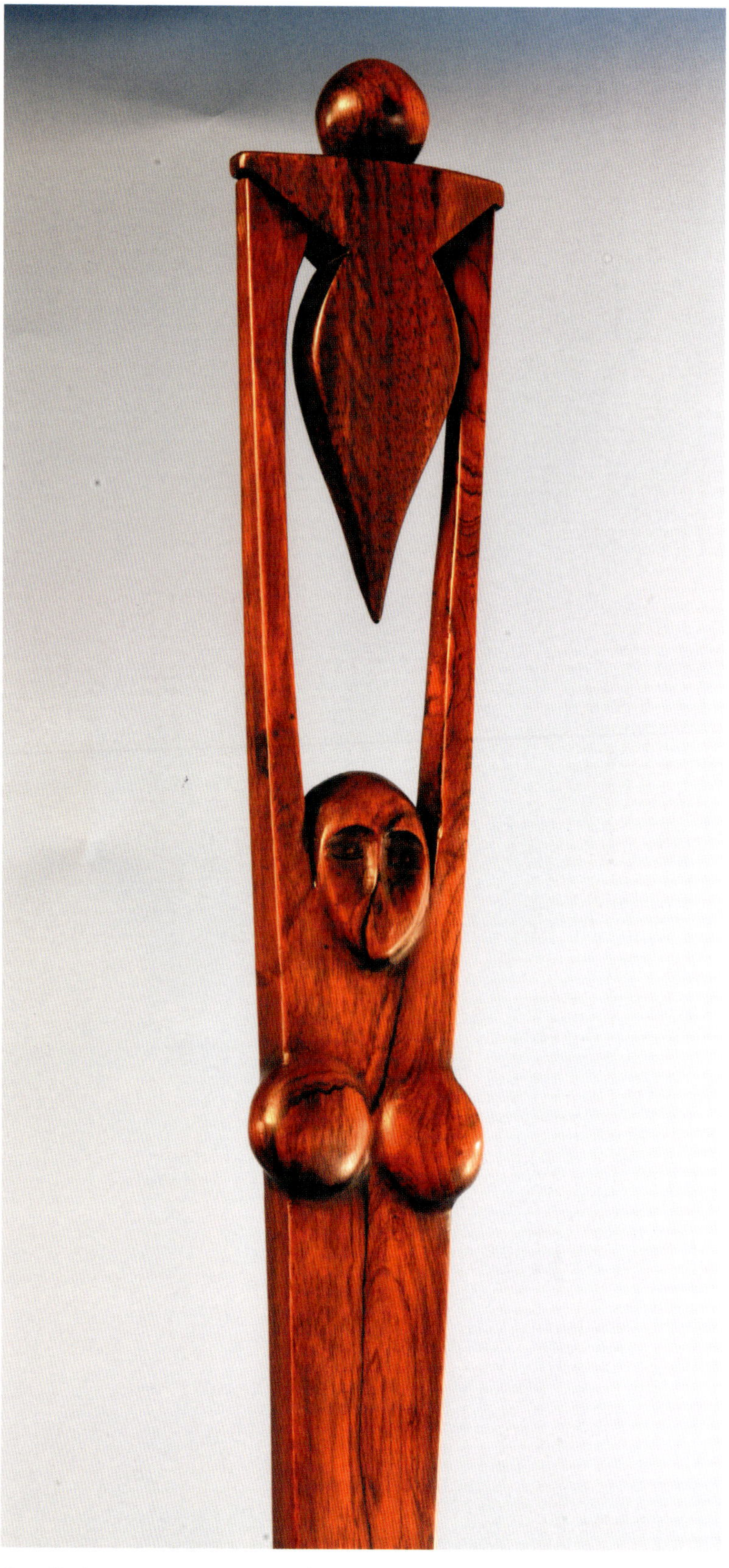

Detail of *First Born*. *Photo courtesy of James Mario.*

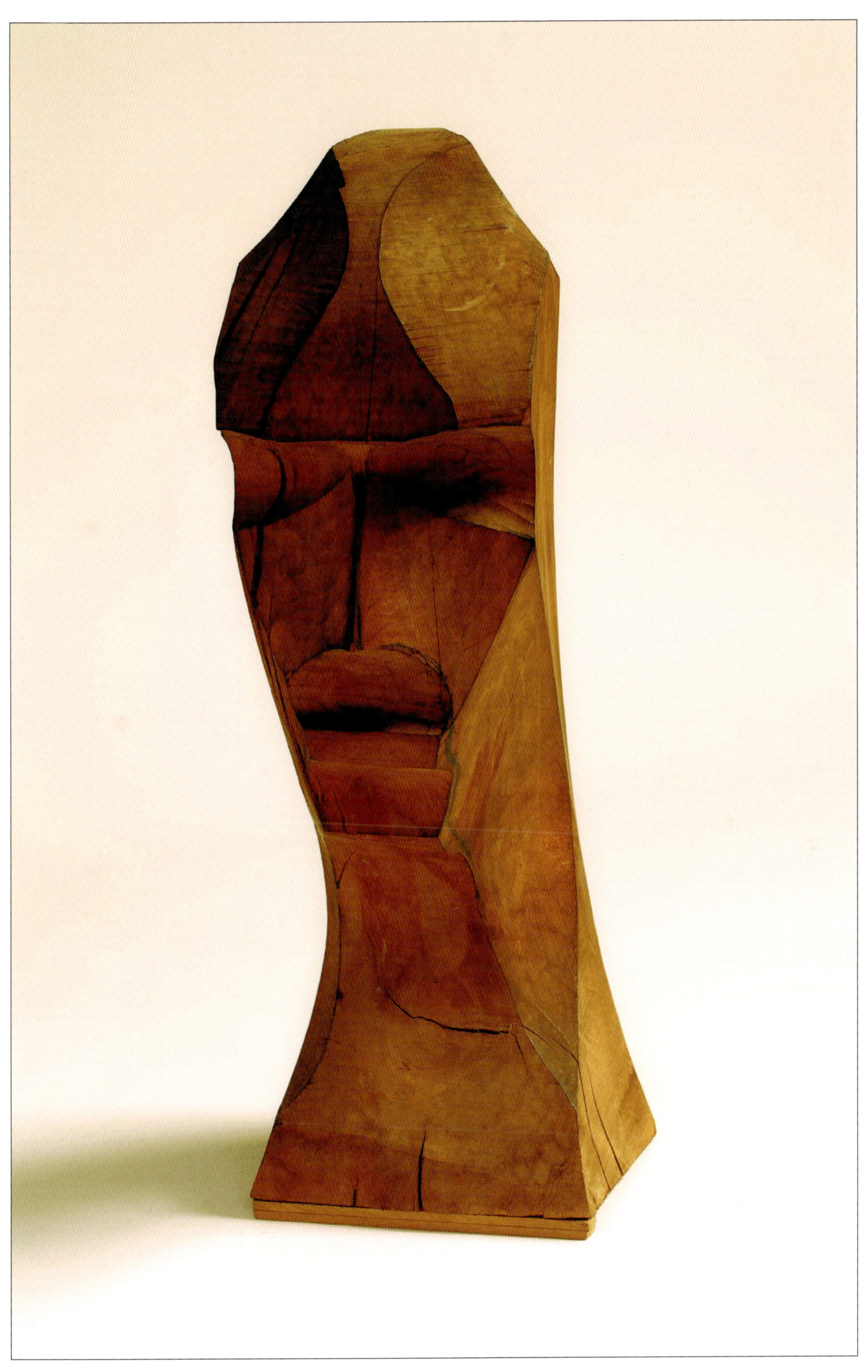

Head of Dreiser, 1927. Pine, 17.5 in. X 7.5 in. X 6 in. Sketch for mahogany *Head of Dreiser*, 1927, that is now in the Rare Book Room of the Van Pelt/Dietrich Library at the University of Pennsylvania. *Photo courtesy of James Mario.*

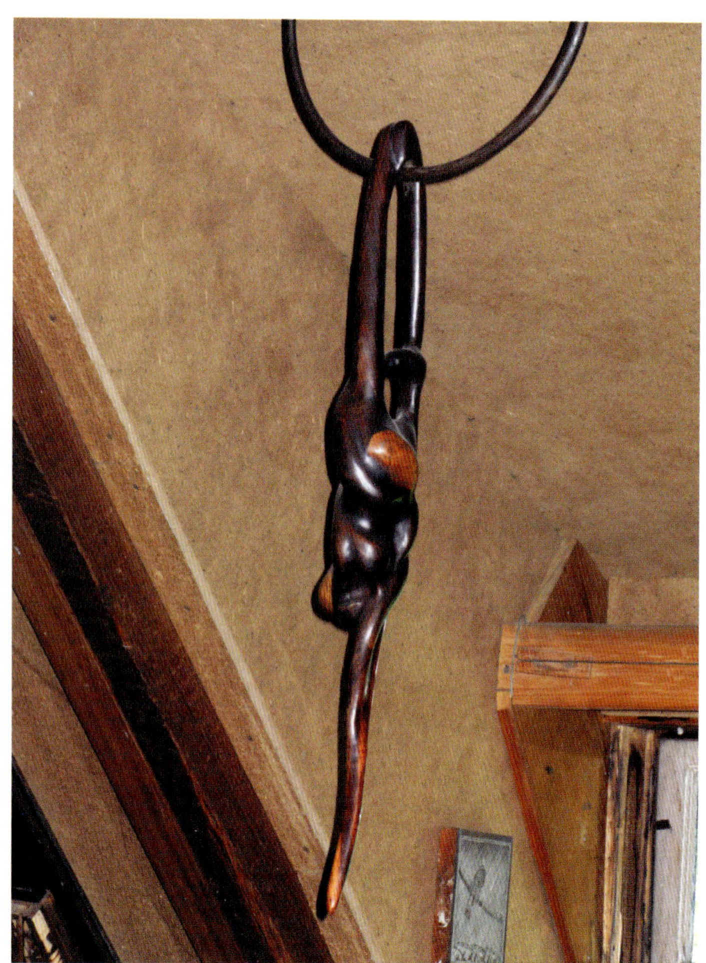

Monkey Business, 1927. Lignum vitae with iron ring, 36 in. high. Signed "W.E. 1927."

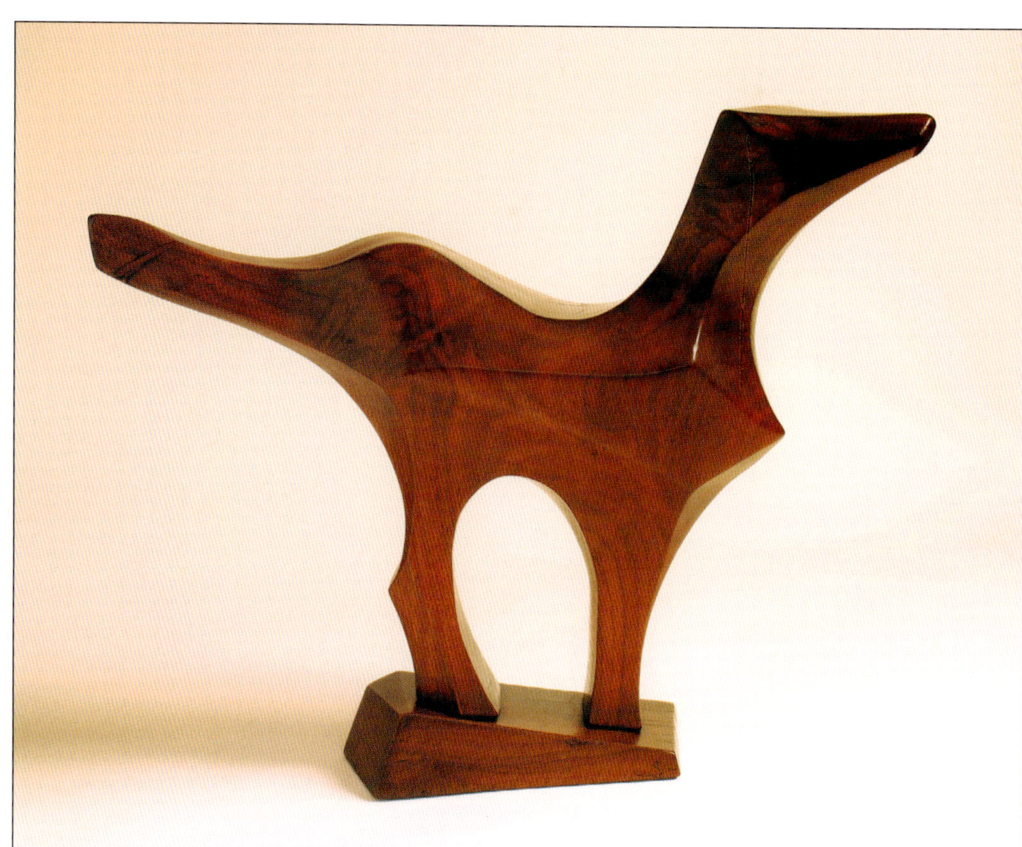

Pup, 1928. Walnut root burl, 20.5 in. X 25 in. X 7 in. Signed "Wharton Esherick MCMXX-VIII." After artist's daughter Ruth's collie pup. *Photo courtesy of James Mario.*

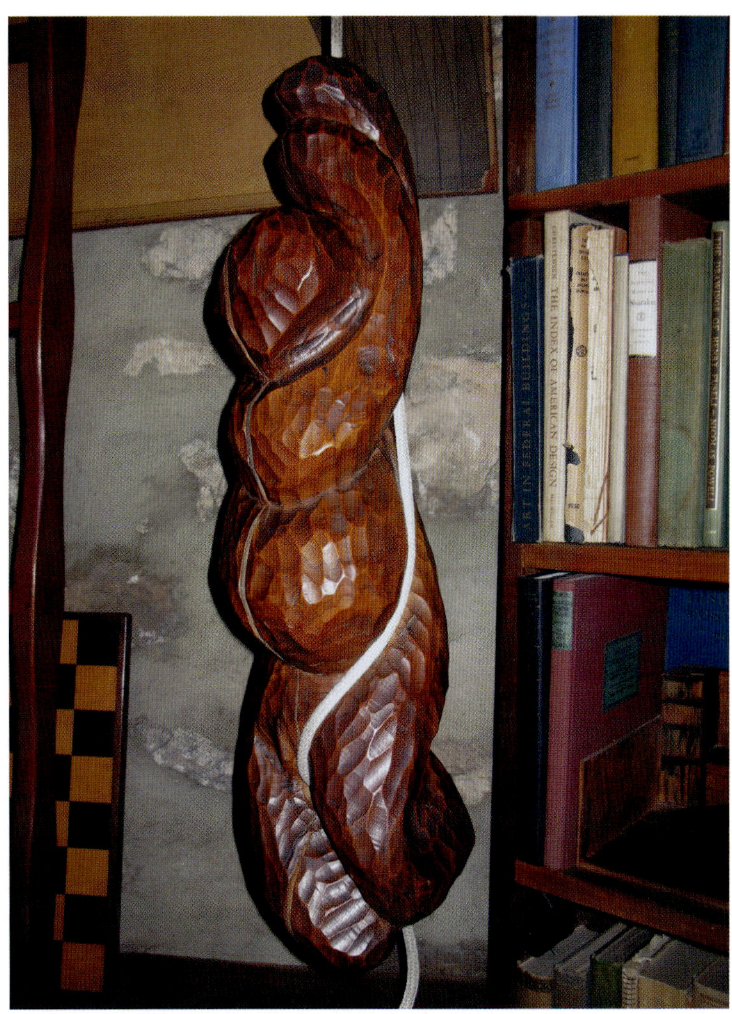

Hanging figure, c. 1928. Tulipwood, 30.5 in. high. Serves as counterweight for the trap door that closes off the bedroom at top of the spiral stair.

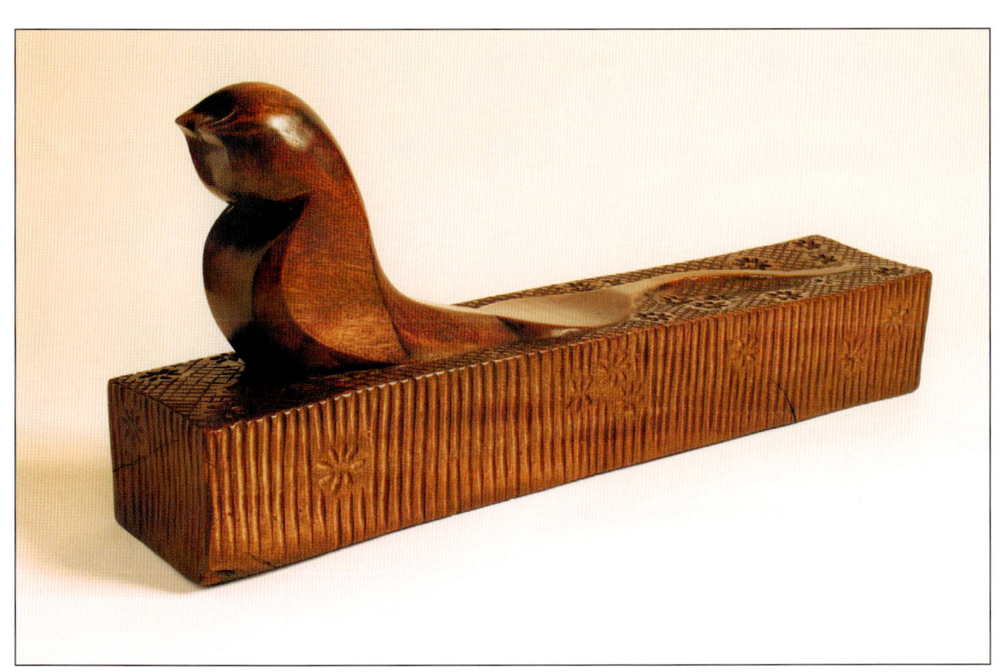

Cat in the Grass, 1929. African mahogany, 13.4 in. X 30.2 in. X 6 in. Signed "Wharton Esherick MCMXXIX." A transition from representational (grass) to abstract (cat). *Photo courtesy of James Mario.*

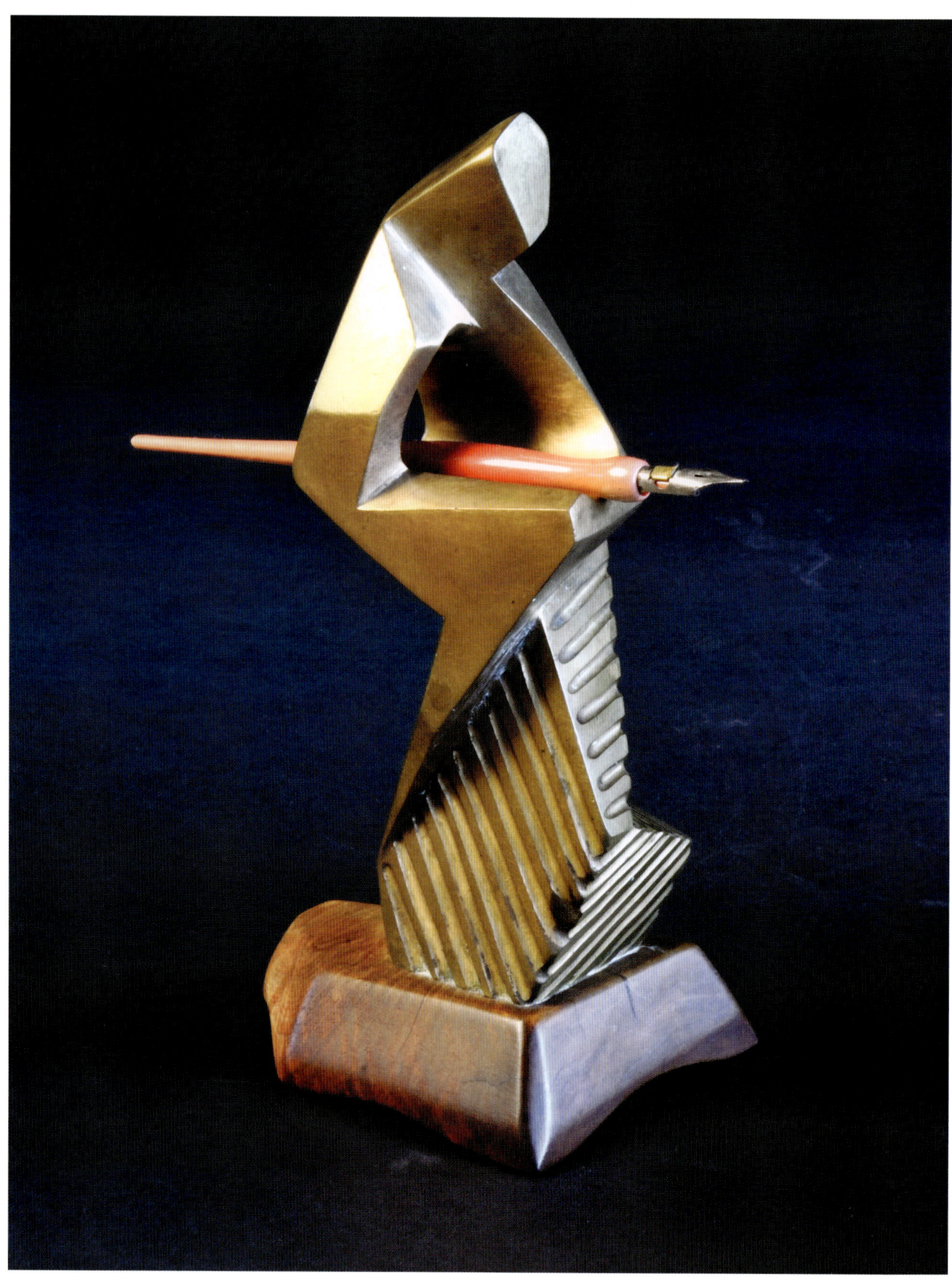

Desk Figure, 1929. Bronze casting from cocobolo original, 8.5 in. X 5.1 in. X 3.7 in.
Signed "W.E. XXIX." *Photo courtesy of James Mario.*

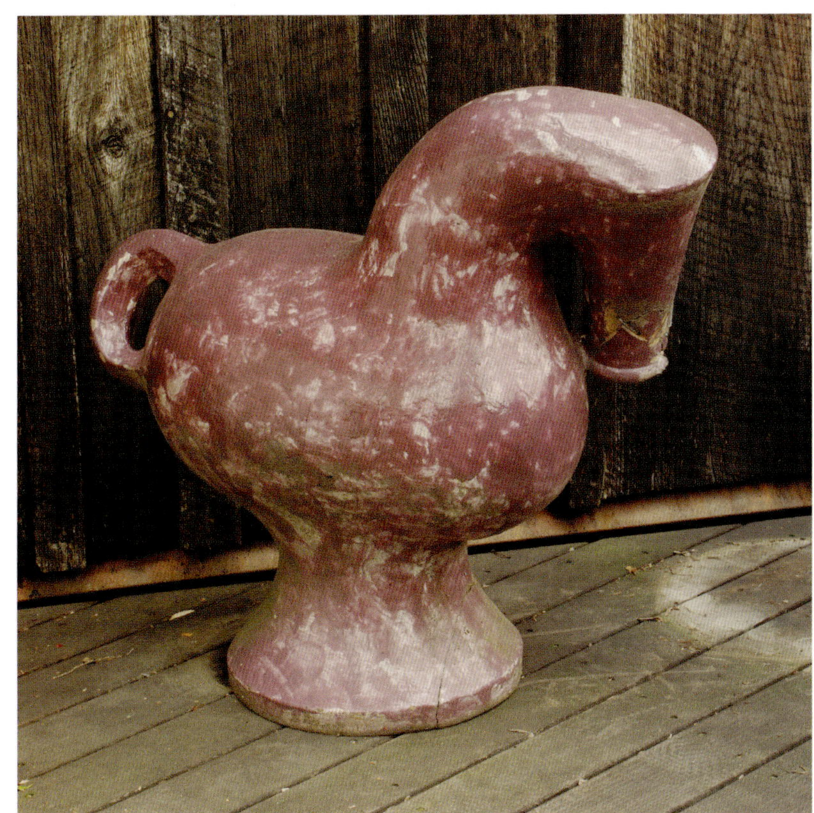

Horse, 1930. Ceramic, plum glaze, 23 in. X 25 in. X 12.5 in. In 1930, while in Daphne, Alabama, Wharton made a series of ceramic sculptures, working with potter Peter McAdams. *Photo courtesy of Mark Sfirri.*

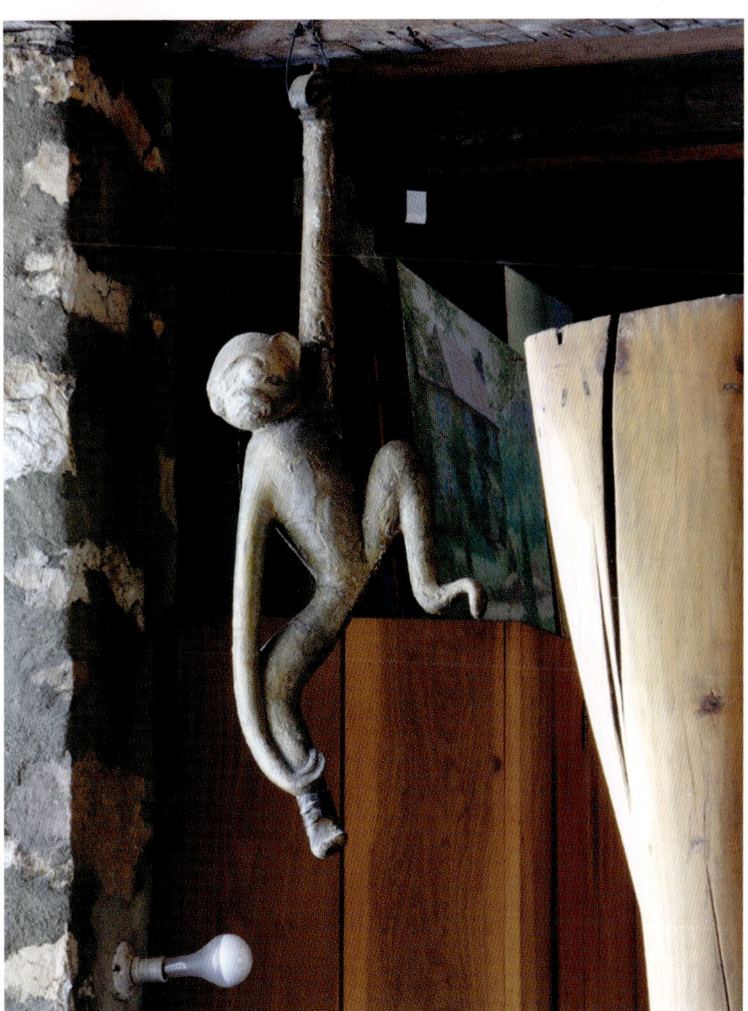

Hanging Monkey, 1930. Ceramic, grey glaze, 48 in. high. *Photo courtesy of James Mario.*

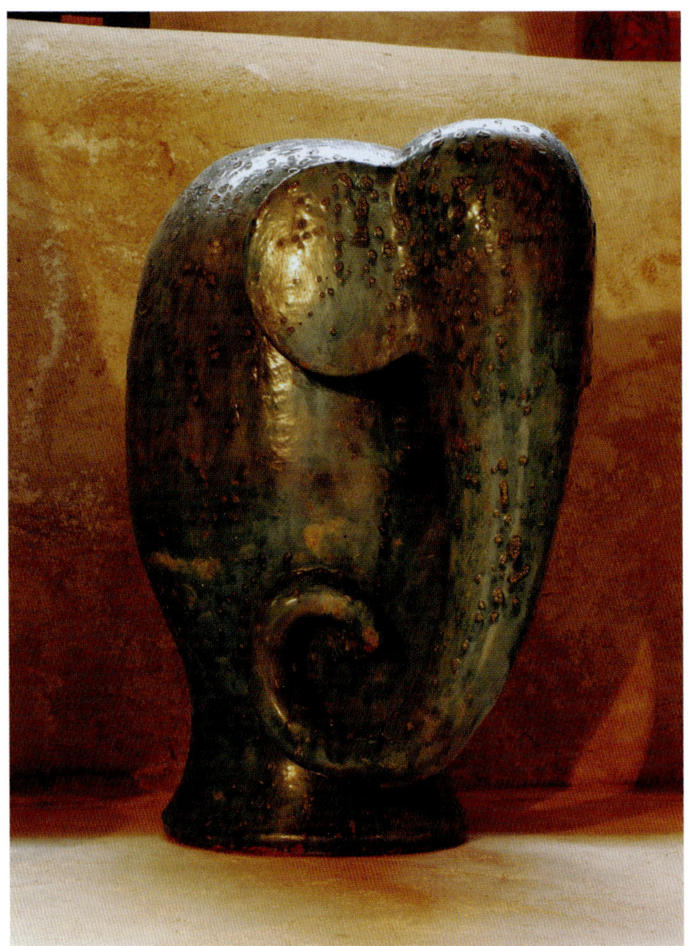

Elephant, 1930. Ceramic, blue-green glaze. Signed "W.E. MCMXXX." *Photo courtesy of Mark Sfirri.*

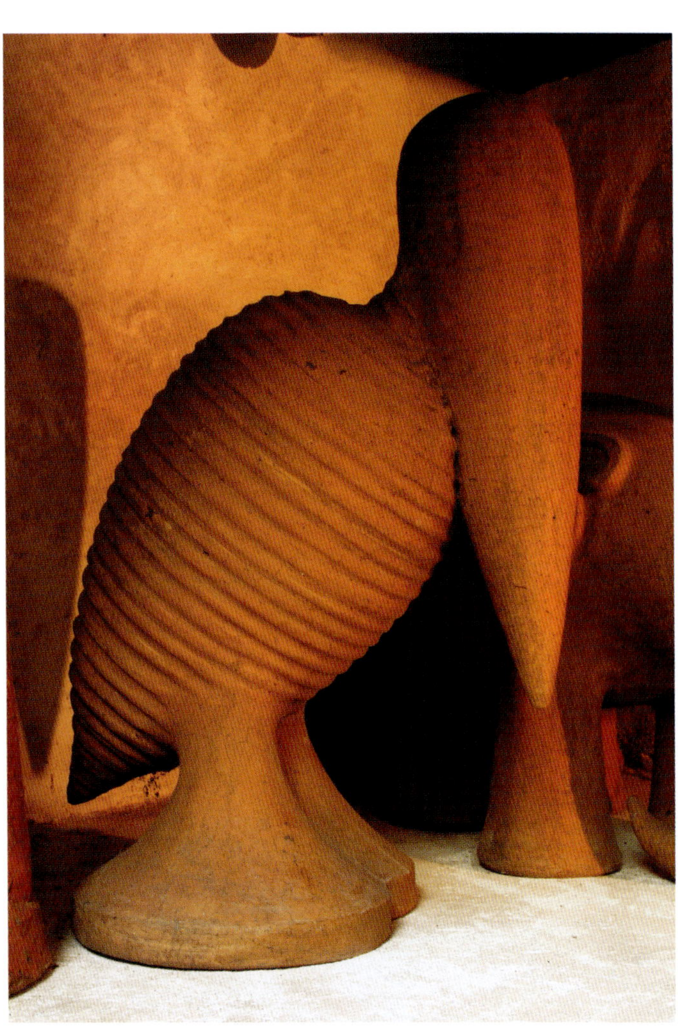

Unglazed Pelican, 1930. Ceramic, unglazed, 15.7 in. X 18 in. X 11.7 in. Signed "W.E. MC-MXXX." *Photo courtesy of Mark Sfirri.*

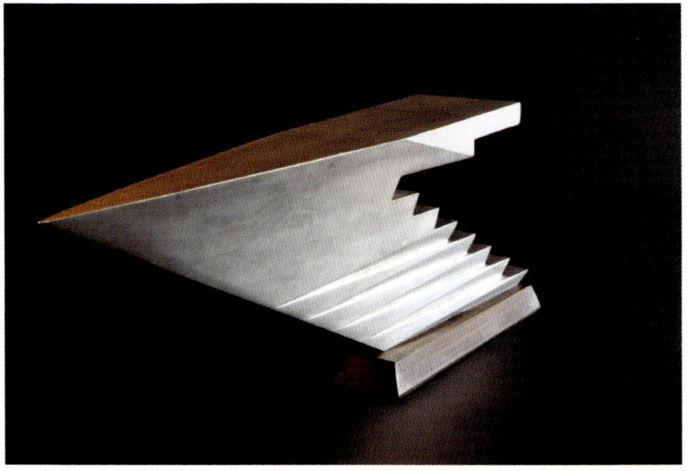

Speed, 1932. Aluminum casting of painted wood original, 10.6 in. X 33.4 in. X 6 in. Signed "Wharton Esherick MCXXXII." Created as a stage prop for Hedgerow Theatre's production of "The Ship." *Photo courtesy of James Mario.*

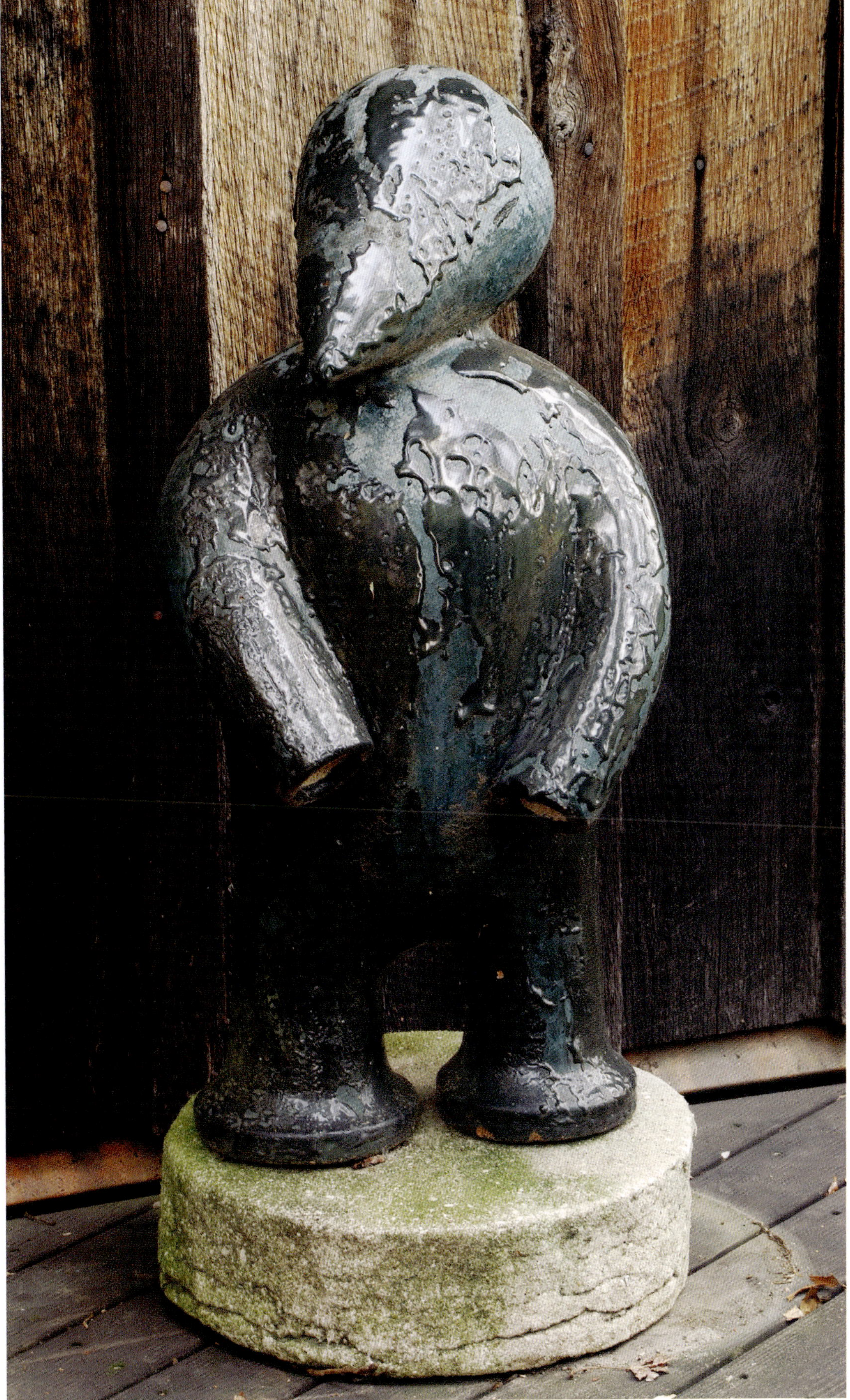

Winnie-ther-Pooh, 1930. Ceramic, mottled green glaze, 26.4 in. high X 12 in. diameter. An aluminum casting of *Pooh* greets Museum visitors outside the Visitor Center. *Photo courtesy of Mark Sfirri.*

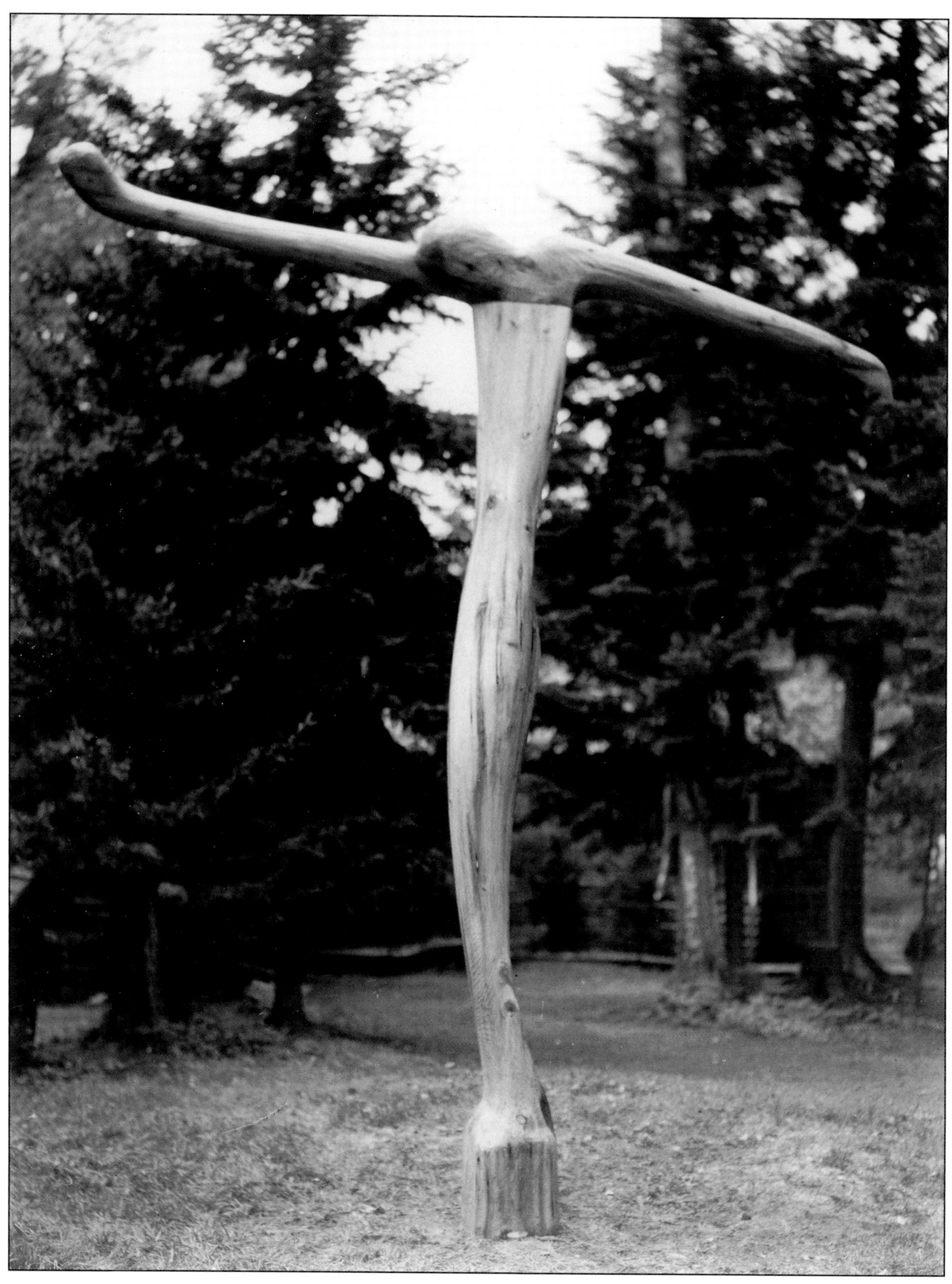

Dance Finale, 1933. Pine, 157.9 in. X 128.3 in. Signed "W.E. MCMXXXIII." Made for the Gardner-Doing Dance camp in the Adirondacks. It depicts a dancer taking a standing bow at the end of a dance. When Wharton brought it inside, he took it apart, placing the torso in the sculpture well and the head and arms above the window.

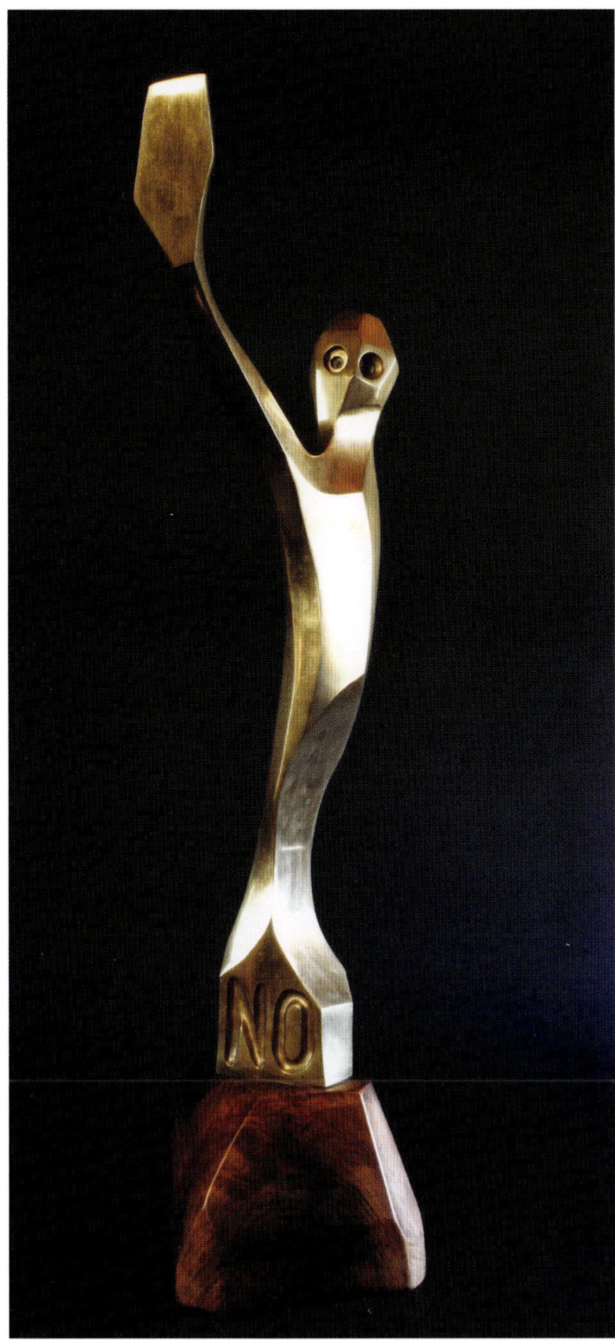

No, 1934. Bronze casting of pearwood original, 41.5 in. X 9.5 in. X 9 in. Signed "W.E. MCMXXXIV." The original was designed to keep people from using the stairs to the balcony at Hedgerow Theatre. The Museum uses it for the same purpose on the stairs to Peter's bedroom. *Photo courtesy of James Mario.*

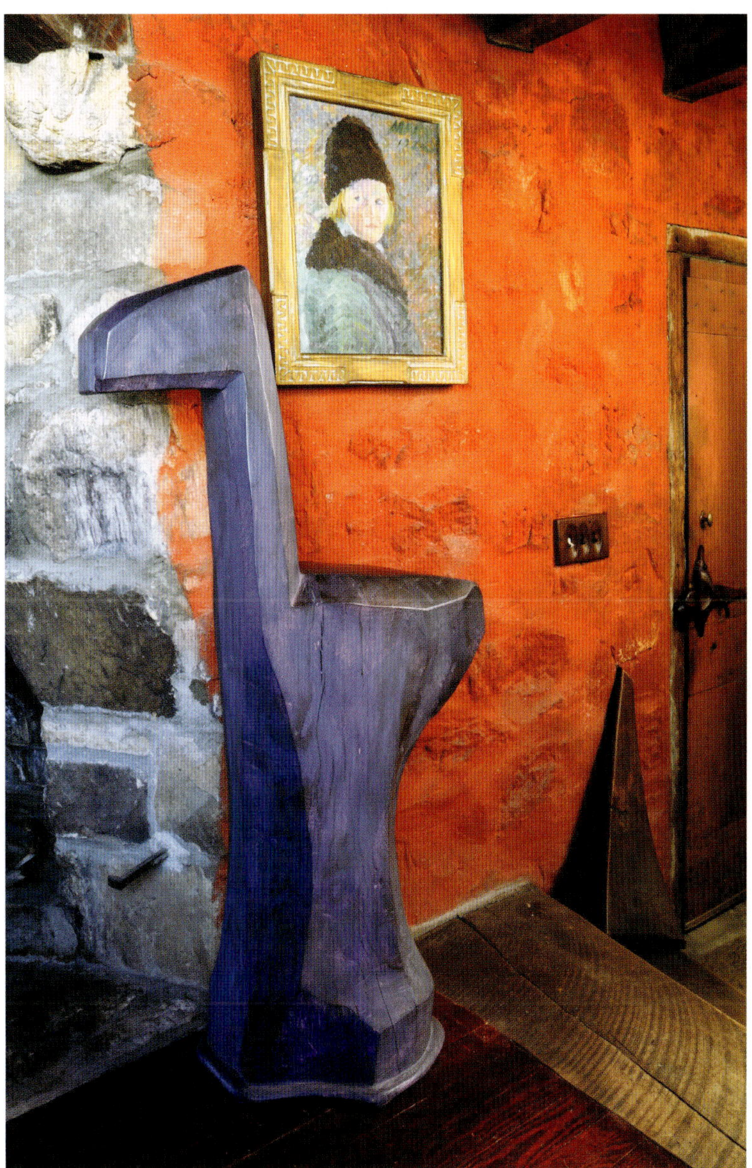

Garden Horse, c. 1935. Painted wood, 55.5 in. X 24 in. X 17.5 in. *Photo courtesy of James Mario.*

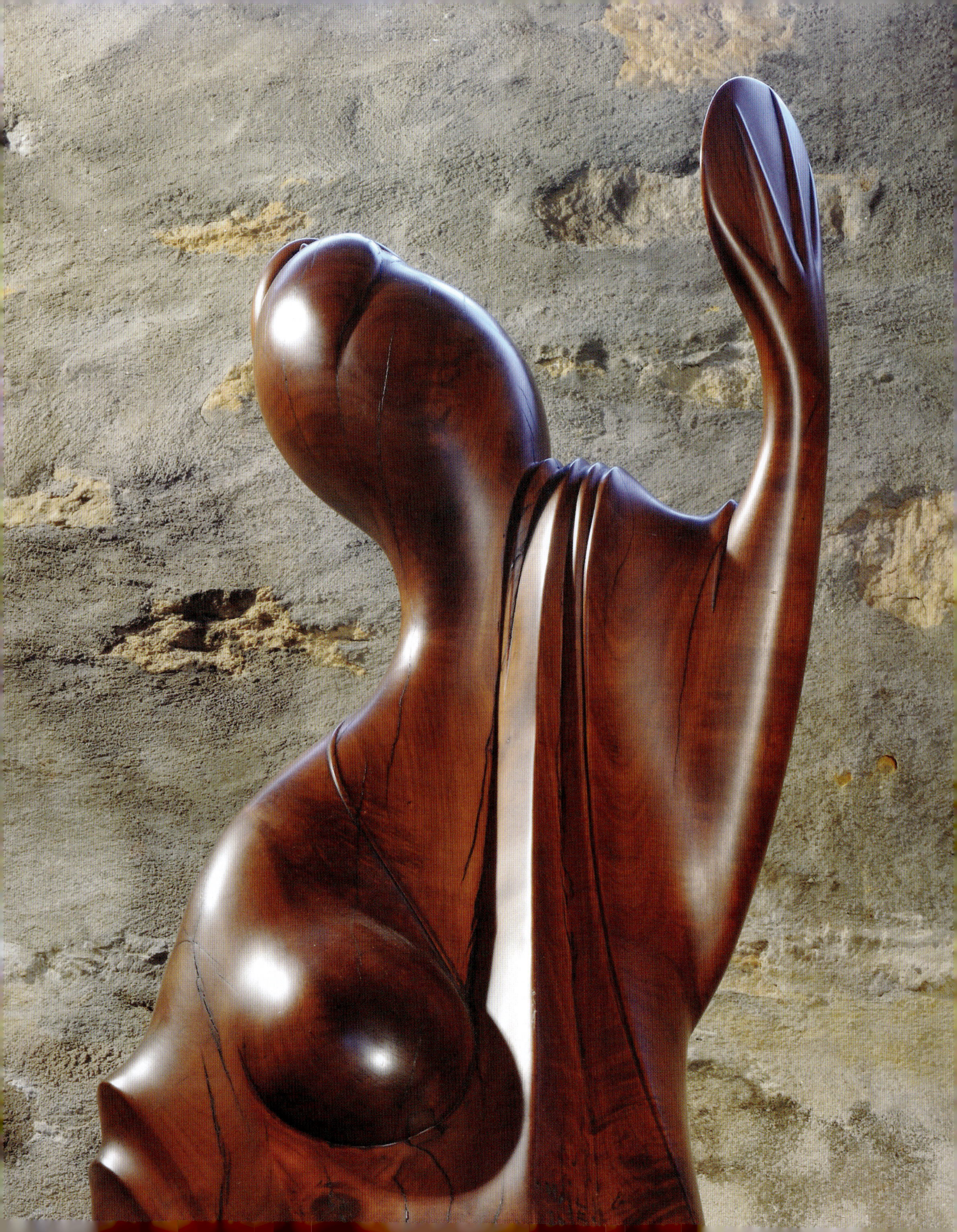

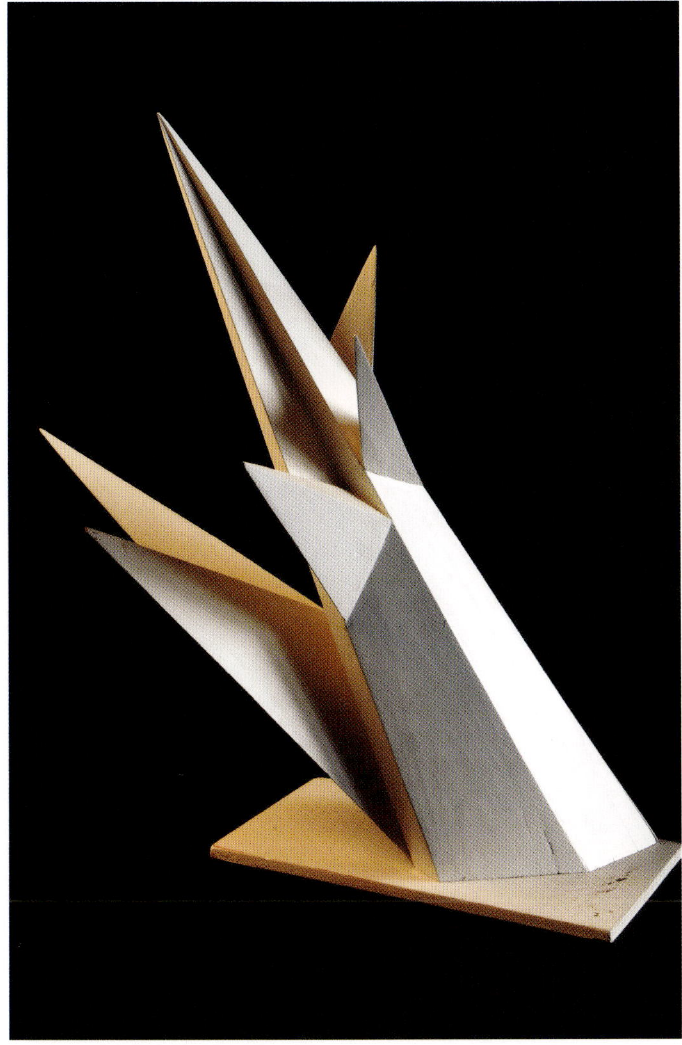

Offense, 1939. Painted wood, 21.25 in. high. *Defense*, 1939. Painted wood, 21 in. high. Submitted as an entry for the U.S. Treasury Department's war memorial competition. *Photos courtesy of James Mario.*

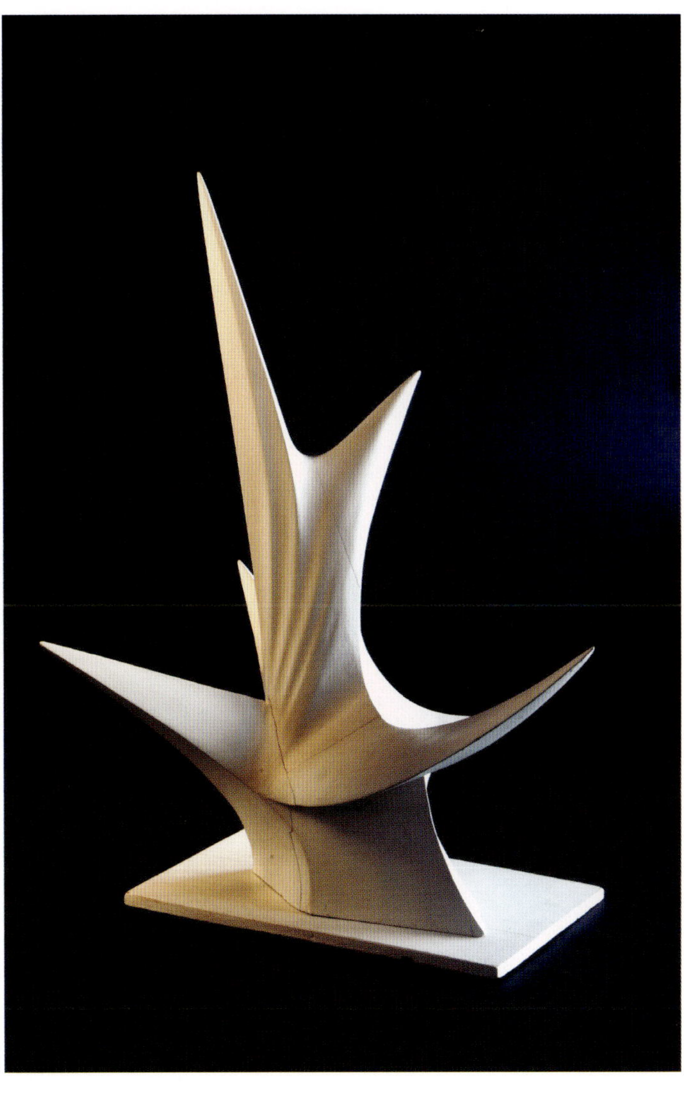

[opposite]
The Actress, 1939. Cherry, 27.4 in. X 17.5 in. X 12 in. Signed "W.E. 1939." Wharton's daughter, Mary, applying her make-up in the mirror. On loan to the Museum from Luisa Lehrer. *Photo courtesy of James Mario.*

Twin Twist, 1940. Red Oak, 181.5 in. high X 20.9 in. diameter. Signed "W.E. MCMXL." On loan from the Pennsylvania Academy of the Fine Arts. Harrison Earl Fund and Women's Committee Purchase 1968.

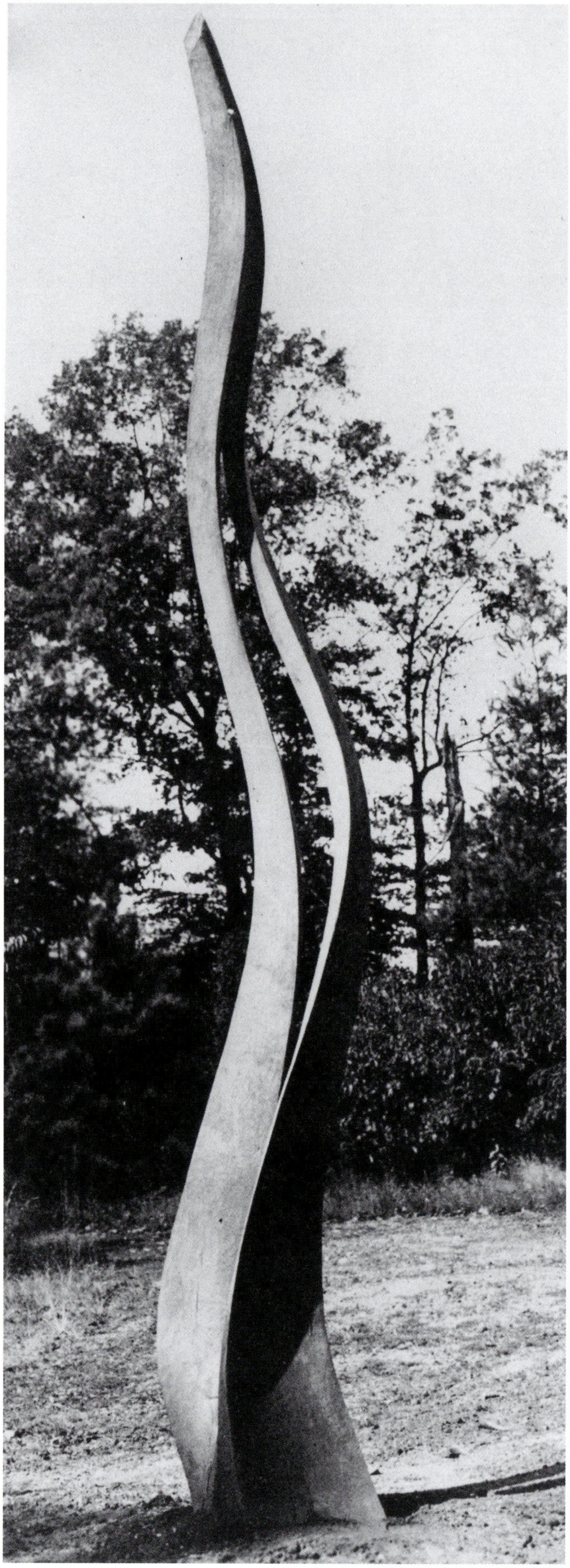

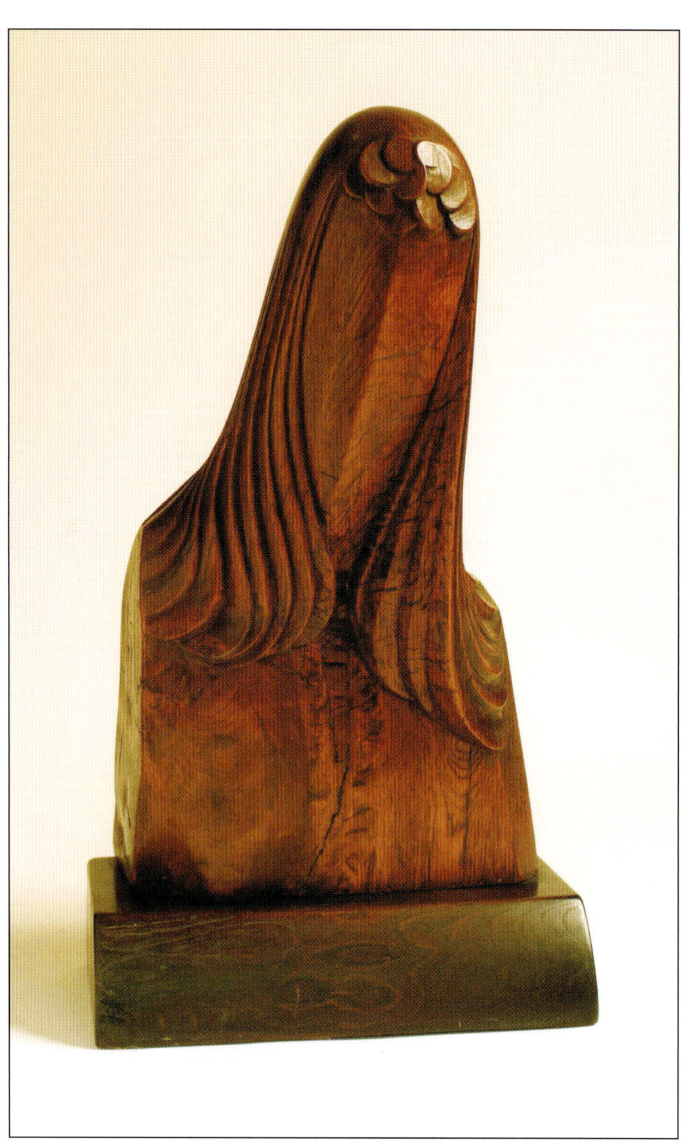

Her, 1942. Crotch oak, walnut base, 22.2 in. X 14.5 in. X 10 in. Signed "W.E. IV II." *Photo courtesy of James Mario.*

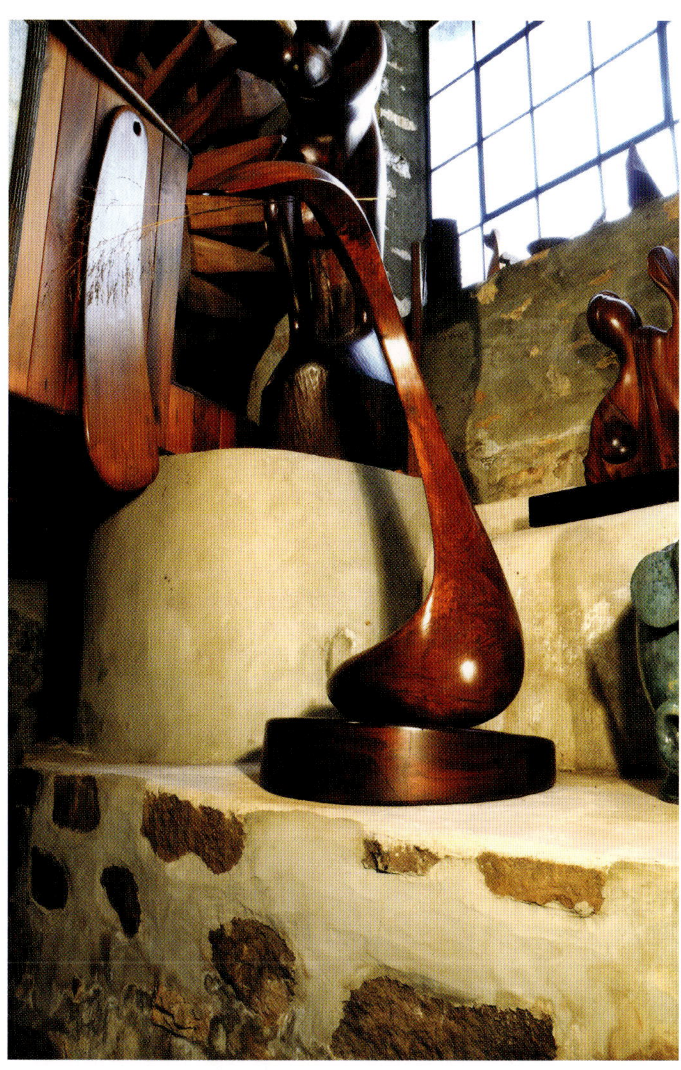

Fun, 1944. White oak, walnut base, 50 in. X 51 in. X 28.3 in. Signed "W.E. 44." *Photo courtesy of James Mario.*

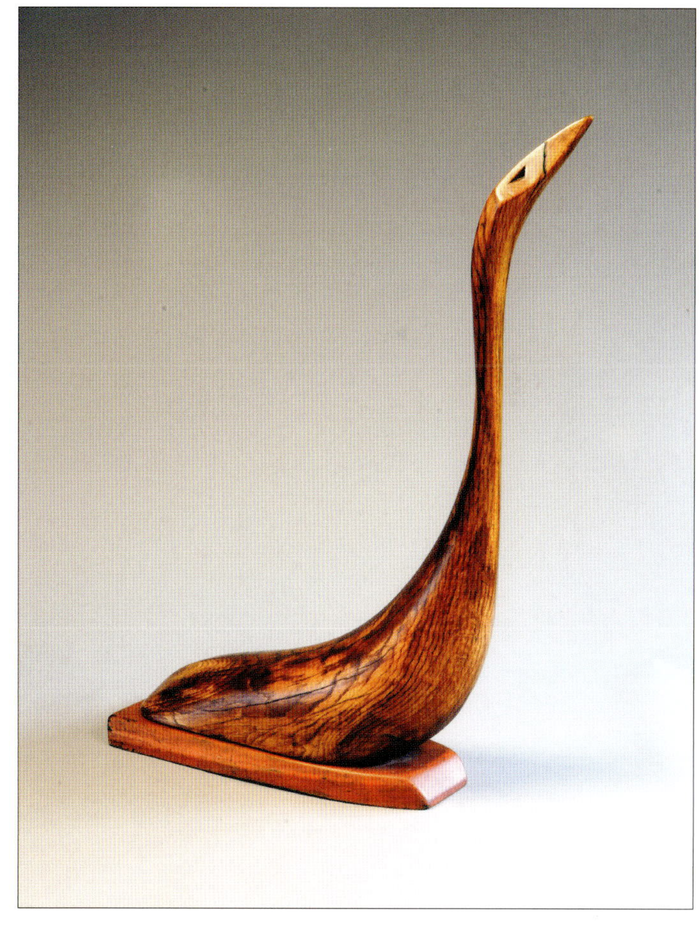

Camille, 1944. Chestnut oak, 29.9 in. X 29 in. X 7.6 in. Inscribed "Hedgerow 1944, Quintine Quintana W.E." Made to commemorate a 'silly-goose' role played by Miriam Phillips. *Photo courtesy of James Mario.*

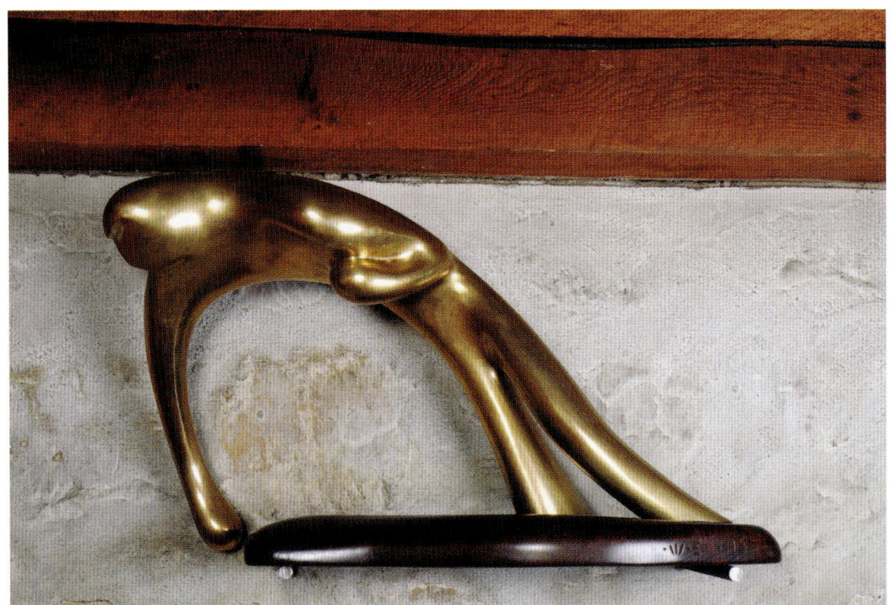

The Wallop, 1945. Bronze casting of the walnut original, walnut base, 19.7 in. X 36 in. X 14.5 in. Signed "W.E. 45." *Photo courtesy of James Mario.*

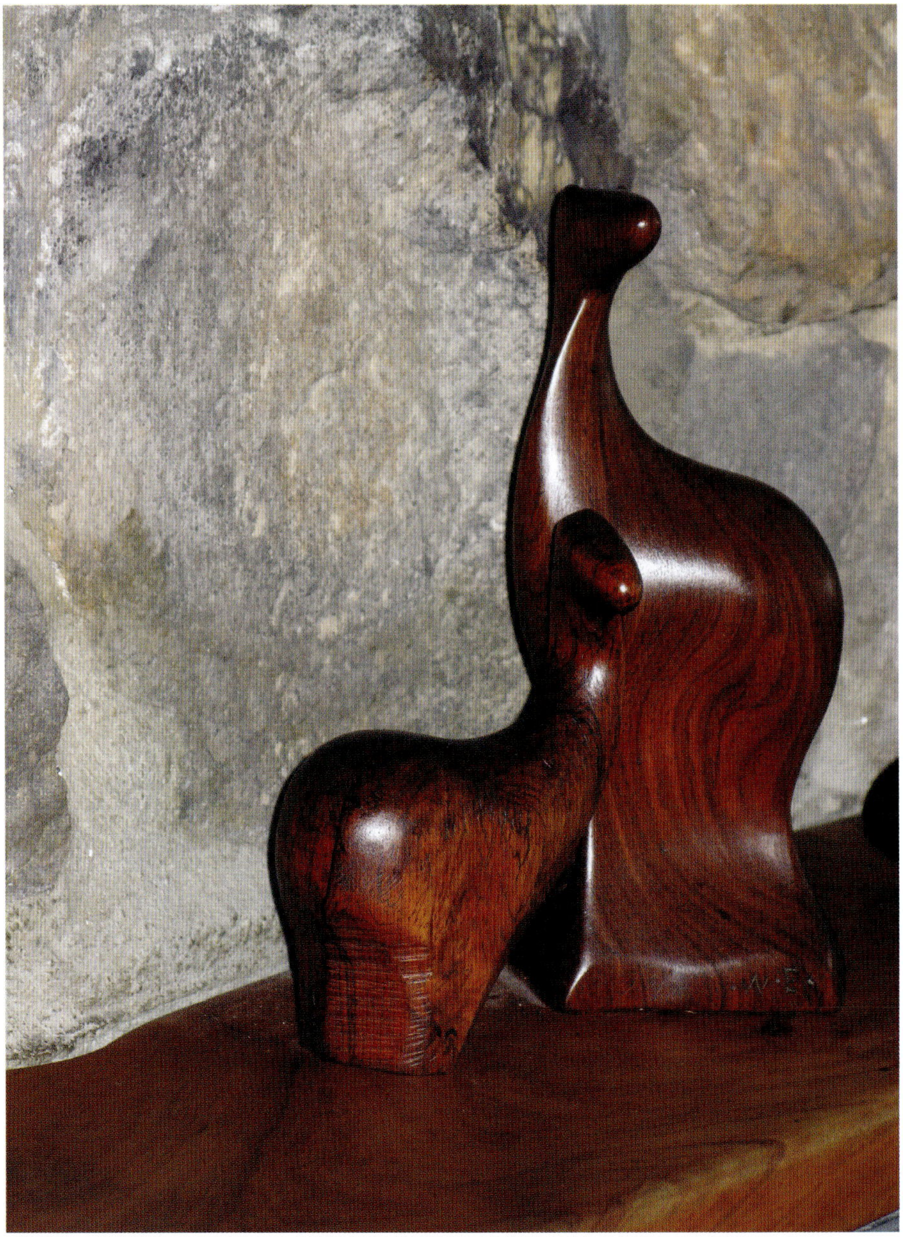

Babbie and Colt, 1946. Cocobolo, mare 8.7 in. high, colt 5.6 in. high. Signed "W.E. 46."

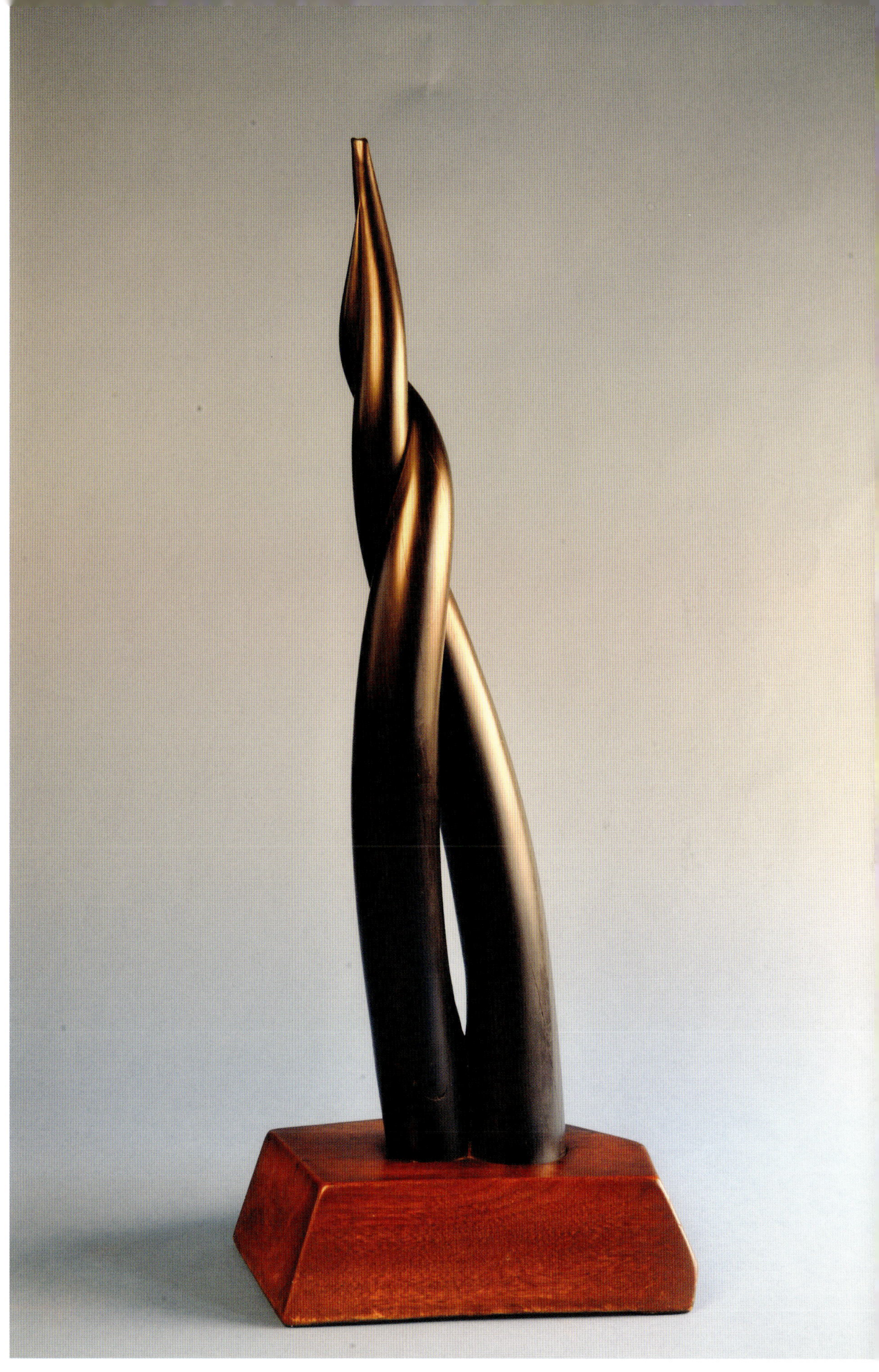

The Pair, 1951. Ebony, walnut base, 32 in. X 13 in. X 9 in. Signed "W.E. 1951." *Photo courtesy of James Mario.*

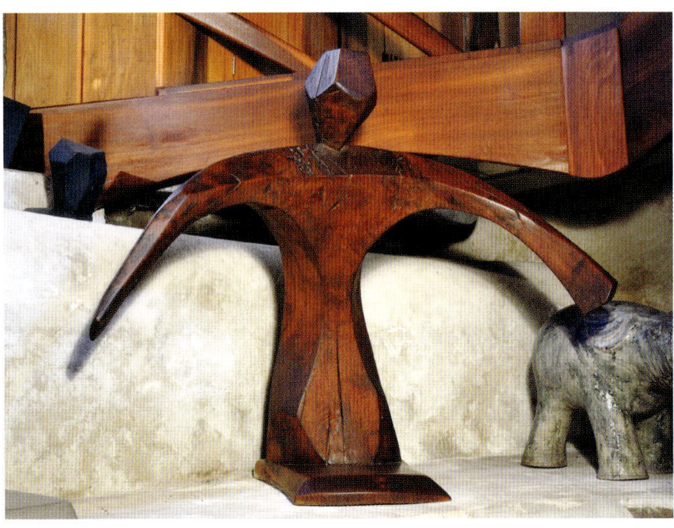

Love and/or Hate, 1940-60. Oak, 40.6 in. X 31.5 in. X 50 in. Signed "W.E. 40-60." Commissioned work often took precedence over sculpture. Wharton would sometimes put a piece aside to work on a commission, returning to it years later to finish. *Photo courtesy of James Mario.*

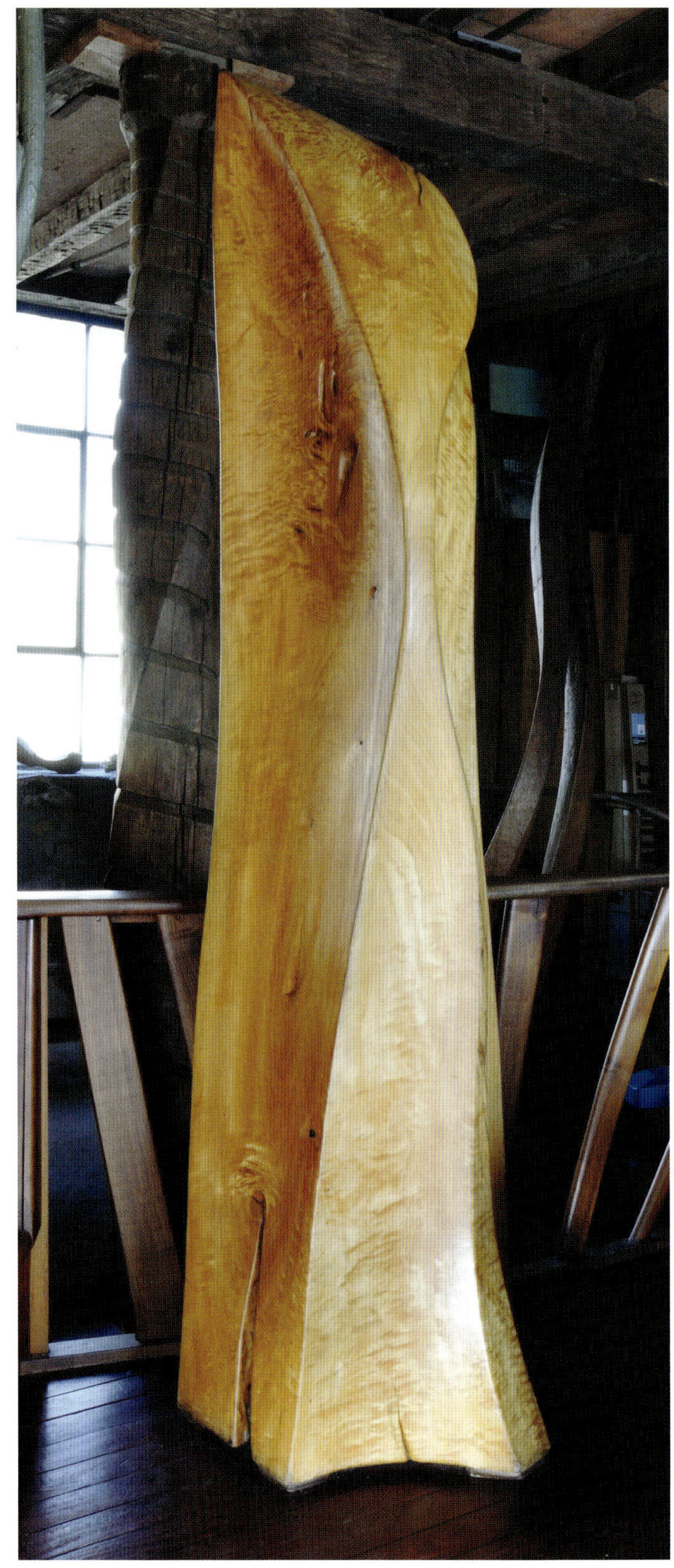

Rhythms II, 1966. Cottonwood, 91.3 in. high. Signed "W.E. 1966." Sculpted from the same tree as the taller *Rhythms*, commissioned for the public library at Broad and Morris Streets in Philadelphia. *Photo courtesy of James Mario.*

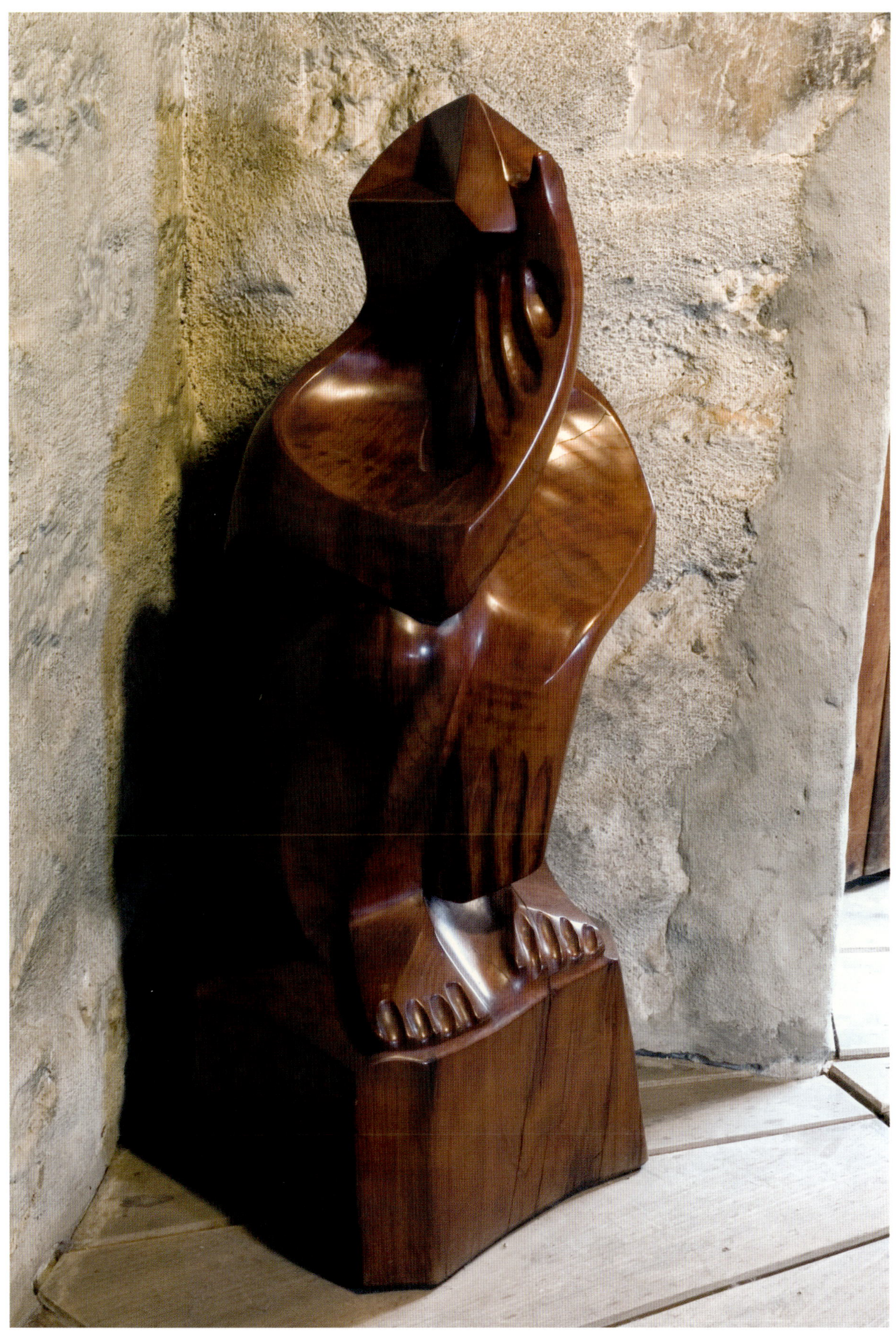

Boredom, 1966. Cherry, 36.2 in. X 13.5 in. X 13 in. Signed "W.E. 1966." *Photo courtesy of James Mario.*

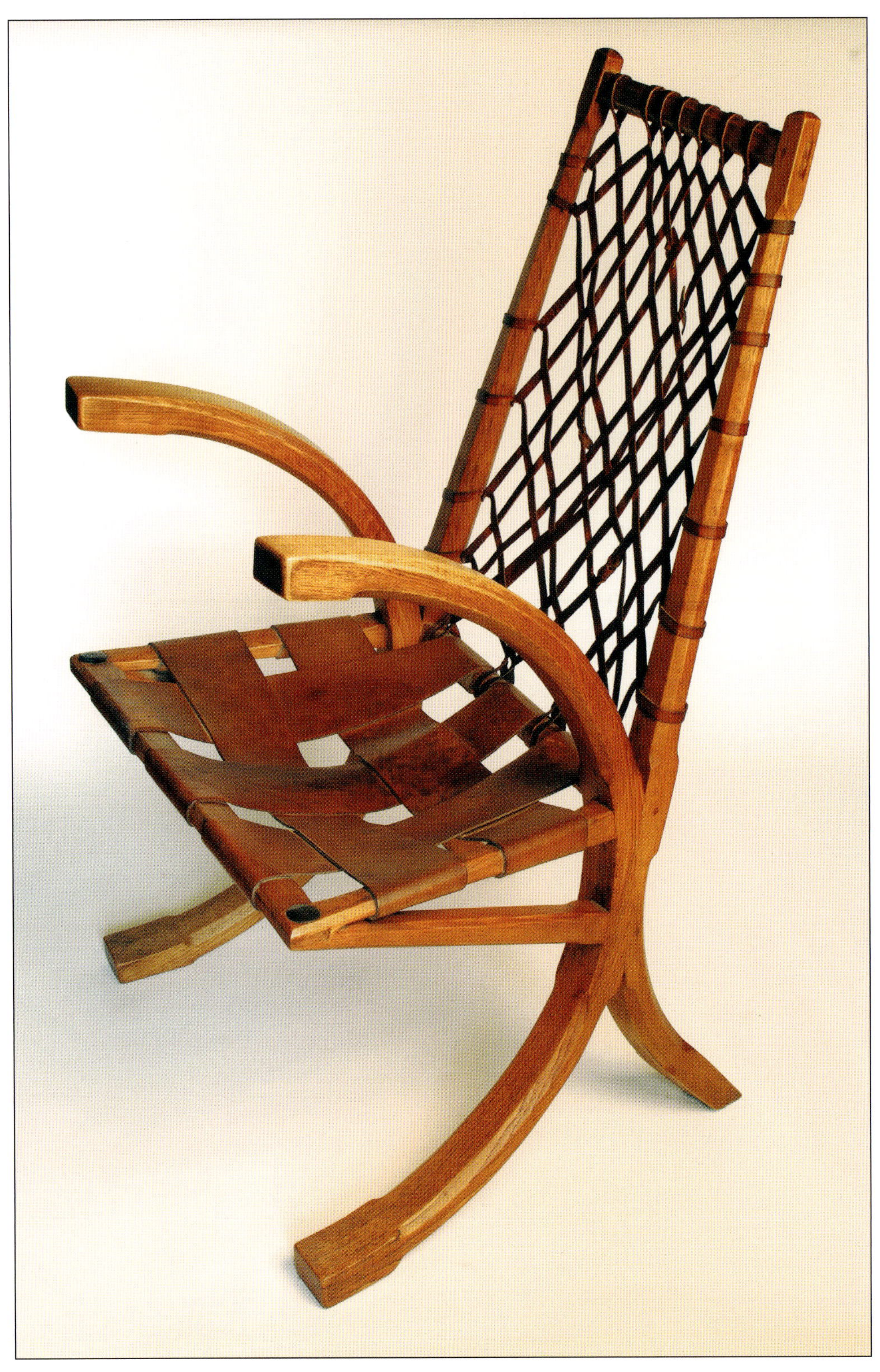

Wagon Wheel Chair, 1931. Hickory, laced leather seat and back, 39.8 in. X 20 in. X 22 in. Signed "W.E. 1931." Design used for chairs in a harness room, Mt. Kisco, NY, using wagon wheel rims. *Photo courtesy of Mark Sfirri.*

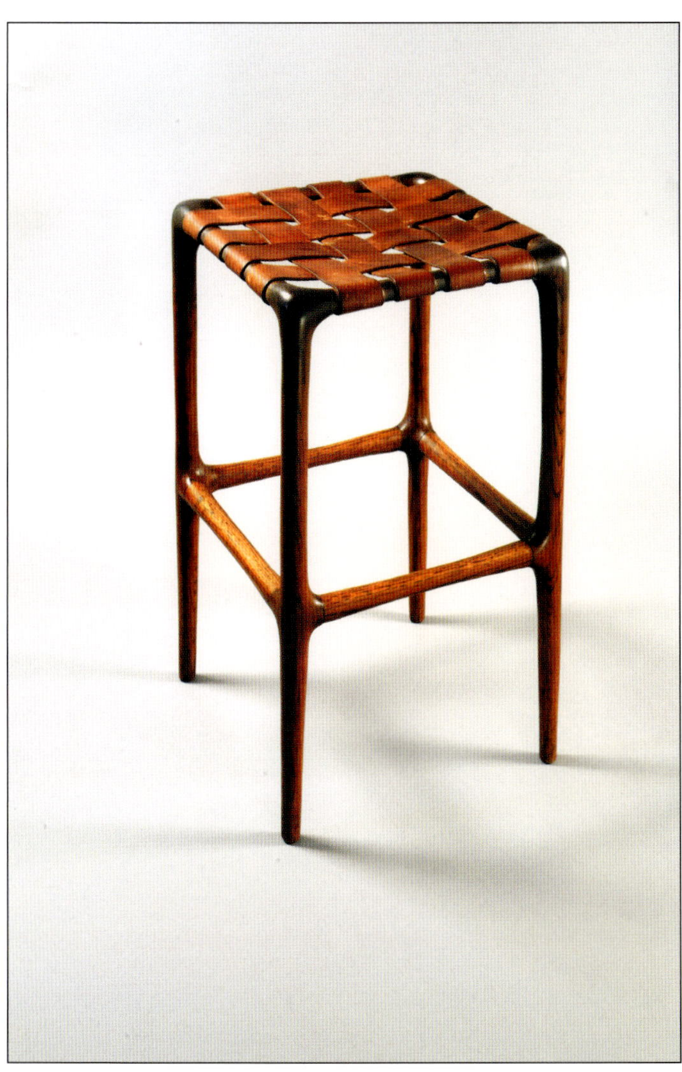

Desk Stool, 1929. Oak, laced leather seat, 26.8 in. X 14 in. X 14 in. Signed "W.E. 1929." *Photo courtesy of James Mario.*

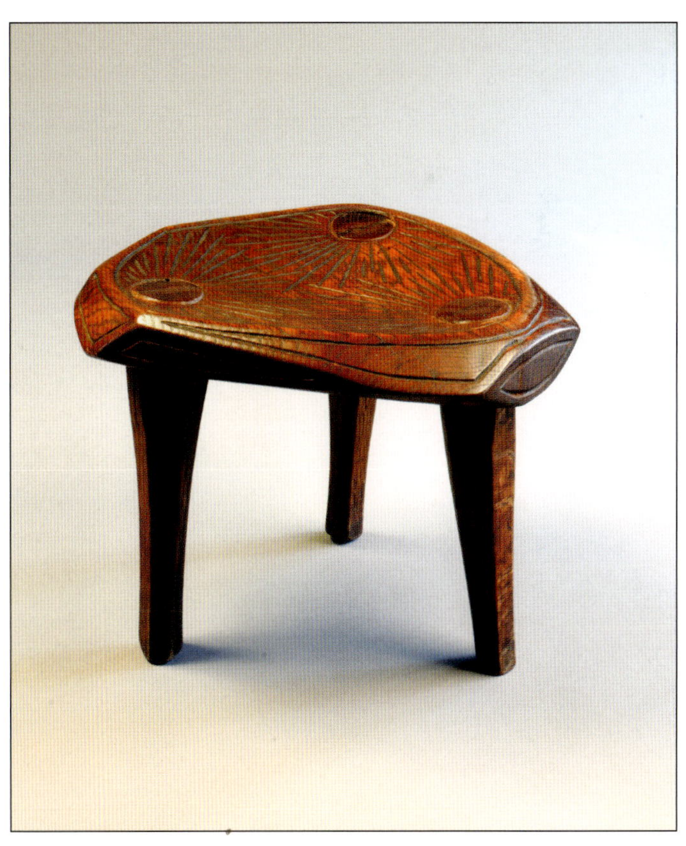

Carved Three Legged Stool, 1931. Oak, 11 in. X 11.5 in. X 12.5 in. Signed "W.E. 1931." *Photo courtesy of James Mario.*

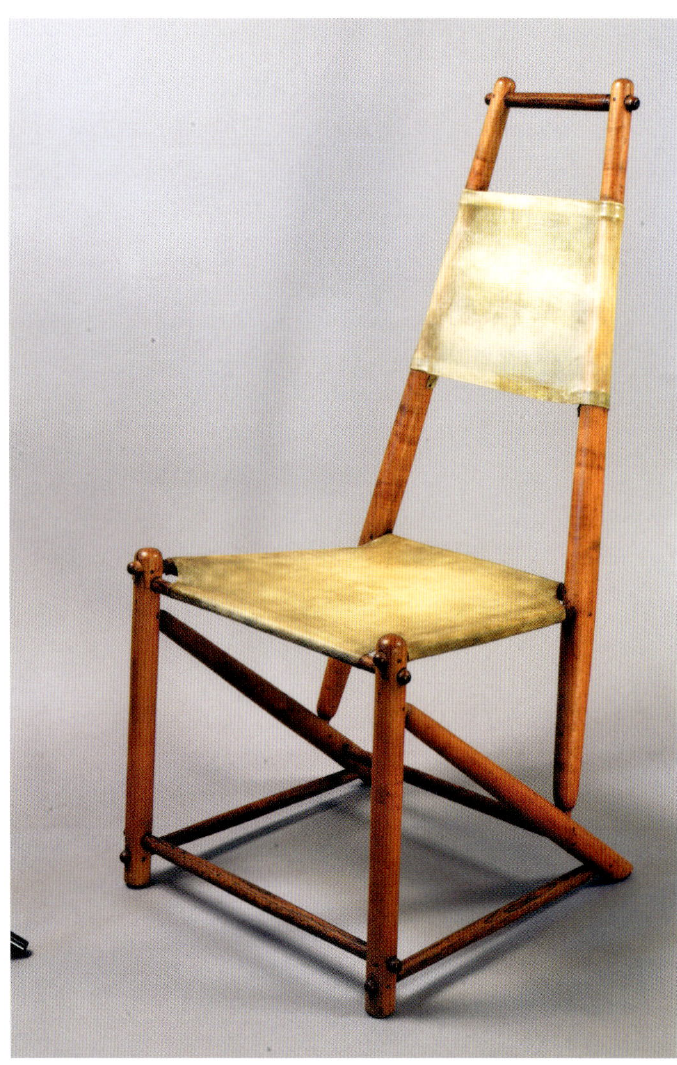

Bedroom Chair, 1932. Maple, rawhide seat and back, 36 in. X 18.1x16.9 in. Signed "W.E. XXXII." *Photo courtesy of James Mario.*

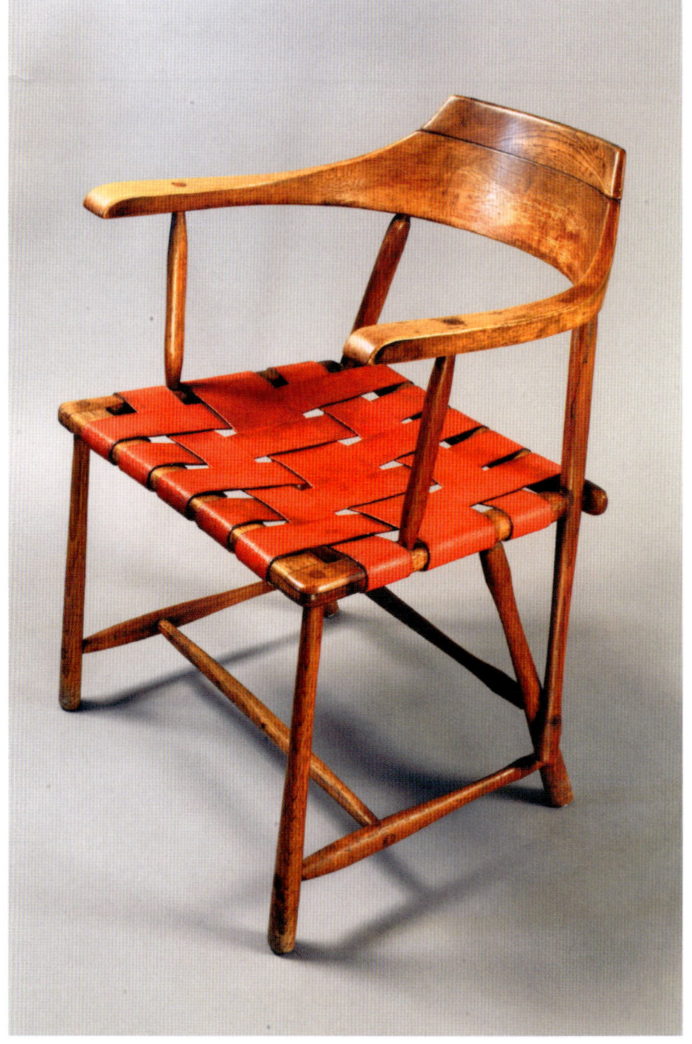

Mate's Chair, 1938. Hickory and oak, laced canvas seat, 28.7 in. X 17 in. X 22 in. Signed "W.E. 1938." *Photo courtesy of James Mario.*

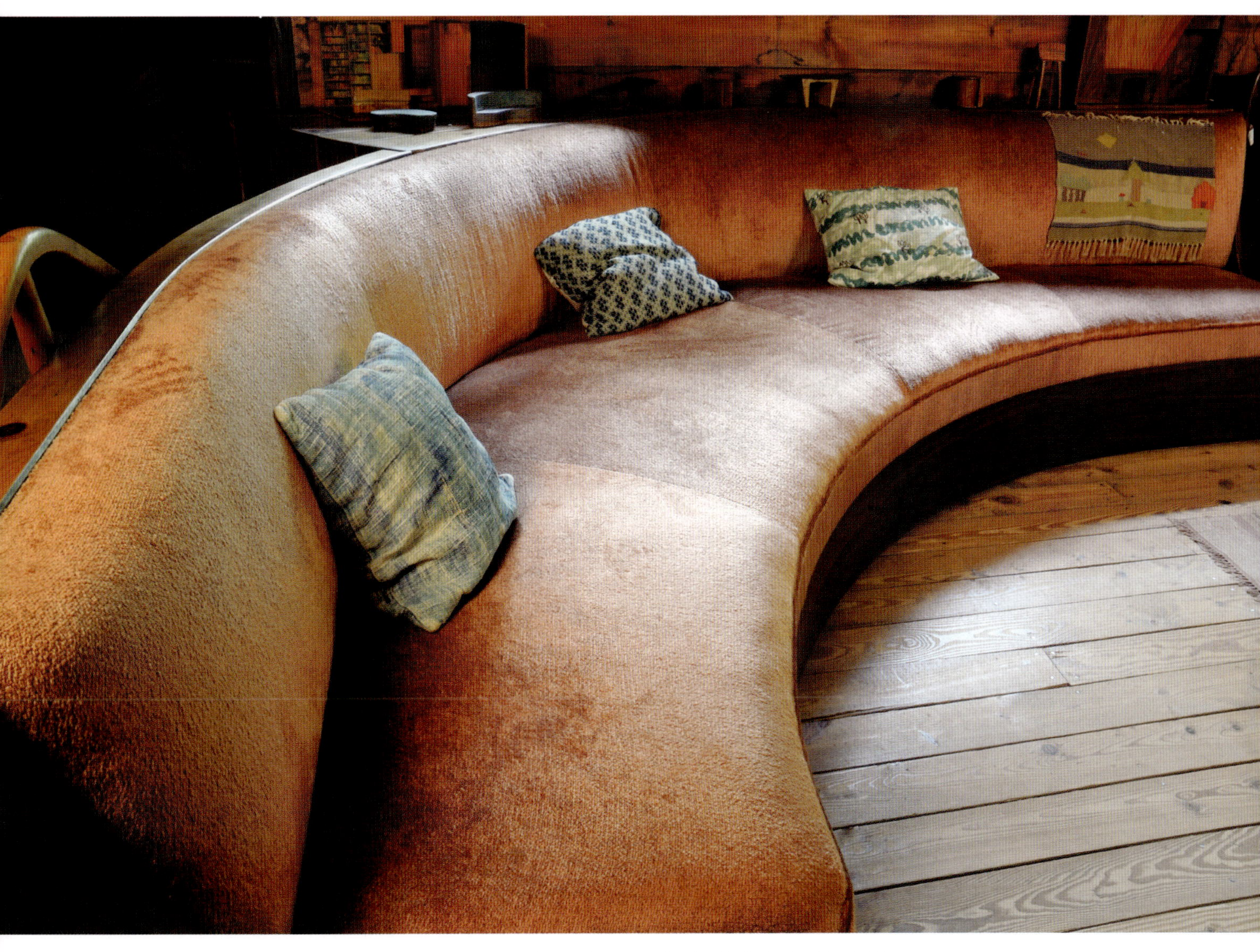

Bedroom Sofa, 1936. White Pine and mahogany, upholstered seat, 34.4 in. X 125.4 in. X 99.6 in. Originally made for the Curtis Bok house, but rejected. *Photo courtesy of James Mario.*

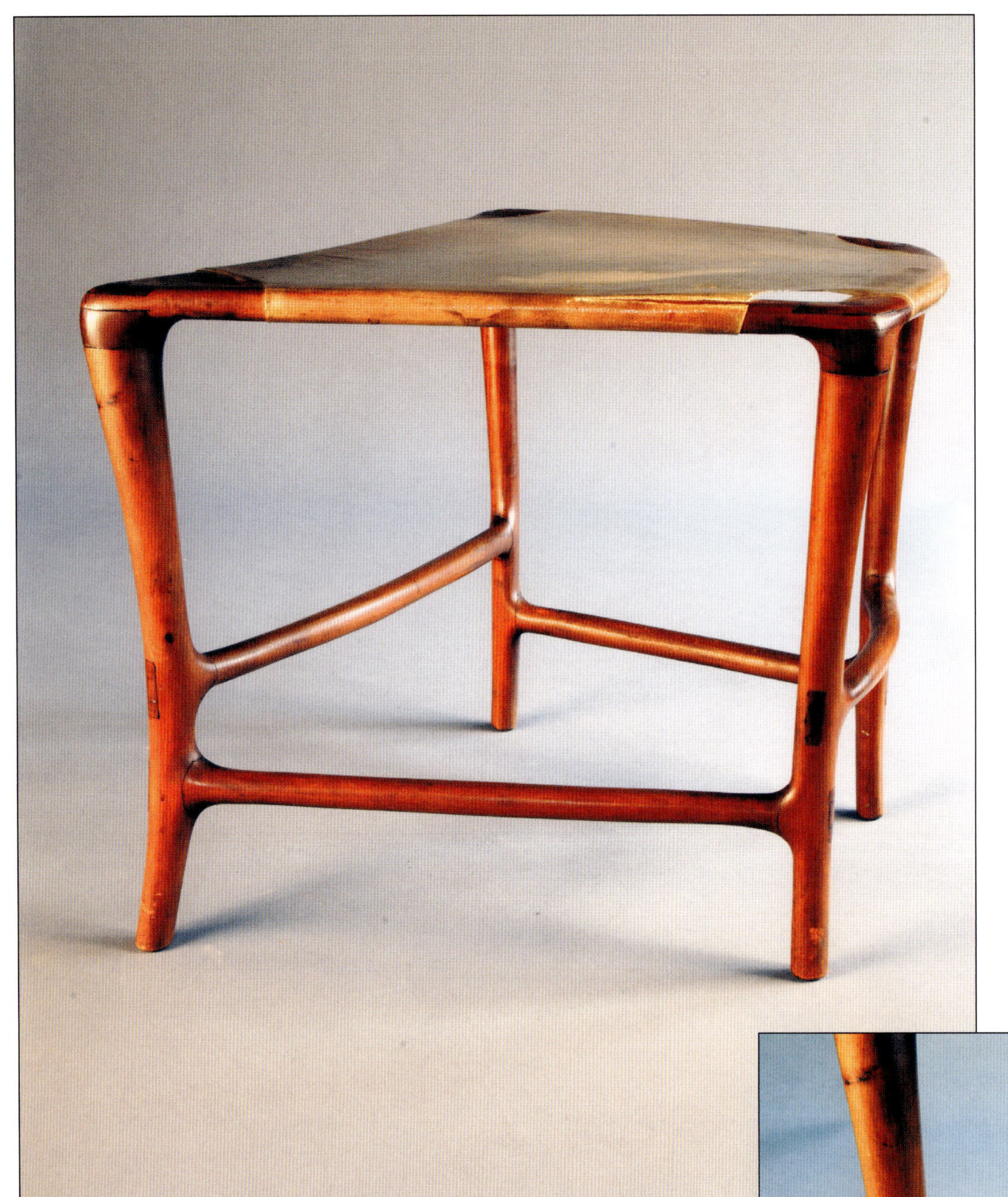

Dressing Table Stool , c. 1947. Dogwood, rawhide seat, 14.6 in. X 16.5 in. X 15 in. *Photo courtesy of James Mario.*

Dressing Table Stool detail of organic leg/stretcher joints. *Photo courtesy of James Mario.*

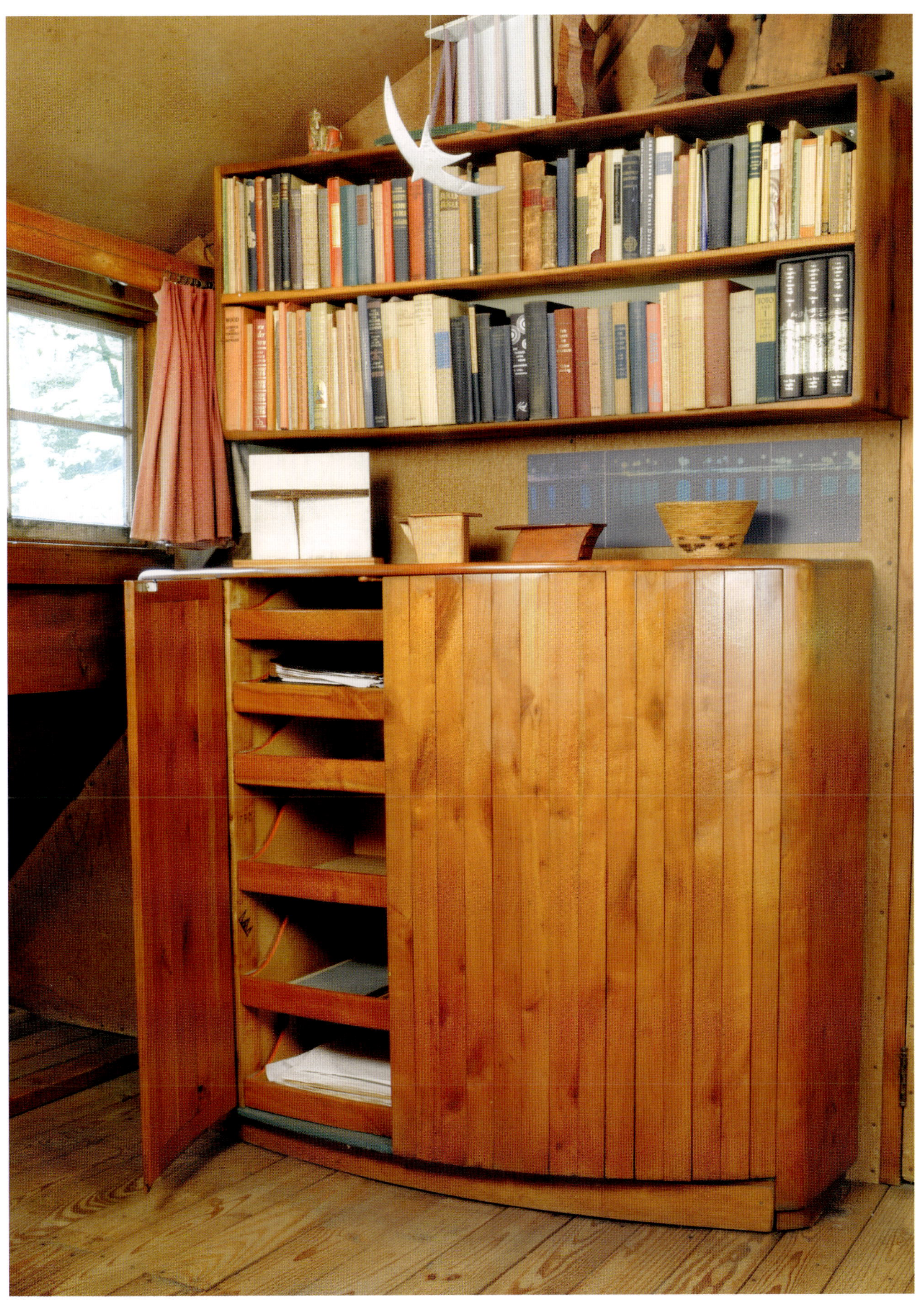

Cabinet Dresser, 1950. Cherry, 50.2 in. X 66.7 in. X 22.5 in. Signed "W.E. 1950." *Photo courtesy of James Mario.*

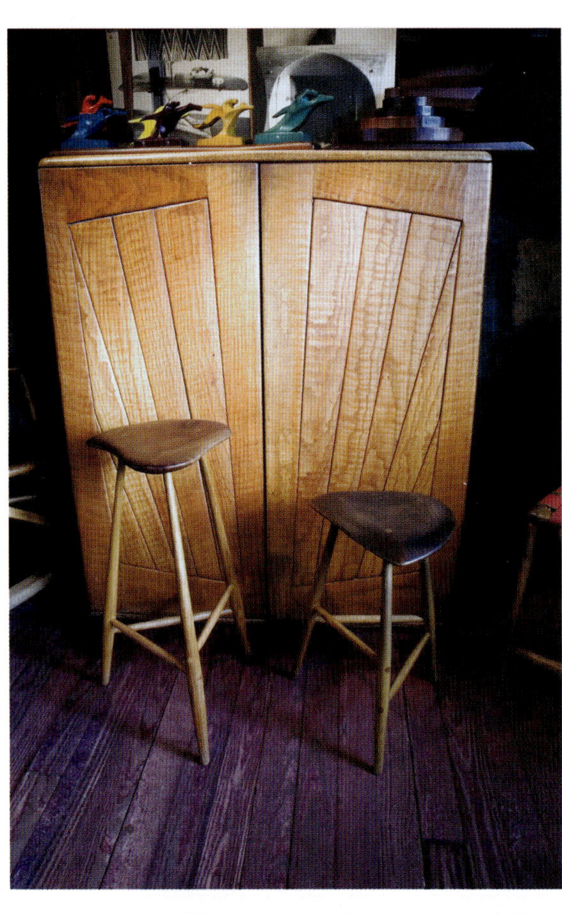

Cabinet Desk, 1958. Curly oak, satinwood, walnut, and fir plywood, 48 in. X 106.7 in. X 23.8 in. Signed "W.E. 1958." *Photo courtesy of James Mario.*

Rail Sofa, 1959. Walnut, cherry, and poplar, 36.2 in. X 116.9 in. X 41.7 in. *Photo courtesy of James Mario.*

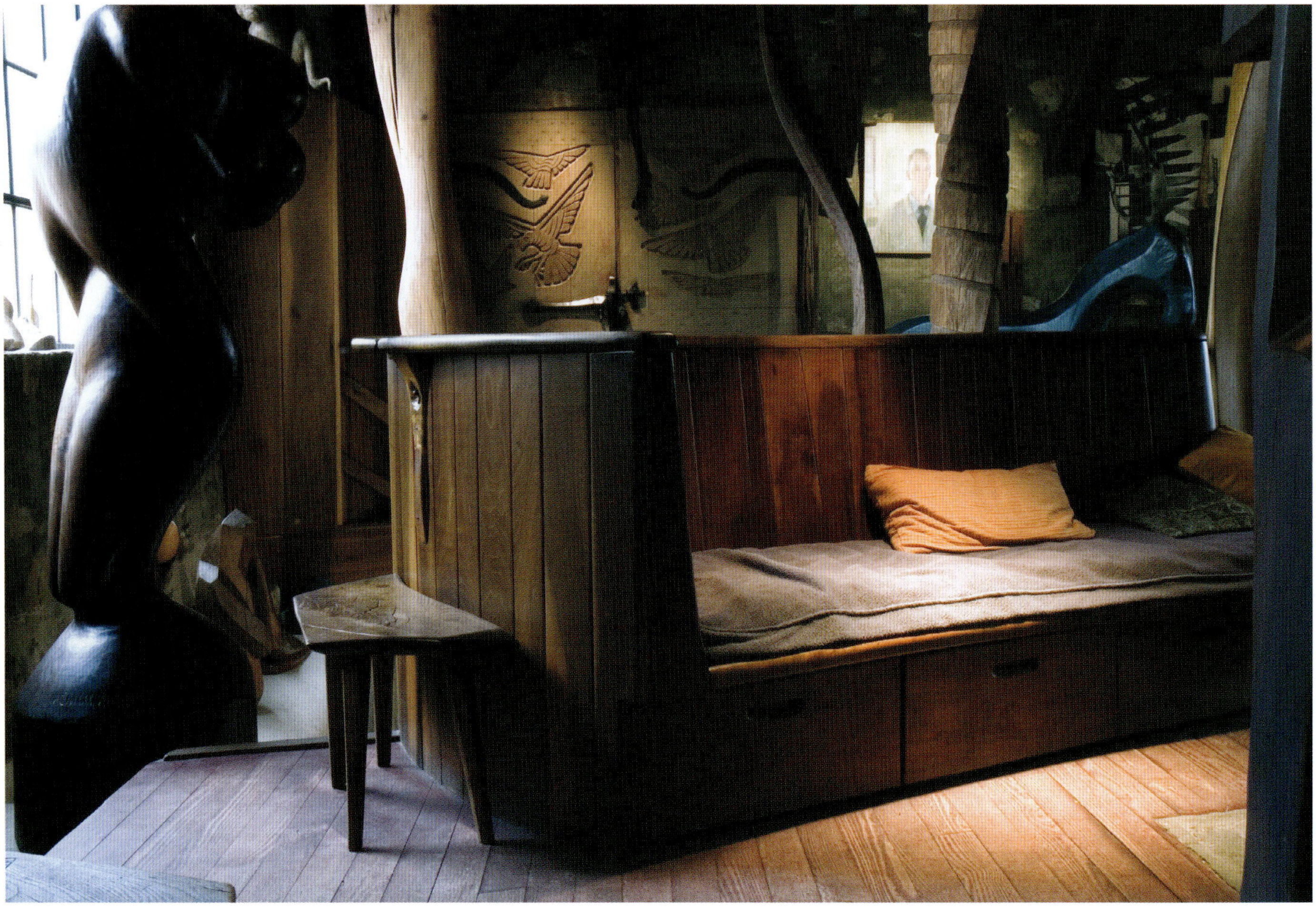

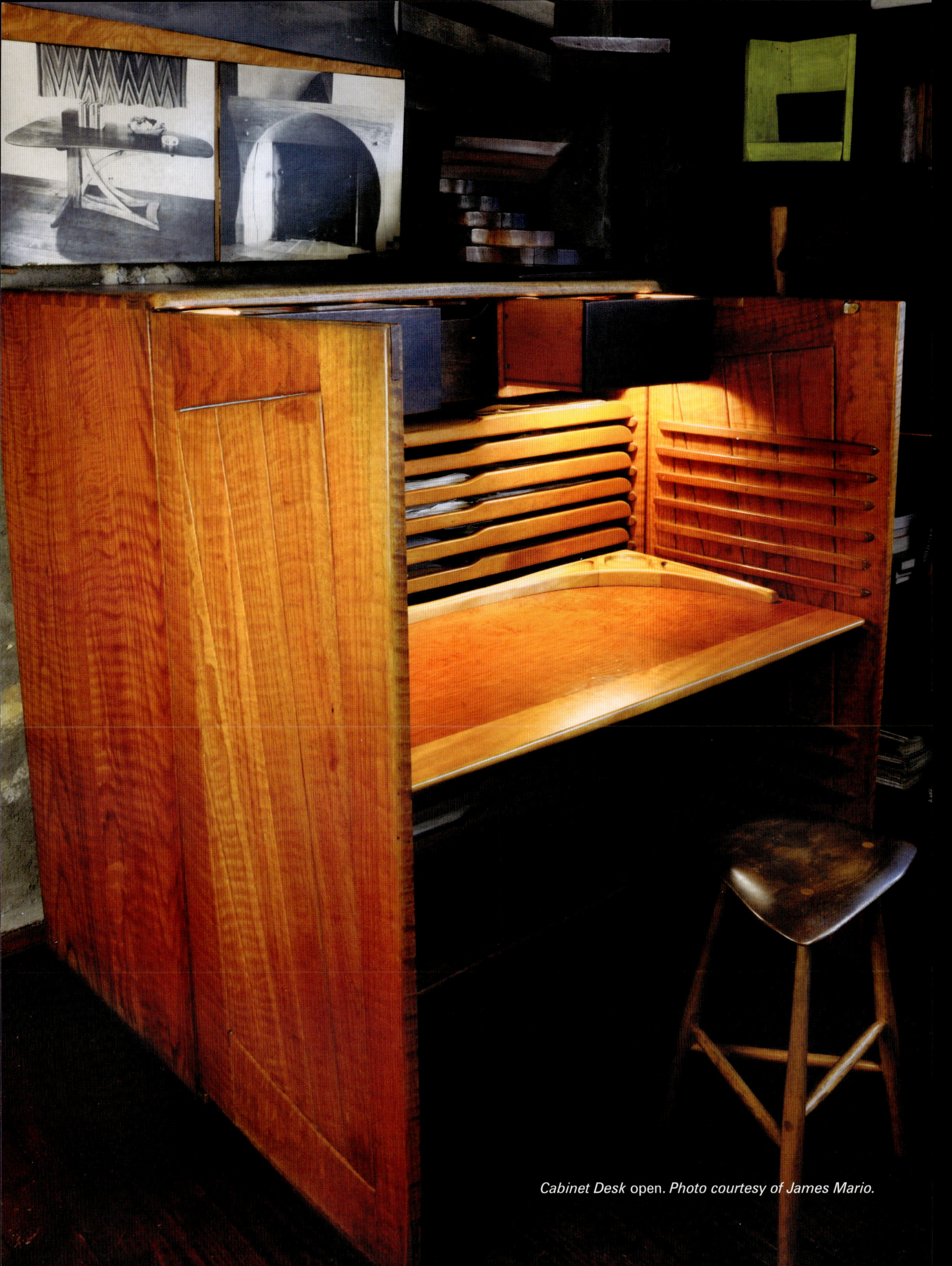

Cabinet Desk open. *Photo courtesy of James Mario.*

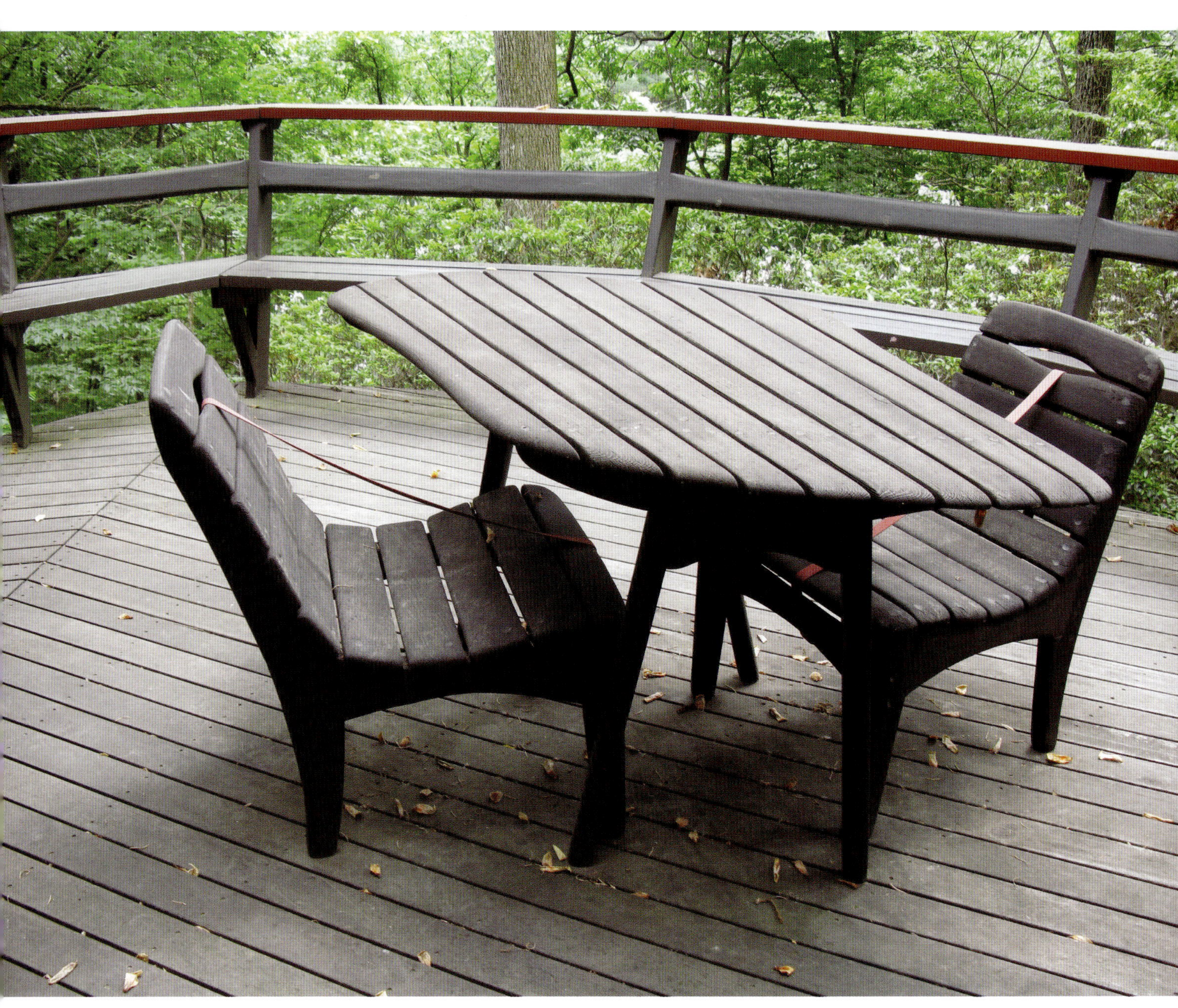

Deck Table and Chairs, 1966. Cedar, 28.7 in. X 63.5 in. X 32.6 in. Signed "W.E. 1966."

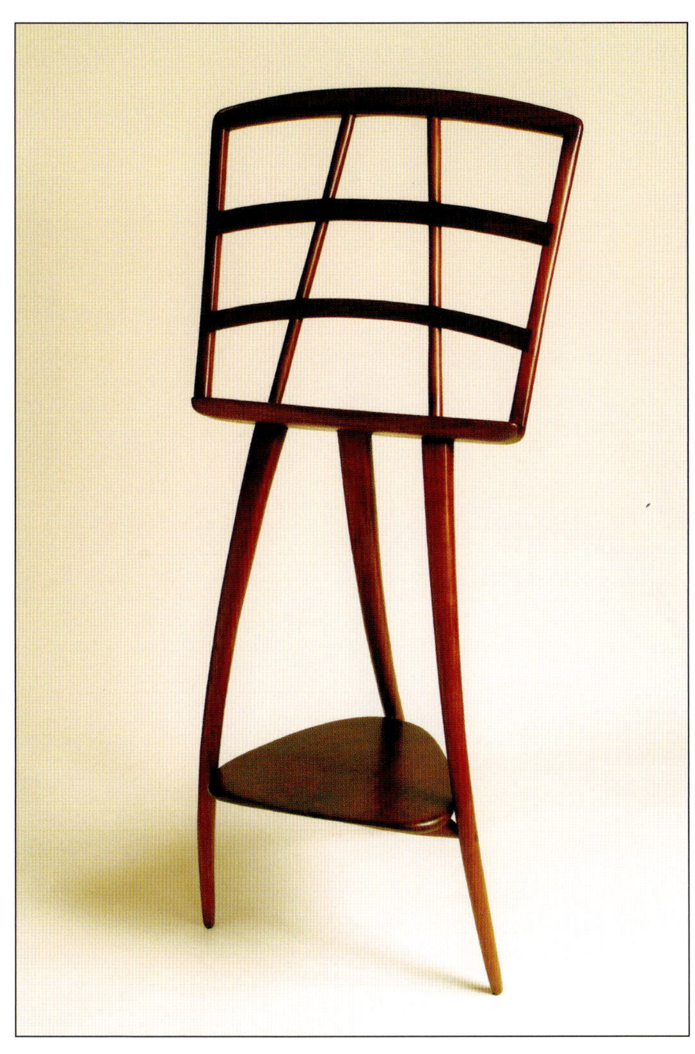

Single Music Stand, 1960. Walnut and cherry, 44.2 in. high. Signed "W.E. 1960." Based on Esherick's 1951 design. *Photo courtesy of Mark Sfirri.*

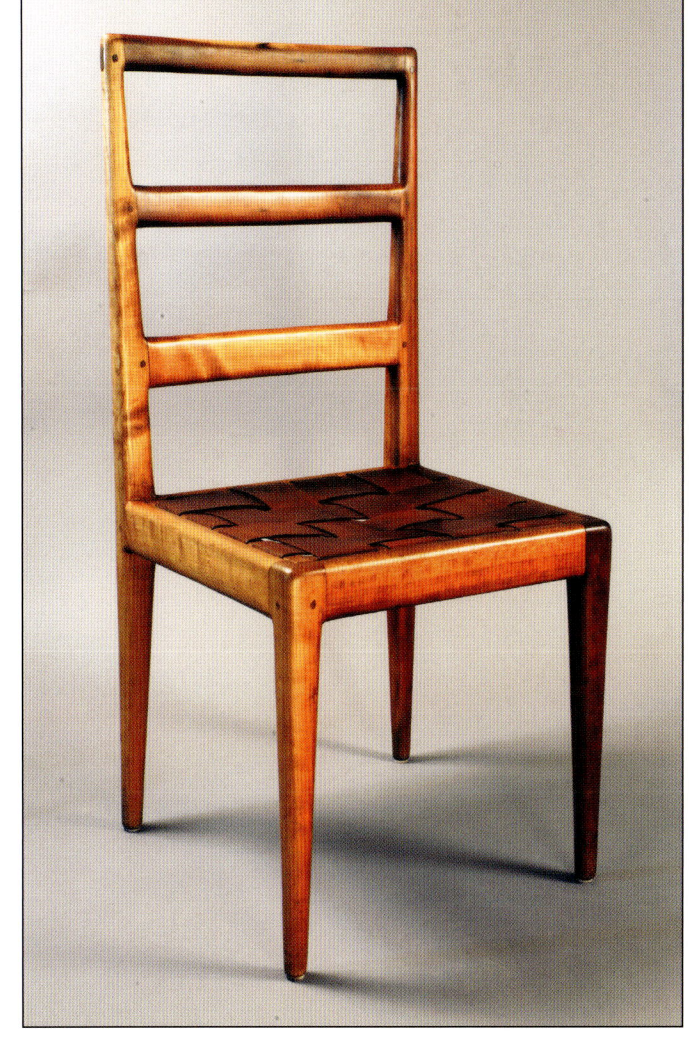

Ladder-Back Chair, 1968. Cherry, laced leather seat, 38.8 in. X 18 in. X 18 in. Signed "W.E. 1968." *Photo courtesy of James Mario.*

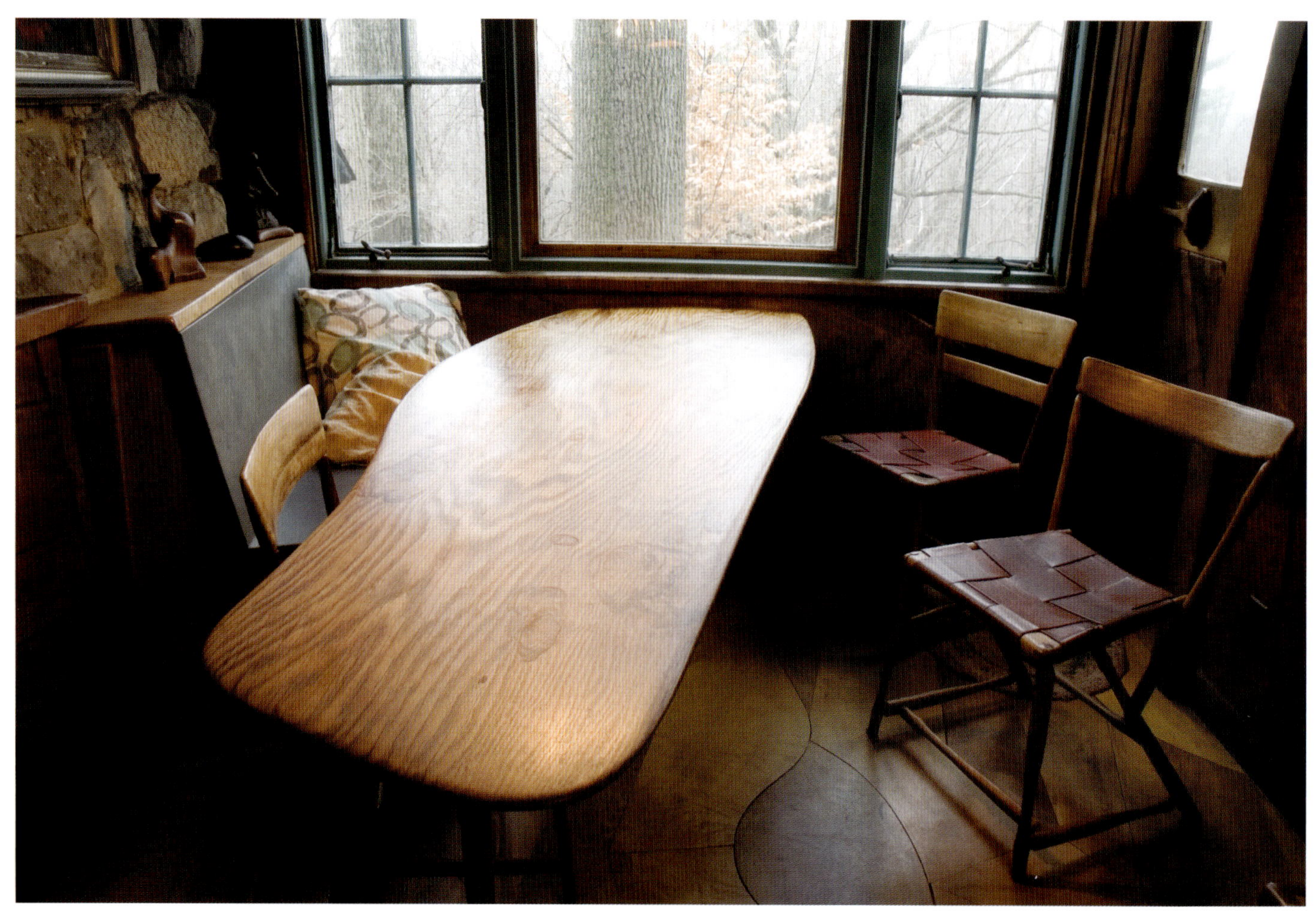

Dining Room Table, 1967. Oak, 28.7 in. X 87 in. X 32.7 in. Signed "W.E. 1967." *Photo courtesy of James Mario.*

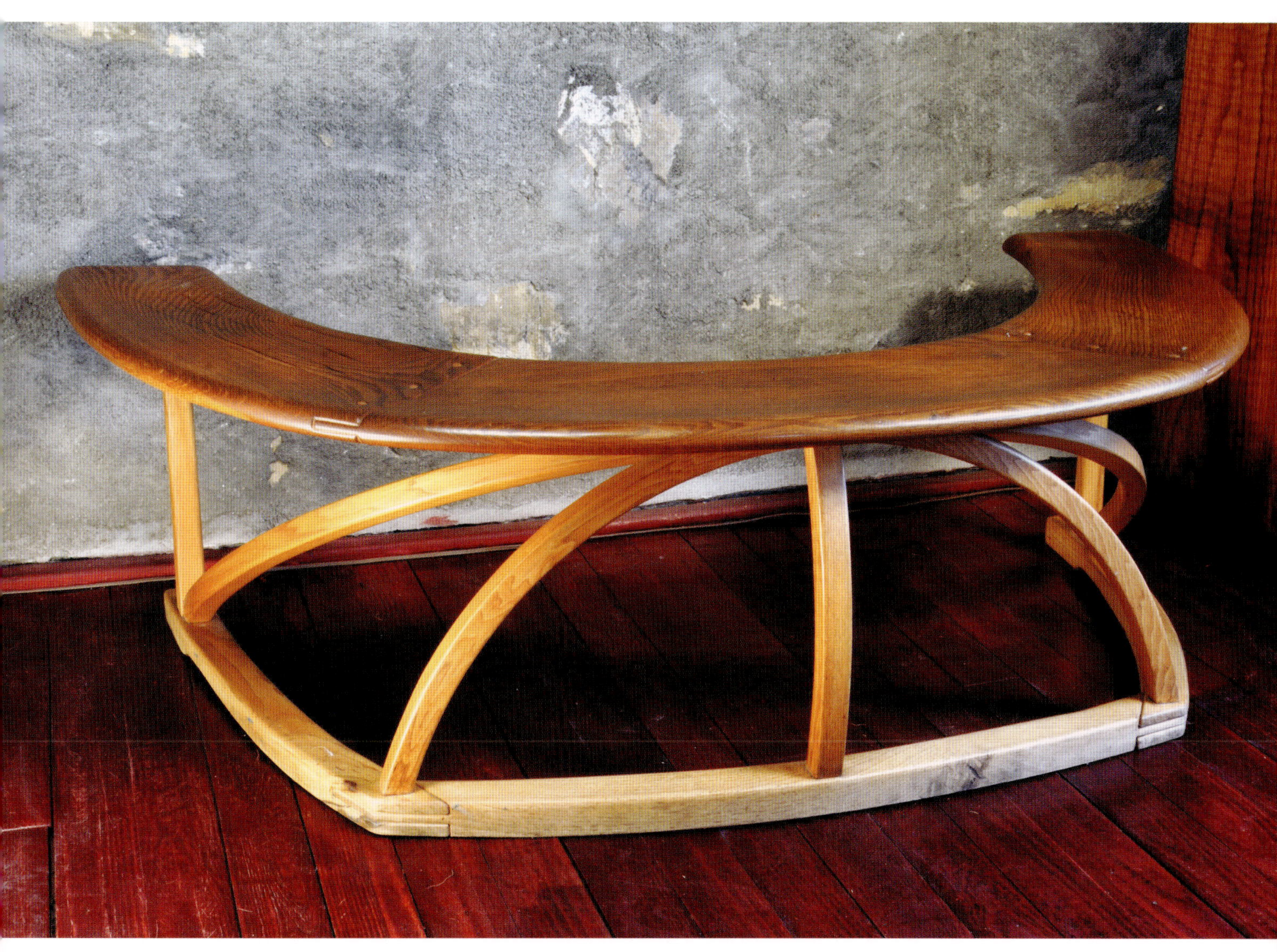

Fireside Bench, 1969. Oak and hickory, 17.5 in. X 61.4 in. X 34 in. Signed "W.E. 1969."
Photo courtesy of James Mario.

Utilitarian Objects

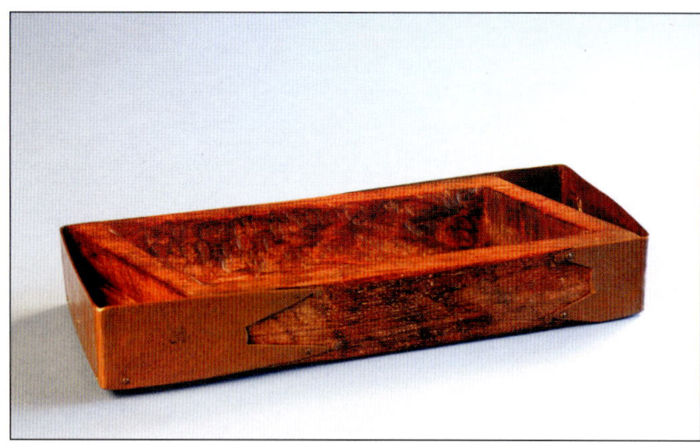

Pencil Caddy, c. 1926. Padouk and copper, 4.1 in. X 11 in. *Photo courtesy of James Mario.*

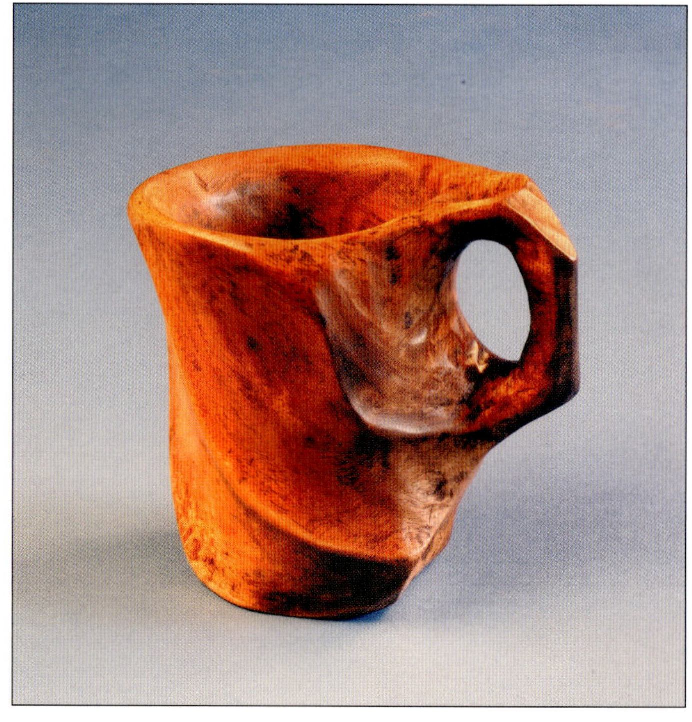

Carved Cup, 1927. Walnut, 4.9 in. high. Signed "W.E. 1927." *Photo courtesy of James Mario.*

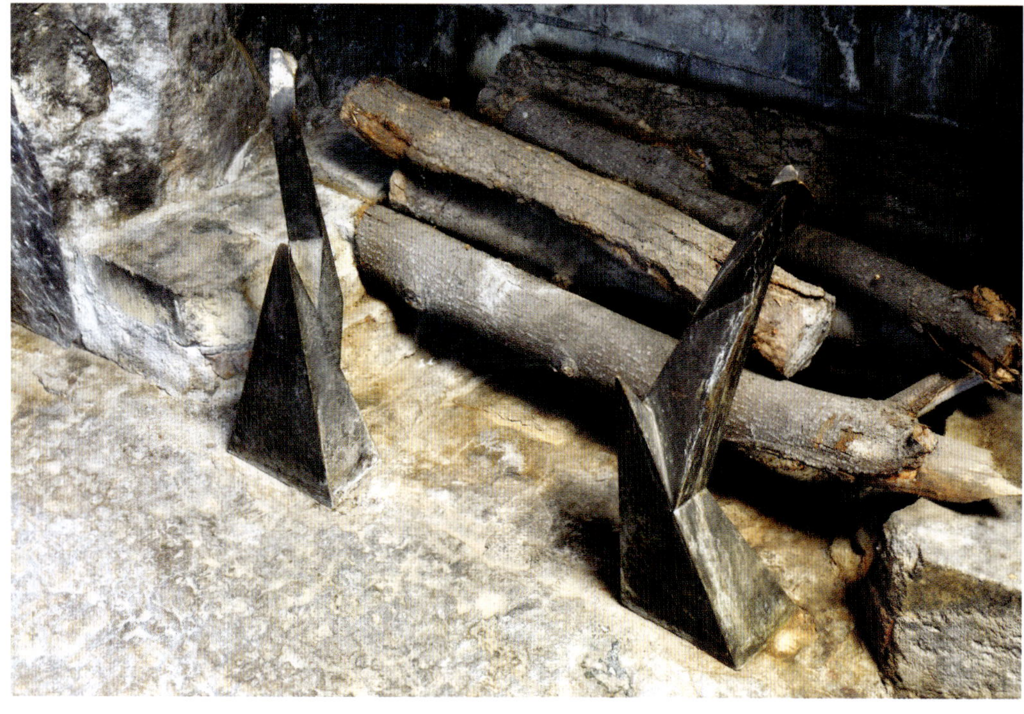

Andirons, c. 1927. Bronze castings from wood originals, 16.9 in. high. *Photo courtesy of James Mario.*

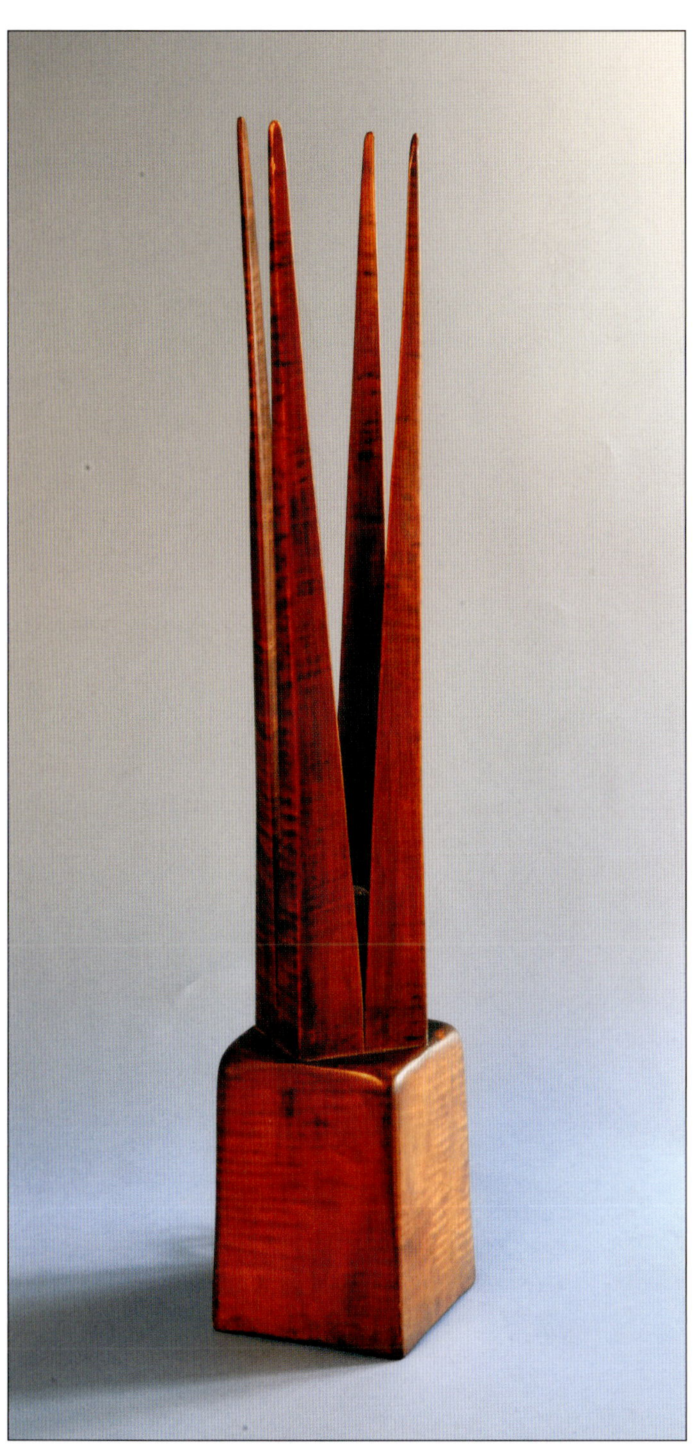

Table Lamp, 1931. Maple, 29.9in. high. Signed "WHARTON ESHERICK MCMXXXI." *Photo courtesy of James Mario.*

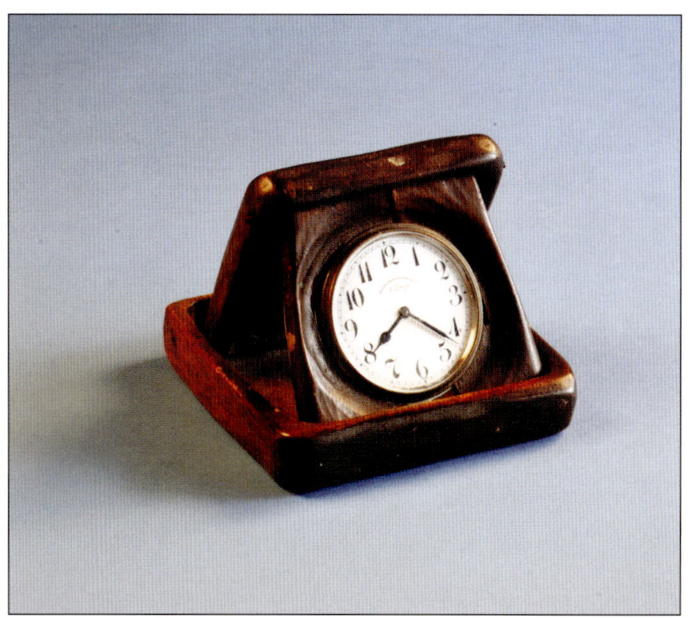

Folding Clock Case, c. 1930. Walnut, 5.1 in. X 4.9 in. *Photo courtesy of James Mario.*

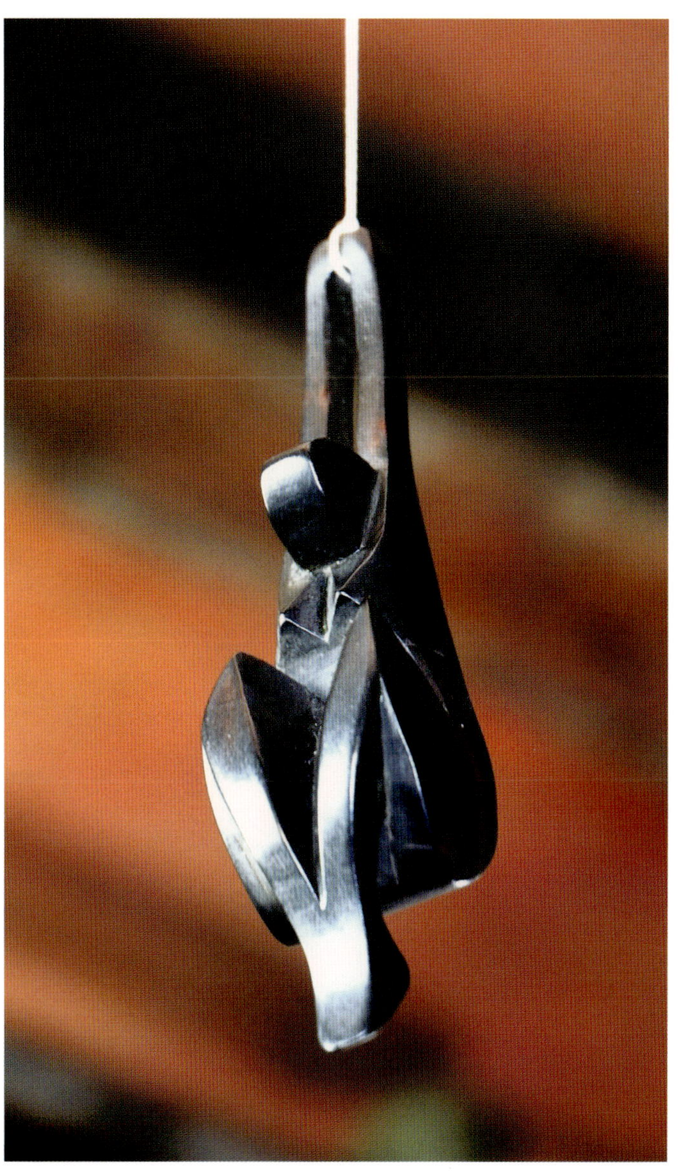

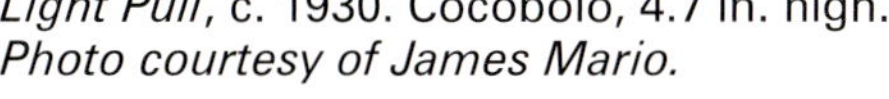

Light Pull, c. 1930. Cocobolo, 4.7 in. high. *Photo courtesy of James Mario.*

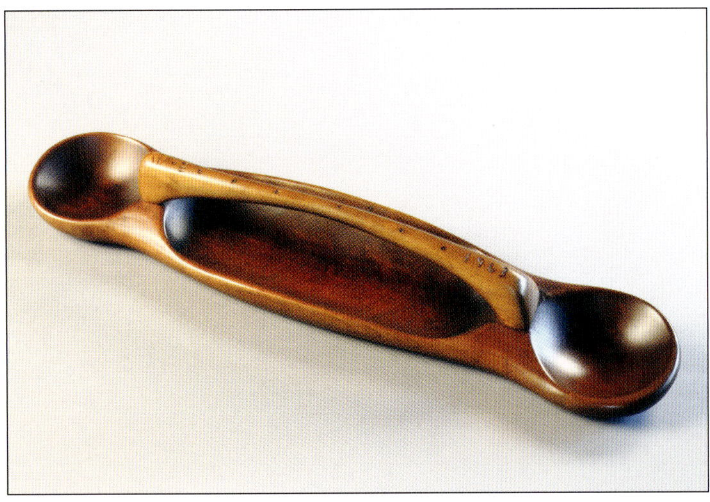

Pencil Caddy, 1963. Cherry, Signed "W.E. 1963."
Photo courtesy of James Mario.

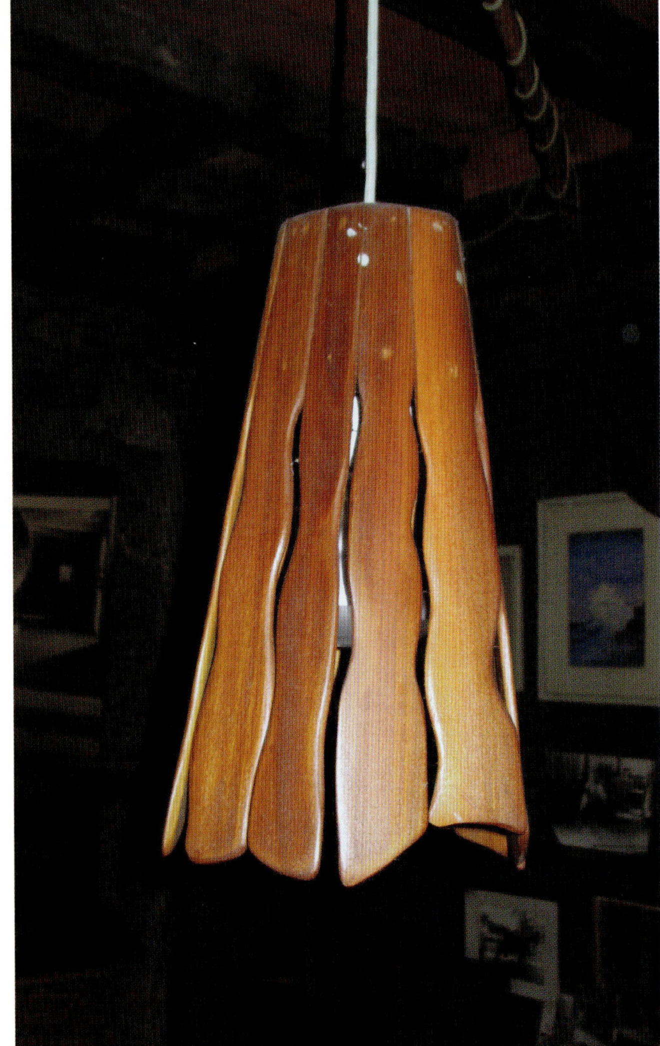

Starboard Swinging Light, c. 1960. English walnut shade, green wire, poplar boom. This light was paired with the *Port Swinging Light*, marked with a red wire. Both hung over the appropriate sides over Esherick's *Flat-Top Desk*.

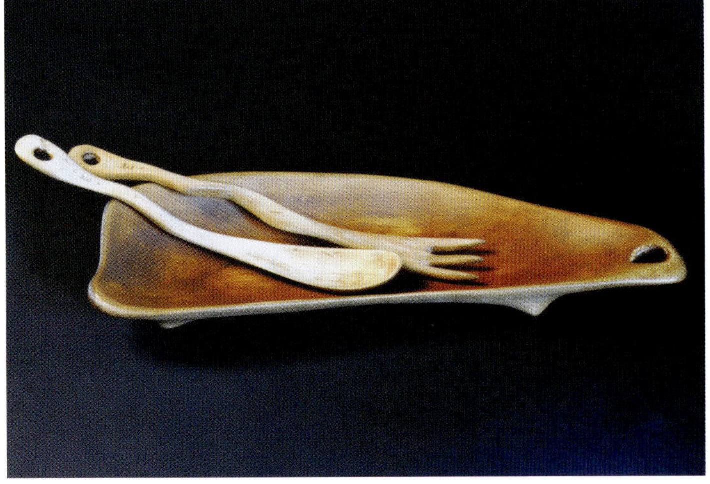

Salad Bowl, 1964. Dogwood. *Salad Servers*, 1960. Dogwood, spoon 11.8 in. long, fork 13.4 in. long. Signed "W.E. 1960."
Photo courtesy of James Mario.